*helio*graphica

As a result of the Heliographica Sustainability Program, 10 cents from the proceeds of this book will be donated to environmental causes that support forest preservation and environmental education for children.

Rescuing God from Christianity:

A Closet Christian, Non-Christian, and Christmas Christian's Guide to Radically Rethinking God Stuff

SvenErlandson

*helio*graphica

Rescuing God from Christianity:
A Closet Christian, Non-Christian,
and Christmas Christian's Guide to
Radically Rethinking God Stuff
Copyright© 2004 by Sven Erlandson

No part of this book may be reproduced or transmitted in any form or by any means, graphic, electronic or mechanical, including photocopying, recording, typing, or by any information storage retrieval system, without the permission of the publisher.

*helio*graphica

For information:
Heliographica
2261 Market St., #504
San Francisco, CA 94114
www.heliographica.com

ISBN 1-933037-41-5

Printed in the United States of America

Rescuing God from Christianity:

A Closet Christian, Non-Christian, and Christmas Christian's Guide to Radically Rethinking God Stuff

SvenErlandson

— To My Butterfly,

For your fire and for loving me even in the hard times; and

— To Dad and Mom,

For teaching us indiscriminate love and the nobility of selflessness.

Moyers: But aren't many visionaries and even leaders and heroes close to the edge of neuroticism?

Campbell: Yes, they are.

Moyers: How do you explain that?

Campbell: They've moved out of the society that would have protected them, and into the dark forest, into the world of fire, of original experience. Original experience has not been interpreted for you, and so you've got to work out your life for yourself. Either you can take it or you can't. You don't have to go far off the interpreted path to find yourself in very difficult situations. The courage to face the trials and to bring a whole new body of possibilities into the field of interpreted experience for other people to experience — that is the hero's deed.

— Joseph Campbell, mythologist, interviewed by Bill Moyers (*Power of Myth*. Joseph Campbell (Betty Sue Flowers, Ed.). Anchor Books, 1988.)

[Acknowledgments]

Thanks to Steve Bailey and Anneliese Boies for your laughter and support.

Thanks to Phil Krikau for believing in my work, and continually showing me what down-to-earth, yet passionate Christianity looks like.

Thanks to my uncles: Rev. Dr. Alden Erlandson, Rev. Paul Erlandson (deceased), Rev. Robert Johnson (deceased), and Rev. John Johnson. Your life commitment to the work of ministry has been instrumental in shaping my sense of personal identity and calling.

Special thanks to Dr. David Fenrick for astute critiques and unwavering belief in my work. Your friendship and your commitment to mission in your own life inspire me.

Special thanks to Eileen "Andy" Andersen, my salty, 80 year-old drinking partner and Christian friend, for giving me a secluded roof during the final stages of writing and editing.

Special thanks to Dr. Jay Bland. Your discipline in life, your generosity of spirit, and your deep commitment to writing as both art and instrument of change inspire me.

Personal thanks to Janice Cronkhite for making this book far tighter and more readable. Thank you, especially, for patiently enduring my walk down the odd paths God has called me.

Lastly, thanks to the Spirit of life for giving me Colbjorn and Svea, and for daily and yearly giving me the courage to do what I believe you have called me to do.

Contents

[Introduction] ix

Chapter 1 [Understand the Playing Field] 1

Chapter 2 [Seek God by Getting Higher] 9

Chapter 3 [Ask Questions to Get to God] 25

Chapter 4 [Separate Truths from "Facts"...
and Focus on Truths!] 41

Chapter 5 [Change How You Think of Jesus] 67

Chapter 6 [Change How You Think of God] 85

Chapter 7 [Listen For God's Quiet Voice ...
So God Doesn't Have to Yell] 95

Chapter 8 [Create a Religious Hybrid to
Increase Spiritual Profitability] 109

Chapter 9 [Build Heaven Today] 117

Chapter 10 [Re-think God, Science, Resurrection, and Greatness] 129

Chapter 11 [Beware: Following Jesus Equals Suffering] 135

Chapter 12 [Create Space for You to Get Close to God:
Beat Christians at Their Own Game] 153

[Epilogue] 173

[Appendix A] 177

[Appendix B] 185

[Endnotes] 193

[Annotated Bibliography] 205

[Introduction]

"I want to believe!"

— Poster behind the desk of Fox Mulder
on the hit TV show *The X Files*

LONG BEFORE YOU EVER BEGAN SEEKING GOD, God sought you. No matter how you think of God, the questions about the great Unknown of life have pursued you, almost haunting you for a long time. God has wanted to be nearer to you long before you knew that God was what you wanted.

God has wanted you to pursue your questions and doubts so that you would find the gifts of peace, power, purpose, love, and so much more on the other side of your questions. When you were first fulfilling your most basic needs, God had in store for you to know the true fulfillment of your highest needs.

But somewhere between then and now your life got off track. And you know it, because you can feel it. It is that sense of being unfulfilled, that sense that no matter how much you accumulate in life, more is just not enough.

All along you have claimed to be a spiritual person. You have been kind when you could be, and loving when you could be. You have believed in God, as well. But you began to realize that to just say, "Oh yeah, I'm spiritual" does not bring fulfillment, joy, and purpose. Somewhere along the line you realized that your own attempts to fill your inner longings weren't enough. You hunched you might need God to find what you sought. You felt the tug of the Divine. And so you poked around different God-sources.

But, very quickly, you hit a glitch. You wanted God, believed in God, and maybe even loved God. But you didn't know how to get closer to God. You knew the Christian church is in the God business. But maybe you had bad experiences with Christianity prior to that, or you just weren't interested in what they were selling or how they were selling it. And, other than a few bits and pieces, no other religions really grabbed you. Because of all this you felt the tension: desire for God, but no way to get there. And that is where you find yourself today.

So, the only choice you have had is to go the spiritual journey alone, with no spiritual community to share it and be aided by, for now. To do this — to go alone — you must now wrestle God free from Christianity's grasp, free from all the standard ways God is thought of and understood. For those do not work for you. You have to claim your share of ownership of God, so to speak.

To begin this journey you must give yourself permission to ask your questions. And you must see the value of your questions as tools for setting God free and growing closer to God. You must set yourself free to question life, question religious institutions, doubt theology, and express the questions that rise up from your own spiritual journey.

And, should you choose to explore the Christian Bible as an authoritative or helpful text on your spiritual journey, what your questions can lead to is a discovery that the Bible holds much more truth and is much more relevant as a spiritual guide when it is read metaphorically and as parable, instead of literally. Once you realize that you have permission to re-think the Bible beyond Christianity's black-and-white take on it, you will find your world rocked by depths of truth and wisdom that you never could've imagined. Should you try this it will become a powerful shift in your life.

All of a sudden, you will begin to sense God moving in your life, speaking life-giving truths to you. You will begin to hear whispers of God's voice inside you, speaking your life's calling, telling you all you can do with who you already are. You will discover a depth of meaning in scripture and in all of life that overwhelms you, challenges you, and pulls you in invigorating new directions.

You will discover the true brilliance and life-saving power of Jesus' teachings and his life example. You will have the freedom to absorb his great teachings, *not because he is Jesus and you must believe what he says,* but simply because the teachings of this man are brilliant, time-tested, and life-changing. You will hear Jesus calling you to a life of loving God and loving neighbor. You will hear Jesus challenging you to speak truth in love, fight injustice, and become a source of love in the lives of others. You will read of Jesus teaching the nobility of self-sacrifice — sacrificing all you constantly seek for yourself so that you may be of service to others, and in turn find God.

And as you follow Jesus' path of compassion and self-sacrifice, and God's voice of new purpose, you begin to discover a new richness in life. You begin to discover the joy of living your calling and breathing life into other people. Slowly, you begin to notice the fading of the spiritual unrest and hunger. Slowly, you are filling up!

You begin to understand what it means to live forever. For you sense inside you the inspiration and power of those who've gone before you, those people you admire who also lived that path of purpose, vigor, and self-sacrifice. Their spirit lives on in you.

You begin also to see that there is room in Jesus' teachings and in God's world for the truths and wisdom of other religions and philosophies. As you bump into and get to know people of other backgrounds, you grow to see the beauty and depth in their beliefs. And, here and there, you incorporate into your beliefs pieces of them that really speak to you.

As you follow on Jesus' sacrificial path of loving God and loving neighbor what you find is that this path, this noble way, brings suffering, just as surely as it brings joy. You realize the higher road is also a harder road. It is infinitely more fulfilling than your old life, but in so many ways it is infinitely more difficult.

But in that suffering you discover the oddest of things — truth. From the dark belly of life's whale you hear life and God speaking wisdom you never knew. And you change. You grow. This wisdom transports you. You begin to see the beauty and goodness of the suffering God sends.

You begin to see the yangs to life's yins. You find a whole new side of life for which to give thanks. In your suffering and from this suffering you discover something you never expected to find here — laughter. It is a laughter you've never known before, the laughter that comes from disengagement from what used to be life's most extreme hardships. You learn the laughter that comes when life is not so serious. You learn the laughter that comes from finally understanding a bit of life, and not being so shaken by it.

It is Divine laughter. It can sustain one through the harshest of times. It is not laughing at the events of life so much as it is a laughter of understanding the context of it all, and that the God of life has times and seasons for all things. And so, despite the suffering, you persist, because the yoke of Jesus' path and God's path is freeing.

With that laughter and understanding comes peace. It is a very deep peace. With peace comes love that franticness and over-seriousness cannot make room for. From peace flows hope. And all of these fruits are the filling of your soul, even as you have become an instrument in the filling of the souls of others.

Just as combating a winter cold with lots of rest and chicken soup might a week later yield the realization, "Hey, my cold is gone. When did that happen?" so also you notice one day as you turn around that, surprisingly, your spiritual longing is gone. You realize it has been replaced by fullness and a welling up inside that never leaves. You have a great "Aha!" moment. You understand what Jesus meant when he said, "I have come that you might have life, and have it abundantly!" You begin to understand that heaven really is right now, here … today, and that you truly do have the power to create it with God, and help others create it, as well.

And in it all you realize that you do know God. You see God in *all* of God's creation. You feel and hear life pulsing with God's own heart. You discover that you are dancing in the richness and beauty of this life. As you discover how beautiful this life really is and how fortunate you are to have known the life you've known with all its peaks and valleys, you find that you no longer fear death. Nor do you fear the God who brings death just as surely as life.

You simply give thanks for all you have known and all you have become. You delight in knowing that you will live on in those who have known you and whom you have touched, just as others lived on in you. Then, somehow, almost magically, you realize that is enough. You discover in your times of peace that the joy, the richness, the beauty, the laughter, and the God of life are more than enough to fill your soul and overcome your fear of death.

And just as life slips from your grasp, you realize you are no longer grasping for life, but that your hand has long been open, letting life in and letting life go. You realize your life has filled you up, and it is time to make room for others. You die neither hungry, nor alone. For you die just as you lived, with God right there in every element of it. You die with the very Spirit of life holding your hand, whispering to you, "Do not be afraid. I am with you. You are my child. In you I am well-pleased."

So walk forward with courage.

God awaits you!

A Few Qualifiers

There are a few basic premises and qualifiers on which this book is built. First, this book uses the term *God* a great deal. America has very strong Christian roots and influences, and much of spirituality in America is either a response to Christianity or somehow in relation to Christianity. As a result, the Judeo-Christian word *God* is a term that most people are familiar with when discussing the great Unknown or the unknowns of life, the Unseen, the Force of life, and so on.

However, the author recognizes that the word for God in Jesus' native tongue (Aramaic) was *Allaha*, a one-letter difference from the Islamic word for God, *Allah*. The author further recognizes that the undefined nature of God is such that terms like *spirit, higher energy, force, power* (and even simply *the universe* and *life*) are all terms for the same, to some greater or lesser degree.

Second, as shall be discussed in Chapter Eight, every religion of the world has the power to bring you into full and life-giving relationship with God, whatever you consider God to be. However, it is not the purpose of this book to give a comprehensive world religions guidebook to you on your spiritual journey. If this is what you seek, I strongly recommend reading the works of the great student of myths and religions, Joseph Campbell.

Joseph Campbell once said that you will never hear the truths learned from other religions and myth systems woven into preaching from Christian pulpits. The reason, he said, is because Christianity doesn't know how to incorporate the findings and wisdom of the world outside its doors, and often doesn't believe it has to.

This book is, in part, a response to that challenge. This book is an attempt to reconcile the Bible with the truths of other sources, including science, other religions, and present-day experience and sensibilities. This book does not attempt to show how this came from this religion and that came from that religion. Instead, it is, in part, an attempt to radically re-interpret the Bible and shift emphases in the Bible so that the Bible makes more sense in light of these other sources. It is the very strong belief of this author that when this is done, the Bible becomes an infinitely more powerful teacher than it ever was under Christianity. It becomes a much better tool for you on your journey with God to God.

Just one more note on that thought: Because America has such strong Judeo-Christian roots and still has such strong Judeo-Christian influences, many people know the symbols, stories, and main players in the Bible. Thus, the purpose of this book is to take that great book and breathe new life into it by showing you how you can re-think it. It is my hope that you will not only find this book provocative and refreshing, but potentially life-changing.

Third, this book uses the Revised Standard Version (RSV) for most Biblical references. Alternate language choices (placed in brackets; and based on Greek, Hebrew, and Latin definitions and allowances) are used when Biblical terminology is not part of common language.

Fourth, approximately 1000 years ago, the Christian Church was a largely unified entity. But, power struggles and theological bickering led to a split, or schism, that created two primary branches of Christianity: The Roman Catholic Church (largely the Church in the West: Europe and parts of the Mediterranean region) and the Orthodox Church (the Church of the East: Africa, present-day Middle East, and parts of present-day Russia). 500 years after that, after Christianity had spread into most regions of the world, the Roman Catholic Church itself split because of the theological issues raised by Martin Luther, a Catholic monk. This was the Protestant Reformation, which, almost immediately, led to the birth of a multitude of Protestant branches or denominations.

It is worth noting that today the Christian Church can be broken into three main sections: The Roman Catholic Church, the Orthodox Church, and the Protestants. Any church in your city that is Catholic or Orthodox will be labeled as such on its marquee. Any other church you may see is, for simplicity sake, Protestant, which only means it does not answer to the Roman Catholic Pope and does not answer to the Patriarchs of the Orthodox Church. For example, Mormons, Presbyterians, Jehovah's Witnesses, Baptists, Unitarians, and non-denominational churches, to name a few, all fall under the Protestant umbrella.

Fifth, there are many hues, varieties, colors, and types of Christians, Christian branches, Christian theologies, and Christian churches. No two sections or branches believe the same thing, but all are Christian. No two churches within the same denomination believe the same thing, but all are Christian. No two Christians believe the exact same things, but all are Christian. Each is similar, yet different; and sadly most believe they are the one true way.

However, despite the many Christian varieties, most people *outside* Christianity either don't know that there are differences, don't know what the differences are, or, more likely, don't care. Many people outside Christianity lump all churches and denominations into one big heap and call it *the church* or *Christianity*. This is a critical point!

Because this book is directed specifically toward non-Christians, Christmas (or non-practicing) Christians, and closet Christians in America, it operates from this understanding of Christianity and its churches as one big undifferentiated heap. Thus, unless a reference is made to a specific church or denomination, terms such as *church* and *Christianity* refer to this Christian heap. These terms also refer to the widely generalized theologies of Christian branches, which, because they are perceived as out-of-touch by a great many people, have also been thrown by non-Christian America onto the pile.

This point needs to be repeated. It is absolutely essential to understanding this book. Because this book is written for people who are *outside* organized religion, **this book is written largely from the perspective of people outside organized religion.**

In actuality, the Christian Church has thousands of ways of interpreting the Christian Bible and story. It is not the purpose of this book to define or defend these interpretations. Each church must do that itself.

But, again, Christian internal differences are largely irrelevant to those outside the church. To many people outside the church, the Christian Church is perceived as having one basic story and theology. It is from this mindset and for people of this mindset that this book is written. This book offers the spiritual seeker of this mindset a radical re-interpretation of Christian scripture.

Sixth, this book is founded upon two basics: One, the Judeo-Christian Bible is an excellent, well-seasoned way (but not the only way) to reach God; and, two, the Bible has far more to offer than Christianity is aware of or willing to admit.

Thus, this book is an attempt to powerfully re-interpret (as metaphor) the Christian Bible in exciting ways for the spiritual seeker who is tired of out-of-date, literalism-based theology. Because of that, there are many references to the Bible that the seeker can pursue for further study.

Some chapters of this book are "to-do" steps to move you forward on your spiritual journey (1-4). Some chapters are designed to help you think of God and traditional Biblical concepts in new ways (5-11). One chapter (12) is designed to simply help you create mental and social space to grow in your relationship with God.

Seventh, Christianity as a religion is not bad. In fact, Christianity is good, beautiful, and spirited, *when it is done well*. When one objectively considers all the good that has been done in this world in the name of Christianity (despite all the bad, which will be addressed in the book), and when one considers those people in Christian history who were really extraordinary Christian people, one can today be somewhat proud to be a man or woman who attempts to walk the noble path Jesus taught. For, when the following of Jesus' teachings is done well, it truly is a remarkable thing!

Unfortunately, it's not being done well in America, right now. Sure, there are pockets of good Christianity and there are a few churches that are really banging out a high quality product. But, all in all, Christianity in America has become a great challenge, and even an embarrassment to many people.

Therefore, this book is written, in small part, as one man's effort to revive a brand — Christianity. It may seem that Christianity is to be torn asunder in these pages. But, while this book is highly critical and at times pokes fun at the church, nothing could be farther from the truth. The primary goal of this book is to bring people to God, not get them into a church. Please don't forget that. But, for those people who are reading this book who are frustrated yet still in their churches, the secondary goal of this book is to help Christianity rebuild itself, making it far better than it is. Then it can once again be equated with creativity, goodness, intelligence, and quality.

Finally, a man named Thomas Chandler once said, "To love someone is to learn the song that is in their heart, and to sing it to them when they have forgotten." I believe that song in the heart is the voice of God speaking an individual message to each one of us, and a collective song to all of us. To love people is to help them hear and follow the voice of God in their lives. May this book help you to do just that.

Chapter 1

[Understand the Playing Field]

"Discontent is the first step in the progress of any man or nation."

— Oscar Wilde

IT IS A GORGEOUS SUMMER DAY. The grass is bright green with that freshly mowed smell. The sky is royal blue, streaked by just the occasional wispy cirrus cloud and the high arching contrails of a jet long out of sight. The only sounds are of birds in the trees and a child in a sandbox nearby. It is the peaceful kind of day that childhood memories are made of.

But there is a problem. The summer serenity is pierced by the shrieks and squeals coming from the sandbox. For, the child is not using his sandbox toy to build sand cities, sand roads, and little sand castles. Instead, he is using his sandbox toy to beat up his little sister. He keeps hitting her and hitting her, to the point where she runs from the sandbox crying to her mother in the kitchen. It is no fun playing with him anymore. He hurts people.

Neighbor kids, after suffering similar beatings, long ago chose the same course, and got out of the sandbox. Now they only play tag nearby, always careful to keep a safe distance from the sandbox boy.

Not content to play alone, the child with the sandbox toy soon gets out of the sand and starts chasing the other children around the yard, hitting them with the sandbox toy and monopolizing the yard. The hitting, he discovers, is far more entertaining than making sandbox cities and sandbox roads.

In truth, this child is not a bad kid. In fact, he is a beautiful, spirited child. He's just one who doesn't know how to play in the sandbox or with other children. In fact, he soon discovers that many other children stop coming around to his yard, despite how cool his yard and toys are. Though inherently good, he is a child who needs to have his toy taken away, get a talking to, and be taught that there are acceptable and unacceptable uses of things in life, just as there are acceptable and unacceptable ways of interacting with other people in life.

Christianity has become the sandbox bully. Christianity is whacking everyone in or near the sandbox of life, to the point where many do not want to play with Christianity anymore.

And the toy? Sadly, it is God. Christianity's God has become a weapon with which Christianity beats on all those who would like to be in the sandbox too, playing the game of sandbox life. While it's a bit of a stretch to call God a toy, you get the point. If God is not being rammed down people's throats, God is being used as justification for callous human living and the ugliest of human atrocities.

Now, as with the child, Christianity is good, beautiful, and spirited *when it is done well*. But today in America Christianity is seldom done well. People are running from Christianity and have been doing so for decades, despite the goodness and life-changing power of its God.

In life the oppressed and the hurting are given new life by taking away the source of the oppressor's power or by empowering those who suffer. Thus, either God must be rescued from Christianity, or people outside Christianity must be given new access to God and the sandbox of life, or both.

That is the simple purpose of this book. It is to set God free and place God in the hands of everyone. It is to create new paths for the children of God to get to God, dance with God, and play with joy and peace in the sandbox of life.

The Other Kids in the Yard

There is a reason you picked up this book. It's not by chance. My bet is that you did it because, for whatever reason, you don't go to church. Maybe you don't like Christianity. Maybe you don't like its theology. Maybe you don't like its past or its leaders. Maybe you have had a bad experience with Christians trying to convert you. Whatever your reason, you probably don't like the church.

American census data shows you are not alone. Despite the fact that approximately 90% of Americans believe in God,[1] only 50% of Americans (approx. 150 million people) are actually enrolled "members" of any religion.[2] That means at least 40% of Americans (approximately 120 million people) consider themselves believers in God but are not members of any faith organization! This doesn't even include the vast number of people who are enrolled members of an organized religion, but simply do not attend or take an interest.

There are a whole lot of un-churched people in America (*Un-churched* is a term the Christian Church uses to denote people who don't go to church.) But, after thousands upon thousands of conversations over the years, it has been my experience that many of these people are not just *un-churched*, but *de-churched*, perhaps like you.

The *de-churched*, I have found, are people who may have had a relationship or membership with a church at one time, but have since either left the church or simply grown disinterested. Whether it was something the church said, did, or didn't do that turned you off, today you want nothing to do with it.

Yet, I believe you still want God in your life. That's the other reason you picked up this book. You may be *not-religious*, but you are also a spiritual person. You desire a greater understanding of God, the great Unknown, the Energy of life, and the Spirit of the Universe. You are interested, to some degree, in the great truths of the highly evolved spiritual thinkers, leaders, and mystics of the past. You are curious about fresh answers to questions you have long had.

Like so many in this country, perhaps you are in a state of deep spiritual longing and hunger. You long for a sense of lasting contentment. You ache for a state of unending joy and hope. You dream of having a sense of purpose that excites you, helps humanity, and inspires your life. Yet you have no way of quelling those longings and achieving that dream.

This spiritual longing is the driver behind America's excessive consumerism, ridiculous levels of waste, and disregard for the health and well-being of less fortunate people in other countries, not to mention our own. We are a culture of anxiety, depression, discontent, and spiritual unrest. Further, America's spiritual hunger is not being fed by conventional means of delivery — religion — nor to any significant degree by any unconventional spiritual means, such as support groups, psychotherapy, yoga, drugs, self-help books, exercise, or overworking. And so we spin farther and farther out of control.

Filling the Void

Still spiritually hungry, Americans have gone looking for something to fill the spiritual emptiness left by the church and organized religion. What we have found are a few highly unusual players to fill at least some of our spiritual needs. The biggest of these are:

1) Starbucks: It is no small coincidence that a sort of coffee revolution has paralleled the American exodus from the church in the last 40 years. Starbucks has become the modern day chapel. The mug has replaced the chalice. For the price of a cup of coffee, one can experience communion, peace, and inspiration, feeling God in a way remotely similar to church.

Starbucks coffee shops, and similar caffeine purveyors, offer an odd hybrid of spiritual community, warmth, peace, and a mood-elevating drug, to boot. In this regard, it is no secret that written into the Starbucks mission statement is the desire to create for people a "3rd Place" — home and work being the 1st and 2nd places — where they can go and just be. In a role formerly occupied by the church, this new 3rd Place is a place where the people are upbeat, the chairs are comfy, there is a bit of a bustle, and the music is cool. Starbucks offers a spiritual experience.

By successfully taking that role of 3rd Place from the church, Starbucks is reaping at a startling clip. Seattle, Starbucks' home, is the new Vatican City with 6,000+ satellite chapels worldwide, and growing at a rate of three new store openings per day ... per day!

2) The Entertainment Industry: Recognizing that storytelling is one of the most vital elements of religion and spirituality (insofar as stories convey a society's values, history, and motivating forces), just as shamans gave spirit and purpose to ancient cultures with their stories, Hollywood has become the great American storyteller.

If Starbucks is the cozy American chapel, movie theaters and multiplexes are the great, new American cathedrals. The chapels offer community; the cathedrals offer a sense of awe. Little different from our ancestors, we have become a people who worship bright light and loud noise. And our new priests dispense the communion wafer in large buckets with lots of butter and salt.

Sending a vast variety of messages and myths, Hollywood has an impact on the collective American mindset that is impossible to overestimate. In particular, movies such as *The Matrix*, *Gladiator*, *Star Wars*, *Indiana Jones*, *The Lord of the Rings*, and *Harry Potter*, while not dealing directly with religious issues and values, per se, have ironically had an enormous impact on the spiritual and theological formation of hundreds of millions of Americans and people around the world.

For many, the modern rock concert has stepped in to fill the need for spiritual experience. The music industry provides us with massive group experiences that transport us and take us away from our miseries and trivialities. But it also gives us gods to idolize and pin up on our children's walls, while we listen to their sacred texts spinning round and round. For some, this has become the modern day religious pilgrimage as they avidly follow such groups as The Dead, The Stones, Phish, Springsteen, and Jimmy Buffett. Some travel to Ozzfest, Lollapalooza, Burning Man Project, or South by Southwest.

Eclipsing even the music and Hollywood behemoths is the video-gaming industry, a fast-growing multi-billion dollar industry. Every new Hollywood thriller release is considered for its gaming potential. Big name writers such as Tom Clancy and Michael Crichton have gaming as an integral part of the production of each new story they produce. Even sports legend John Madden has become a titan in the video-gaming industry.

Gamers are the ascetics and monks of today. Isolating themselves from the rest of the world or gathering in small groups, they spend hours in a form of, almost, meditation, navigating the labyrinthine worlds of discovery, destruction, and adventure.

3) Oprah: Billy Graham of the 21st Century, Oprah has become the great American evangelist. Open for worship and a good message every day at 4pm, the Oprah Evangelistic Association has deliberately morphed from being just another broken-family talk show to the highly evolved, almost slick, "house of spirit" for tens of millions of people, particularly women. Choosing inspiration over entertainment, she has almost single-handedly

re-infused a great portion of America with desire for and conversations about spirit and spiritual growth.

In exchange for her relevant discussions of spiritual matters and her down home integrity, America has rewarded her with an average income of almost $100 million per year since 1990, making her net worth roughly 1 billion dollars! This is the most telling measuring stick for how great the spiritual longing is that she has tapped into.

The Root Cause

At the heart of America's cultural unrest and at the heart, also, of why people will not enter Christian churches to address that unrest is a series of theological problems. People take issue with Christianity's history, practices, and image, but underlying all of these are severe problems in thinking and beliefs.

Christianity clings to concepts of God, Jesus and religion that are not only ineffective in bringing people today into relationship with God, but also continue to do damage to America's spirit and soul. And, insofar as American culture is still somewhat shaped by its Christian roots and stories, even non-Christian Americans are affected by these theological problems.

Christian theology has long asserted that we humans are captive. We are in bondage to sin, hardship, and a life of misery, all as a result of our own broken and degraded nature. However, today, there is a much bigger problem. It is God who is in bondage — captive to a religion that:

1) Makes God a "being" that is floating around in somewhere in space, distant from humanity;

2) Insists followers believe in a list of beliefs, often at the expense of ever fully knowing God;

3) Makes Jesus the end goal of religion, rather than a path and a guide for drawing closer to God;

4) Is adamant that the Bible is a factual, literal account of God's activity in ancient days (Thus, the sacred book becomes the point of the religion, and the God plays second fiddle ... or third); and

5) Limits God's power, influence, methods, and complexity; refusing to believe that God may be far, far more than Christianity's ability to understand.

Christianity is holding Jesus and God captive in a cookie-cutter, one-size-fits-all mentality. In the eyes of most people, according to the church there is one way to interpret the Bible, one way to believe, and one way to follow God. If you want to know God, you must do it the church's way. The keepers of Christian theology (which include not only theologians and bishops, but also everyday Christian folks who cling to beliefs handed to them by Sunday School teachers, who were taught by clergy, who in turn were taught by bishops and theologians) cling tenaciously to a sense of exclusive ownership of God and religion.

This only serves to drive people angrily away from anything that even smells of Christianity. Because God is captive, all of the people the Christian church wishes it could reach — i.e. the 90 to 120 million who are spiritual but not religious — are without a viable source of spiritual inspiration and leadership. America is depressed, anxious, and wandering because it has no God, no spiritual leadership, and no sense of purpose.

Imagine Nike Corporation deciding that from now on it is only going to sell size-7 women's shoes. No longer is it going to sell size-9 or size-4. No longer is it going to sell men's shoes. No longer is it going to sell sweat suits, windbreakers, jock straps, football helmets, decals, jerseys, or socks. Nike is only going to sell size-7 women's shoes. If you want Nike, you gotta buy size-7 women's shoes.

With that, the world sort of furrows its brow, and says, "What is *that*? That's ridiculous!"

And that is precisely America's response to Christianity's size-7 God. America is furrowing its collective brow, and saying, "What is *that*?"

So, God must be rescued and set free, odd as that may sound. It is our responsibility, as both non-Christians and non-practicing Christians, to break the Christian chains that oppress God, so that God may be set free to do God's work in you and the world. This book is a tool to aid you in that process. If there is one thing Christian history teaches, it is that God speaks different messages to different people. And, God speaks in different ways to different people. Thus, your task is to find what and how God is speaking specifically to you.

This Book is for You

This book is nothing more than one man's attempts to set God free; free from Christianity's control; free from the very literalism that Jesus railed against; free from the scriptural laws that Jesus tried to imbue with spirit; free from those people who are convinced they have him all boxed up and pretty with a pink ribbon on top; and free to love the world God created.

So, whether you are one of the *de-churched* or are a person who has simply never known much about Christianity, this book is for you. This book is for the millions of Americans in 12-Step groups and other self-help groups, many of whom find themselves caught between wanting to know God better and not wanting Christianity's version of God. It is for the "closet Christians," who like God and maybe even like church, but, because of the Christian image problem, are loathe admitting it. It is for "Christmas Christians" who have a fondness for God, but can only tolerate the church on major holy days. It is for the many people inside Christianity who long for more from their church and their spiritual-religious life, but who cannot bring themselves to leave. In frustration, these folks often settle for "good enough."

This book is written for you and God. It is written to set free how you think of God, so that the two of you may meet. For, only when we have changed our understanding of God — personalizing God — will we know the peace, power, purpose, joy, hope, love and fulfillment that we seek. These are the fruits of relationship with God.

Chapter 2

[Seek God by Getting Higher]

"Seek me, and live."

— God (Amos 5: 4)

*Some men die by shrapnel,
And some go down in flames.
But most men perish inch by inch,
Who play at little games.*

— Unknown

IN THE 1950s, ABRAHAM MASLOW, one of the great minds of modern psychology, developed a concept for explaining human behavior, which he called The Hierarchy of Human Needs. Maslow believed that human existence is fundamentally about getting our needs and longings met. All of life, from birth to death, is spent fulfilling one need or another. And it is the drive to meet our needs that determines our behaviors in life.

To illustrate this he envisioned an upside-down triangle, and said that at the very bottom point are our most basic physical needs — the needs for touch, security, food, etc. The highest levels of self-actualization are those that cause us to step beyond ourselves and live for something greater — spirituality, God, and assisting others in the development of their character and abilities. The rest of the triangle looks like this:

GOD

Spirituality · Love · Intimacy with God
Truth · Beauty · Goodness
Caring · The need to be needed
Creativity · Generativity
Self-actualization · Individuation

Self-value · Sense of mattering
Curiosity · Exploration
Experience of pleasure/pain
Structure · Stimulation
Space · Recognition
Belonging
Mirroring
Food-Shelter
Security
Warmth
Touch

Maslow called the lower tier the "Basic ego needs" and the upper tier the "Being needs." The lower needs are those that life starts with, ends with, and always comes back to. These are the ones we can never escape, the ones we constantly need refilled. They are the basics of life — food, water, stimulation, self-value, and so on.

The upper tier ("Being needs") revolves around the human need to feel truly alive. These are the needs that set humanity apart from the rest of the animal world. Once the Basic needs are met, these Being needs are the ones that give life meaning and a sense of vitality and spirit.

Every person, Maslow asserted, is somewhere on that pyramid. Some are fulfilling base needs. Some are fulfilling higher needs. Some can never seem to get one need met. Some have abundance in the realm of other needs.

All of us, over our lifetime, move up and down the pyramid, doing the work of getting our needs met. But life's general direction is the movement from bottom to top. It is the movement from securing base needs toward fulfilling the more elusive and intangible needs that fill the deepest parts of our souls.

In contrast to this general movement is the path of the proverbial starving artist. The artist seeks first to meet his or her spiritual needs and self-expression needs, often at the expense of love, community, shelter, and even food. When most people are working their way up the pyramid, the artist is generally trying to work his or her way down it. The artist can self-express but seeks greater skill to become generative, thereby achieving a feeling of self-value. If others appreciate the artist's work, he or she gets recognition and a sense of belonging. Then, one day, long down the road the artist achieves his or her dream — to be able to buy food and a home with money earned from his or her art and creative self-expression.

This top-down movement is mirrored in the spiritually grounded, but financially poor person. This person, like the artist, has a deep relationship with God yet struggles to meet the Basic needs of life.

Whether life is spent moving up or down the pyramid, the needs are the same. Fundamentally, Maslow was describing the spiritual journey, whether he realized it or not. It is the path of the spiritual seeker. Spirituality is not a state, but a movement toward the fulfillment of our ever-evolving needs. And each one of us, simply by being human, is a spiritual seeker.

With our inherent tendency to push too hard, work too long, extend ourselves too far, and desire too many "things," we find ourselves, ironically, always to be lacking. We are always reaching but never fully attaining; always striving, but never "there." That is why people keep wanting more things (and things more powerful) in order to be fulfilled. This whole longing for fulfillment, the longing to fill the holes inside, by definition, *is* spirituality. It is the human condition.

Yet, eventually, the human beast is not content with simple abatement of base needs or even advanced needs. At some point, we all have the desire to know the greater powers, energies, wisdoms, and truths of life. We all have a desire to live for something greater than ourselves. That is self-transcendence.

In short, the path of the spiritual seeker will eventually become a quest for unity with God. Life, from its most basic quest for food, really is all about the quest for God.

"Lower" things may quiet the unrest temporarily, but they do not last. Regardless of where the spiritual journey starts or passes through, it always eventually becomes a quest for the principle (or Principal) that underlies the universe. Maslow acknowledges this quest. God, as Maslow sees it, is the summit of the hierarchy of needs.

See, we quickly learn that food is not god. Shelter is not god. Family is not god. Spouse and child are not god. Community is not god. Even self-actualization and the Self are not god. As we achieve these goals, as the needs are met, we quickly long for more. We are not content. And that is the most obvious indicator that these are not God. We may make them our gods, but none are the Principal. They are not God.

These are lesser gods in the sense that we worship them endlessly, but we always still come up wanting more. For example, one fabulously popular American god is the quest for fame. The Roman philosopher Tacitus wrote, "The desire for fame is the last infirmity cast off even by the wise." Yet, fame, like money, still leaves one feeling hungry inside. It is like a drug. Once had, more is always frantically sought. Whereas, a god, it seems, should release us from that mad and frantic chase.

Consider another god: The most popular deity in America is the god of food.

We worship this lesser god, because she is the one god who can always make us feel good... at least momentarily.

It is the god of the masses. Food is so accessible that everyone can come to this god's altar, three times a day and once before bed. Our worship and total intoxication with this god is the result of our great wealth, our great boredom, and our great lack of purpose. And so, we supersize and big gulp our helpings of this god as a way to forget the emptiness of our spiritual stomachs. And all the while we get fatter and fatter.

All of the gods may bring excitement, but the excitement is fleeting. The gods don't bring lasting contentment. There is always a feeling that something is missing.

The reason we continually feel this hunger inside, this sense of not being fulfilled, is because we equate "more" with greater fulfillment and moving higher up the pyramid of life. We think more food, more shelter (bigger and bigger houses, and more than just one), more stimulation (note America's fixation with entertainment!), and more pleasure (lots of leisure, toys, drugs, and sex) are the answer to getting happier. It is about getting more!

But that is not the answer. Money, for instance, is a good strong god; one we have such an infatuation with in America. Yet, we continually hear the wealthiest of the wealthy saying there is never enough. Money, we discover, can't quell the unrest. That is why we are so confused when we hear rich people and movie stars say that they are not any happier than they were before their wealth. We are confused when they say, "For once, I wish I could have something money can't buy!" We wonder: How could a person have so much, and not be happy!?! It seems impossible!

John Stossel of the television news program *20/20*, in an account of ten American myths, reported this interesting finding:

"We get a lot of messages from television and movies telling us that more money will make us happy. Lottery winners have press conferences. Reality shows have pretty women lining up to marry rich guys.

"One lottery winner told us she was very happy for several days, then the thrill wore off.

"Millionaire hip-hop promoter Russell Simmons told me wealth didn't make him or his friends happy either. 'If I know 15 billionaires, I know 13 unhappy people,' he said.

"Simmons' brother, Reverend Run, was the lead rapper for Run DMC. He said he suddenly realized money wouldn't buy happiness when he was at the peak of his career.

"'I get to L.A., and I've got the presidential suite,' he said, 'and it all came at once ... and it was too much. I realized, "Okay, I got it, God. I got it. I got it. This will not work. It is not gonna make me happy." ... The only thing that's gonna make me happy, is the joy that's on the inside of me.'

"Research suggests that Reverend Run and Russell Simmons are right. A survey of 49 of the *Forbes* richest found that they weren't any happier than the rest of us.

"*Money* magazine columnist Jean Chatzky polled 1,500 people for her book, *You Don't Have to Be Rich*, and found that more money makes people significantly happier only if their family income is below $30,000, but by $50,000, money makes no difference.

"'Once you get to that $50,000 level, more money doesn't buy more happiness,' she said. Happiness researchers agree with Simmons and Chatzky: Purposeful work is what makes people happy. And finding religion. And family."[3]

"More" is never enough. The path to greater joy in life lies not in getting "more" of one level of the pyramid, but in moving "higher" up the pyramid. It is about moving farther along the spiritual journey, rather than thinking that simply more of one spot on the journey will be enough to fill all of our needs. More stimulation (TV and movies, for example) will never substitute for fulfilling your creative needs, just as more generativity (creating and building something(s) — a business, a family, a house, etc.) will not substitute for intimacy with God and union with God.

What is need-fulfillment, really? It is the desire to feel content. It is the desire to not feel like you need anything anymore. We all seek that contentment. That's why we want to win the lottery. Addressing this longing for contentment, Buddhism takes a different approach. Rather than seek to satisfy the needs, Buddhism teaches release from needs by simply letting go.

The Four Noble Truths of Buddhism, on which the entire Buddhist ethic[4] is built, are:

1) All life is suffering.

2) Suffering is the result of clinging.

3) By destroying desire we become free from sorrow.

4) By following the Eight-Fold Path, one can overcome selfishness and sorrow, and gain perfect freedom and peace.

According to Buddhism, "clinging" is that grasping tightly at things, people, and experiences we think we need to feel content. Like a squirrel nervously forages for acorns, we constantly forage for more cars, newer houses, and bigger toys for us and for our children. Driven by mad clinging, our cultural anxiety rages out of control. Buddhism steps into this age-old tendency and says only in letting go of everything will there be release and satisfaction. This is what Buddhism calls Nirvana.

Jesus agrees, in part. Jesus teaches that it *is* necessary to let go of smaller "needs." Jesus states, "Therefore I tell you to not be anxious about your life, what you shall eat, nor about your body, what you shall put on. For life is more than

13

food, and the body is more than clothing" (Luke 12: 22b-23). Yet, satisfaction only comes from first and always seeking God with all your heart, mind, and soul.

Whatever your opinion on Jesus might be, it is nonetheless interesting to note the great teacher's words on this matter, "...It is easier for a camel to go through the eye of a needle than for a rich man to enter the kingdom of God" (Luke 18:25). The "eye of the needle" was a term used in Jesus' day for the very small door adjacent to or set in the very large gate to any walled city. It was used as a security measure when it was not safe to have the large gate open. Through this low door all entering had to pass. And it was particularly difficult, if not impossible, for a packed and loaded camel to duck low and pass through it. Jesus' point, then, is not that money is bad, per se, but that it is extremely difficult to be oriented to the kingdom of God (whatever you conceive that to be) when you are oriented toward accruing wealth. You cannot simultaneously have both.

This is what the phrase "less is more" refers to. To be oriented toward having more of the Basic needs means that you cannot be oriented toward achieving higher, Being needs. Having "more" keeps you from climbing "higher." You are bogged down. So, to move higher to greater fulfillment you must let go of having more of the lower needs. In other words, you must have less. Thereby, you make room for some of the higher things of life.

At the core, the reason we still experience so much spiritual hunger in the U.S. is because these gods we chase are not God. These are not God, we come to realize, because a god, a big god — a god with a capital "G" — should satisfy us. A big-G God should make it so we are not left saying, "Is that all there is?" or "What next?" There should be such a thing, such a fulfilling thing, in life. And whatever it is should definitely be named God of all gods.

This, you may recall from Sunday School, is what Jesus was talking about when he said he gives the living water of God, after which you will never thirst again. Jesus promised to take us to the god of the big G.

So you see, the quests for food, for love, for money, and for prestige are all really the singular quest to fill our souls with something that will satisfy. At their root, all are a quest for the god of the big "G" — the god who brings lasting contentment. This is the spiritual journey. Yet, because we cannot reach God without God's help, and because God is in all that God created, the quest to God is also the quest with God. The spiritual journey is the path with God to God.

"But, y'know," people think, "Jesus and his God would be great. They really would. They would be awesome if they just weren't all tied up in Christianity and what it has turned them into."

If only there was some way for God to be more accessible. If only there was some way to seek God without having to go through Christianity and all its demands and baggage. If only that, then there really might be hope for approaching this God of the big "G." For, as it stands, a great many in our society won't go near God if it means wading into Christianity.

Christianity in the U.S. is equated with arrogance, naiveté, cowardice, narrow-mindedness, over-zealousness, hypocrisy, corruption, and so many more negative attributes. It has become for many the very definition of all that is offensive. As a result, a great many people have no desire to get involved.

If only there was a way to set God free to work for people like you and me; folks who want the living water that satisfies all thirst, but who would rather not go through the Christian Utilities Company, which claims to be in charge of metering living water. The United States is the wealthiest country in the world. Yet, there is a deep spiritual longing here because the pipes have rusted, the wells have gone dry, the employees have been laid off, and the Board of Directors at the Christian Utilities Company have traded living water for profit, and run the company into the ground. America is spiritually longing and wounded because there is no one to bring living water to a thirsting nation.

The Two-World Tension

This tension between wanting God but not wanting the church that claims to own God (or at least own the path to God) is one that so many Americans live in. It is particularly pervasive in the younger generations. It is the tension between (a) loving God and perhaps wanting to express and share that love with others in some sort of spiritual community, and (b) not wanting anything to do with the main spiritual community presently on the market in America — the Christian religion.

A massive survey on America's spiritual-religious tendencies was completed in the 1990s by University of California researcher and religion professor, Wade Roof Clark. He determined that 42% of the 76 million Baby Boomers — or roughly 32 million people; one tenth of the American population — are people who have left their church or synagogue. This figure does not include the huge number of people in the younger generations that have either had a similar departure or were never raised in the church to begin with (and therefore don't have any internal pro-church sentiments).

A recent Gallup Poll shows that 26% of Americans view religion as both old-fashioned and out-of-date.[5] That is roughly 75 million people.[6]

At the heart of these numbers is a very real problem: Many people in the U.S. are caught between two worlds. Daily, people are struggling in the tension between wanting more God in their lives and wanting to just be normal human beings in the world.

For example, many people want a deeper relationship with God, but don't want to become the super-moral, super-perfect, super-God people that Christianity seems to say you have to be. Their heads and bodies are in the non-religious world we all share, but their hearts are desiring God, or some relationship with that which transcends everyday life.

As another example, many people in this country are vibrant and active Christians (in their deep love for God and Jesus), spending hours each week in prayer and Biblical study, yet they admit it to almost no one. They don't want people to think of them as Christians. They don't want to come out of the closet as Christians, because the price is so high — social ostracism. Or, on that rare occasion they do admit being a God guy or a Jesus person, they quickly qualify it by saying, "...but I'm not *that* kind of Christian." This is said out of fear of being identified with the pervasive American generalization of Christians, which views them as uncool, unkind, and unliked.

Conservative Christianity has made religion seem arrogant and intolerant, while moderate Christianity has made religion seem spineless and confused. In response, the culture of liberal America, even while it attempts to foster a world of greater respect and tolerance (specifically, religious tolerance) has deemed anything beyond mild religious interest passé and irrelevant.

In addition to this American indifference to the varieties of Christians and Christian theologies, the Christian brand has become thoroughly equated with two very narrow types of churches. One is the church that is large, beautiful, and near-empty. It is led by old white men in long white robes. This is the Christianity of mainline Protestantism, as well as much of Catholicism and the Orthodox Church. It also includes a great many little churches peppering the American landscape. This Christianity is seen as old, spineless, irrelevant, and flaccid.

The other church is upbeat, new, and slick. Churches of this ilk are full of well-groomed, eager, almost cookie-cutter-like Christians, who are often quite comfortable being called religious conservatives (mostly Protestant, but also includes many Catholic churches). In stark contrast to the large and old church, this version of Christianity is seen as pushy, divorced from modern sensibilities, saccharine, naïve, and full of *Jesus* in every sentence.[7]

With these two versions of Christianity branded into the American consciousness it should come as a surprise to no one that in America today Christianity is viewed with either love or hate. Most Christian insiders love it. Many outsiders strongly dislike it. There is little neutrality.

Just as Christianity adamantly condemns worldly immorality, American culture has fought back, openly expressing great contempt for flaming Christians who are so caught up in their Christianity that they have no concept of living in the world and being a normal, down-to-earth person. To quote the phrase, "They are so heavenly-minded that they are no earthly good."

In the spring of 2004 the #1 movie at the box office is Mel Gibson's *Passion of the Christ*. Two of the top ten books on the *New York Times Bestseller List* (fiction) are *Glorious Appearing: The End of Days*, by Jerry Jenkins and Tim Lahaye, which is an interpretation of Christianity's interpretation of end times; and *The DaVinci Code*, by Dan Brown, a story which raises titillating what-ifs about Jesus and those around him. *The Purpose Driven Life*, by Richard Warren, a book offering a fresh Christian answer to the pervasive American sense of purposelessness, is in the top 5 books on the non-fiction list. Despite a drop in sales in nearly every segment of the music industry, Christian worship music experienced a 5% increase. On top of this, we have an openly conservative-Christian President. Yet, despite it all (or because of it all), Christianity still can't get over the negative image it has in this country.

In this vein, despite their popularity, praying athletes are ridiculed by armchair quarterbacks. Religious actors and singers have to closet their Christianity as they grow in popularity, because America will mock them and distance itself from them. Overly religious politicians stir religious conservatives yet annoy the American mainstream.

The spiritual-religious scene is a mess — a mangled, tangled, hairy, confusing mess. The essence of the problem is that no one anywhere on the spectrum has given people permission to be both secular and Christian — worldly and godly. It is always a black and white, either/or, in-or-out proposition. It is always a living in one world with contempt for the other. No one has found a both/and. No one has found a way to make it acceptable in America to be both a God/Jesus person and a salty, regular person of the world.

Biblical Roots, 2-world Theology, and Why Christians Appear Unattractive

Underlying this tension between the church and the world is an enormous theological issue that blocks the gate to the spiritual journey for a great many people. It is a problem that goes all the way back to the very beginning of the Judeo-Christian story. For it is in the Biblical story of creation that God and the world began their mutual hatred and mutual love for each other.

Before addressing how the Christian story of creation is the underlying root of the two-world tension, it must be re-stated that this book is written from the perspective of the Christian outsider. When this book says, "The Christian Church thinks..." or "Christianity believes..." it is stating what many non-Christians and non-practicing Christians perceive the Church to believe and say.

As most Sunday School children know, the entire Bible starts with the words, "In the beginning, God created the heavens and the earth" (Genesis 1: 1). The rest of the first chapter of Genesis goes on to describe how God created everything from light and dark to water and land, from beast and fish to plants and trees, and eventually man and woman. And each new creation is punctuated with the words "God saw that it was good." God was creating life and having a ball.

But then something happens. In verses 28-31 of the first chapter, God said to his new male and female, "Be fruitful and multiply, and fill the earth *and subdue it*; and *have dominion over*[5] the fish of the sea and over the birds of the air and over every living thing that moves upon the earth. And God said, 'Behold, *I have given you* every plant yielding seed which is upon the face of all the earth, and every tree with seed in its fruit; *you shall have them* for food. And to every beast of the earth, and to every bird of the air, and to everything that creeps on the earth, *everything that has the breath of life, I have given [to you]* every green plant for food.' And it was so" [emphasis mine].

From the story of creation up to the present day, humanity has had the mentality that it is our RIGHT to use and abuse the earth and all its resources, as we see fit. Inherent in that story is the notion that earth is less important than humanity, and that the earth and "everything that has the breath of life" exist for our needs and us. Inherent in that story is a condescending view of the world. Earth and its other inhabitants are an integral part of human existence, but they are clearly less important than humans.

17

Now, whether you buy into the Judeo-Christian creation story, or not, isn't the point. It doesn't matter. The point is that all of Western society, and even much of Eastern society, has been built upon this story. Christians have so dominated the world for the last 2000 years that this notion of the earth being subject to humanity is woven into the very fabric of our being. All of us are caught in it.

This is why the Gaia Principle — "The earth does not belong to us, but we belong to it"— and even environmentalism are still viewed as peripheral and even flaky, and have taken so long to even begin to catch on. We'll recycle our cans and our newspapers, but we still believe the earth exists to meet our needs. The trees, the ore, and the oil: All of it is ours.

Then something else happens. In Genesis 3: 14, after Adam and Eve have eaten the fruit of the forbidden tree, God gets angry. The sequence of events that follows is what is known as *the Fall*, or humanity's fall from grace. We fell out of full favor with God.

In the verses that follow, God punishes humanity for its disobedience. God gives to humanity both suffering and hard work as consequences of the fact that Adam and Eve refused to play by God's rules. On top of that, and perhaps most hurtful of all, God removed Adam and Eve from God's presence. God kicked them out of the Garden of Eden! And, to insure they wouldn't try to sneak back in, God "placed [an angel] and a flaming sword which turned every way, to guard the way to the tree of life" (3:24).

By putting the angel with the flaming sword at the gate of the Garden, God was not only guarding the trees (the other forbidden tree in the garden was the Tree of Immortality), so that humans would not live forever, but was also insuring that the humans would be far from God. Because we humans had pissed God off, God didn't want us around. God was in the Garden; humans were out of the Garden.

Christianity has spent the last 2000 years trying to get back into the Garden. All of the church's theology is crafted around this one point (see Chapter Nine). To Christianity, the Garden is, for most intents and purposes, heaven. It is to be with God, in God's good graces, enjoying the fruits of knowledge and immortality.

That little story is the source of a great many of our spiritual problems today. For, we are still stuck with this Christian notion that everything out in the world stinks and is bad, and everything inside the Garden (or heaven) is godly and good. This, as the Christian story goes, is the whole reason God sent Jesus to the world — to redeem it, to bring humanity back into God's favor.

This "earth is bad" mentality is not just a Christian notion. Any religion or philosophy that includes reincarnation or life after death is based on the notion that this world is bad, and hopefully, after we die we'll go to a better place, even if that "other place" is simply non-existence.

This creates a tension between God and the world. God and God's creation are not one, but are in opposition to each other.

Christianity has created an all-pervasive mindset in America that God condemns the world, and believes that the world disregards and even hates God.

The belief is that you cannot live happily in both the world and God's kingdom. You have to pick which world you choose. Then you must join in the fight against the other. As a result, those two worlds have been doing battle for a good long time.

The worst effect of this condemnation of the earth/world and exaltation (or "lifting up") of God and heaven is the old guilt by association. Anyone on the path to try to get back into the Garden — that is to say, anyone who is Christian — is good. Anyone not on the road back to the Garden, anyone who actually enjoys the world and finds God's creation good is "of the world" and "worldly," and is therefore bad. And the job of people on the path is to get everyone else on the path, or fight them.

You may or may not hear this preached explicitly from pulpits or taught in Christian classrooms, but that isn't the point.[9] The point is that this is how Christians act! Christians are seen as acting as if they are good and everyone else is bad.

Those who are trying to get back to the Garden look down on the people of the world. They view the world's thinking as flawed and less than Christian thinking. Christians condescendingly think they must educate the world and get the world on the path to the Garden, or heaven.

One of the most respected Christian theologians of the 20th Century was Reinhold Niebuhr. In his seminal work, *Moral Man and Immoral Society*, he perfectly articulates this concept by saying that Jesus was *in the world*, but not *of the world*. Jesus participated in the world, but came to take us to something better. Christians, Niebuhr said, are to do likewise. Christians are to exist in the world but not become sucked into the becoming one with the world. Again, world is bad; God, Garden, and heaven are good.

Surely God is not in the suffering of the world, Christians think. Surely, God is not in the death and destruction that go on in the world. Surely, God is about something far greater than this, they say.

The bottom line for Christians is that God is not here. Jesus was here for a while. But even after his resurrection he got out of town as fast as possible by floating up into the sky. The simple Christian notion that God *sent* his Son (Jesus) implies that God is somewhere other than here. Otherwise, why would he need to be "sent" anywhere? Jesus' spirit is here, but that's about it. The earth is a place to escape from. God is somewhere else. God dislikes the world (outside the Garden), the thinking goes. Thus, Christianity's God will always be a sky-God, never a personal and everyday God, until creation is re-interpreted and re-understood.

Not only does the Bible begin with this earth-is-bad mentality, but it ends with it, as well. The book of Revelation, which is the Bible's final chapter, speaks of the badness of the world, the evil one who will come to rule it for a time, as well as the destruction of it. Eventually, it will be restored as God's good creation. It will be the Kingdom of God — the world as God intended it to be. Again, implicit in this is that how the world is now is bad and not what God wants.

At nearly all points in the Bible and in Christian thinking, the world and all

19

who are associated with it — such as you — are damned.[10] This is why Christians continually offend people. They look down on you. Though few admit it, and despite their nice words, they arrogantly believe that they are better than you. They are the people on the path to God; you are not. In actuality, few Christians realize that both their underlying philosophy and their Garden-driven behaviors indicate belief of their superiority. That is a harsh fact.

They might say, "Oh, Christians are no better. For, we have all sinned and fallen short of the glory of God." But they will go on to try to convince you that they are better because they have found a way out of life's mess, a way back to God. And if you don't get on their way, you are going to hell.

They will tell you that you must decide — the Garden or the world. Either your life is about striving to heaven, which is another way of thinking of the Garden, or it is about living in and enjoying the world. Choose, sinner!

Because Christians believe their Garden-centered, or heaven-centered, thinking is the one true belief system, they treat non-Christians with contempt. In turn, non-Christians volley back contempt. The two-world tension is born. Non-Christians desire to have a relationship with God, but want nothing to do with the religion that arrogantly claims to own God and the path to God.

The non-Christian then throws out Christianity, throws out its Bible, and often throws out its God, all because of the contemptuous Christians and their bad theology. Non-Christians are left to explore other ways to God, other concepts of God, and other religions. Non-Christians and non-practicing Christians are left trying to ascend Maslow's hierarchy toward God, but must reject one otherwise great way of doing it.

The First Steps on the Spiritual Journey Toward God

But, what if the Christians are wrong?

What if the Christians got Christianity wrong?

What if there is another way of looking at it? What if there are ways to the God of Christianity that don't require Christianity the religion? What if it's not about getting back to God, but getting God back here? What if God doesn't hate the world?

What if there is no Garden but this beautiful, rich, good earth God gave us?

At the core of these questions is the essence of what it will take for you to move past your Basic needs as you draw closer to God. The first step is to reject the notion that Christianity owns the one way to God. More than likely, you already think this way. That is part of why you are contemptuous of Christianity and Christians.

Thus, at several points in the following chapters traditional Christian theology is debunked and deconstructed so that you can better understand the Bible and God. ("Traditional" theology is that which is generally understood by most people outside the church to be the thinking of the Christian Church about God, Jesus, and related matters.) Deconstruction of traditional theology is also done so that you can have room and permission to create a theology (based to some greater or lesser degree on the Bible) that makes sense to you!

The second step is to realize that you can have a rich and full relationship with the God of Christianity without having to go through Christianity. In other words, you can throw out Christianity, if you desire, without having to throw out its God. Maybe you do this already, too. But this is a bit of a sticking point because you may not know how to get to God all by yourself. It would be nice to have a leader or spiritual community to help you. But, because you are not interested in Christianity's way, you have to figure out a way to do it alone.

However, despite your rejection of Christianity, the point that must be emphasized is that the Bible does not have to be thrown out, as well. This is the third step: To recognize that the Bible can do good. If the Bible is interpreted in fresh and invigorating new ways, the Christian Bible can be a highly effective tool in building a fulfilling and strong relationship with God. This is the most important point of this chapter. It is the point on which the rest of this book is based.

The point of this book is to draw you into relationship with God (or enhance your existing relationship) using radically new interpretations of the Bible as the primary vehicle. It is to help you in your individual quest for the Spirit of the Universe.

The purpose is not to stick new interpretations of the Bible down your throat, as that would really be the same crime of which you accuse Christianity.

The underlying point is to give you permission to doubt and ask your questions, and to then see those questions as the very key to your greater relationship with God. Further, the purpose of the following chapters is to teach you how to interpret scripture by yourself in ways that make sense to you. The purpose is to teach you methods for interpretation so that you can create your own content, based on the Bible and the God of the Bible.

At different points in this book new interpretations of the Bible are offered for your consideration. You can accept or reject them based on whether they resonate inside you as true.

The perfect starting point for considering fresh interpretations of the Bible is the beginning — creation. It is to open to new ways of understanding the very text we have been looking at in this chapter.

Re-interpreting Creation

What is missing from the whole perceived Christian scenario is memory of the fact that God created the world and found it to be good! The flaw in Christian thinking (apart from the fact that Christians actually believe that this was literally the way the world was created, as if someone was there to document it) is the belief that God is not in the world and of the world even though it was God who created the world.

Creation is the single most visible and tangible contact we have with our creator. Even if you believe the Bible is the actual word of God, the Bible passed through human minds and human hands before it came to its present form. It is dependent upon human translations and interpretations. As will be explained in later chapters, the Bible is in need of fresh interpretations if it is to be a source of life and growth to you on your spiritual journey toward God.

In contrast to the Bible, creation is pure God. It is, to a very large degree, as it was in the beginning. It has evolved, but it is still clearly God's creation. Whether God used clay, a big bang, evolution, or smoke and mirrors really isn't the point. The Spirit of the Universe created this world, and it is good, beautiful, and majestic. It has hardship, suffering, destruction, and death, but that doesn't change the fact that it is good. In fact, as we shall see in Chapter Seven, even these elements of life are blessings from God.

God is very much of and in creation. To begin the spiritual journey is to seek the big-G God. And to seek God is not to look beyond what is. It is not to long for a heavenly Garden. Seeking God begins with the realization that God is in God's creation just waiting to be discovered and embraced.

God longs to speak to us through the roar of the waterfall, the swaying of the wheat field, the wail of the child, the ferocity of the tornado, the smell of peonies, the bite of the winter's cold, the death of a pet, the vastness of the deserts, the warmth of fire, the love of another person, and so much more. All communicate God.

This is what is behind our cultural fascination with Native American spirituality. Native Americans, the thinking goes, live fully in the world and fully in the spirit world. There is no tension or discord between the two, only perfect union of spirit and matter. And that enchants non-Native Americans. That is what we live for — that unity, that integration of life and spirit.

To seek God is to see God. To go forward on the spiritual journey — ascend Maslow's pyramid — is to see the fullness of God in all things, right here and now. In Maslow's upper tier of Being needs are "Truth," "Beauty," and "Goodness," not to mention "Caring, Creativity, and Intimacy with God." The point of relationship with God is not to claim to hold the one truth of how the world was created. Instead, it is to live in harmony with that creation. If God is the Spirit of the Universe, then to become intimate with God is to increase your level of communion with creation and nature. It is to see the beauty, goodness, and truth in all of life.

The spiritual journey is not to go anywhere, per se. It is, instead, to walk in this world forever seeing God everywhere and hearing God communicate through all of life's experiences. To seek God is to see God as in the world and of the world. It is to understand that God lives in harmony with God's creation, and that we are called to live in harmony with God, creation, and all things.

You've heard it a thousand times, but it still holds true. We begin to find God by slowing down. God is in all things (or *is* all things), but God of the big-G is only to be fully found when you let go of your fascination with lesser needs. Only when you step out of the chase for more money, more prestige, more highs, more thighs, and more stuff will you make room for a fuller understanding of God. It is not to negate the beauty and importance of these things, but to see them as only part of the larger puzzle of life.

Until you let go of lower levels of existence, until you let go of lesser needs, you will not begin to see God in all things. It is a paradox of life; you must let go of things in order to see God in those things.

To seek God is to re-orient life. To seek God is, first, to desire God. Second, it is to rebuild your life around finding God and living out God's calling to you. It is to orient your life to higher things.

While you personally may not be able to seek and find God as part of a Christian spiritual community at this point in your life, your own spiritual hunger demands that you begin to seek God, somewhere, somehow. Your soul will not find rest and contentment until you do. To that ends, this book is an attempt to re-work and re-invent Christian theology so that you may have help in your quest for God.

So these are your first steps. If you desire to find the water that will quench your spiritual thirst, get off the treadmill of life. If you desire to climb "higher" to God, you must relinquish obsession with the lower.

Quit going so fast. Begin to see the beauty and richness in more than just toys and stuff. Open up to finding God in all things, and all people. Listen for the message, truths, and wisdom God speaks through all things in the world. Recognize that God is both in and of the world, and that you can be, too. You can be with God and at peace in the world. You can be a salty person of the world, and an intensely God-loving, kind and gracious person. You don't have to pick one over the other. You begin by simply believing it is possible. Then take your first baby steps away from lesser things toward higher things — toward God.

Chapter 3

[Ask Questions to Get to God]

"There is more faith in honest doubt, believe me, than in half the creeds."

— Alfred Tennyson

"Reexamine all that you have been told or read in any books, and dismiss whatever insults your soul."

— Walt Whitman

"Gimme somethin' to believe in!"

— *Poison* (music group)

IN THE QUEST FOR GOD, in the quest for new paths to God, and in the quest to find the fruits of relationship with God there is nothing more important than your questions.

Questions and doubt are what move us higher up the pyramid of needs toward God. They also help us find even greater fulfillment from life at all points on the spiritual journey. They help us understand the roots of our discontent and longing, and the solutions for getting past them. Thus, this chapter is a collection of snippets designed to help you understand the necessity of your questions in drawing closer to God.

Since my childhood, there has been one piece of Christian theology that has been exceedingly difficult for me to understand. Ironically, it is the one portion of Christian theology that is most frequently tossed about by Christians. It is the answer to the question, "Why did Jesus die?"

The answer, as many learned in Sunday School, is that he died for our sins. Specifically, he died to take away our sins. Even more specifically, and I learned this only much later in life while in seminary, the answer to why Jesus died is quite complex. I will attempt to lay it out in the paragraphs that follow.

Ancient societies (right up through the Middle Ages, and even still today in certain parts of the world) were organized in hierarchies: From slaves up to laborers, then up to merchants, landowners, and princes. Finally, at the top of the socio-economic chain was the king.

Interestingly, in these hierarchies if you in any way brought harm to a person below you, short of death, you were not required to apologize or even give it a second thought. However, if you harmed or even offended someone above you, you had to not only beg for forgiveness, but pay for it somehow. Your offense immediately put you into the debt of the one you offended. The greater the offense, the greater the debt. The higher up the chain the person was whom you offended, the greater the payment required of you.

If a laborer stole fruit from a merchant it would require not nearly the high price as if that same piece of fruit had been stolen from a prince. The first might cost you a finger or a pig. The latter might cost you a hand or a life of imprisonment, or both. But if you offended the queen in some way, you and your family might pay with your lives.

In Christian theology of the past 2000 years it is believed that we humans have offended and gone against not just the king, but against the God who is over even the king. Adam and Eve, the original humans in the Christian creation story, disobeyed God and we humans have been disobeying and offending God ever since. This is sin and we are stuck in it. God has historically been considered an angry judge who will punish and smite us for our sins.

Basically, because we are mere mortals and God is... well... God (and quite above any king), there is no way we can possibly repay the debt we owe for all we do and have done to offend God. Not our lives, nor our families, nor our ancestors, nor our descendants' lives and the lives of our pets can possibly atone for our offense of God.

So God, being merciful, sent his only son to die as payment for our offenses. By doing so, God insured that we would not have to die and rot in hell (even though our dying and rotting would not pay the debt, anyway). You can now live knowing that God is not mad at you. If you accept Jesus Christ as your personal Lord and Savior, you will not go to hell when you die, the thinking goes.

The great problem I had with all of this hierarchy-offense stuff was that I was never taught it. When I should've been learning the angry judge stuff, I was being taught that God is our loving Parent who only wants good for us. God was never someone I had to be saved from. And, though my father was a pastor, my parents never planted in me the notion that I am a wicked person. I may do dumb or bad things, but I am neither a dumb nor bad person. They told each of their children that each is a child of the great creator — a good person of a loving God.

Put plainly, the notions of an angry God who seeks to punish me, Jesus dying for my sins, and my burning in hell were just gibberish in my younger years. They made no sense to me, despite how hard I tried to understand. I wanted to be a Christian so badly. I wanted to fit in, but I just didn't get it. I had so much respect and love for Jesus as the master teacher of love and God, but the Savior stuff was literally beyond my comprehension. So, I felt like an outsider. I went on to spend the bulk of my childhood, and later a four-year bachelor's degree and a four-year master's degree genuinely attempting to make sense of it all.

I tried to answer questions like, "If God owns the bank, the FDIC, and the government that sets the lending rates, why waste a son making a debtor's obligation go away? If God wanted the debt gone, why not just write the debt off? Poof, it's gone." I fought with questions on other topics, such as, "If God is even remotely familiar with psychology and human behavior (and God would be, cuz God created it), then wouldn't God know that placing a tree in the middle of the Garden of Eden and saying, 'Don't eat it" would automatically make any naked garden couple go right to that tree and eat?" And, "In that case, wasn't God really just setting humanity up for failure? I mean, could they really be expected to resist such an obvious temptation?" These were just a tiny sampling of the questions I wrestled with for years.

Slowly, years later, the hard work paid off. I began to understand what the church taught, what I believed, and where the two met and didn't meet. The problem then became finding a spiritual community that believed what I believed, or could at least meet me where I was at. Unfortunately, I was taught God's love long before I developed an appreciation for the dogma. Thus, no matter how much I loved the music, the gorgeous buildings, the good people, and the Sunday morning centering it brought to my life, the Christian worship of the hierarchy-offense-angry-God story always got in the way. As a result, I never really fit in Christian circles. But that is another story for another book.

The point is that finally the Christian beliefs began to make sense. I did not buy into them all, but at least I understood some of them and could decide whether to accept or reject them in my own walk with God.

And *this*, I discovered, is what the Bible and Jesus are all about. No one ever teaches it to you in Sunday School, or confirmation, or from the pulpit on Sunday morning. The point of all Christianity is to draw closer to God. It is not to just accept a list of beliefs (as is implied in the reciting of creeds during worship services). *Drawing closer to God means asking questions.* Through the questions we reach greater understanding and nearness to God today. Our questions are what drive our movement on the spiritual journey. They move us higher.

Getting to God means asking the questions that your own personal curiosity and doubt give rise to. It is to then pursue them, no matter where they lead, until they give rise to a new batch of questions, and so on. To draw closer to God means to not be satisfied with simply accepting somebody else's answers when they don't make sense.[11] We begin to resolve the tension between God and world by allowing God to address our worldly questions, by creating space for God to fit into our worldly dilemmas.

This is the walk with God that every human takes, in some form or another. Questions have driven men and women to prayer, to church, to read, and to inquire of Jesus as ways to draw closer to God. Similarly, questions have driven men and women out of the church, away from Jesus, away from prayer, and still, oddly, closer to God.

Permission to Ask Questions

I recall many hours as a child sitting at our kitchen table talking with my mom as she prepared meals. On one particular late Sunday morning I returned from church to find mom busy in the kitchen once again. I had just spent the morning in robes as an acolyte at two services and in Sunday School during the third. I plopped down in a kitchen chair and chatted with mom as she busily prepared the Sunday noon roast.

While I have long since forgotten the exact topic of the conversation, I do know we were discussing what I had learned that morning in Sunday School. Feeling great frustration with what had been taught I blurted out, "Mom, it just doesn't add up. It just doesn't make sense." No sooner had I said it than I winced, uncertain of how my exasperation would be treated.

My mother, who would herself go on to be a nationally recognized educator in her denomination and also teach early childhood education at the seminary level, slowly set down the paring knife and the carrot she had been peeling. A look of grim seriousness came over her as she turned to me. She leaned her six-children-later weight against the counter, as though needing greater support for what was about to be said. As if somehow knowing that a rare and sacred threshold was about to be crossed; as if somehow knowing that her life and the life of her youngest son were about to change forever, she quietly said, "Sven, don't believe everything you hear in church."

The journey began. With those few words spoken by my mother — the pastor's wife! — my spiritual journey, which would lead me far, far from the beaten path, was given permission to take its first wobbly steps. At the age of ten my life began.

What my mother said was just short of heresy. Yet, in deference to how my parents work, I know she never would've said it if it didn't agree with the general spiritual and parenting principles my parents lived on. Tacitly, I understood at some point afterwards that my father doubted too. But here was my mother explicitly encouraging me to not accept blindly what I was being taught, and to begin to pull it apart and decide what works for me. She was teaching me to personalize God.

She did not say, "Well, you should believe this instead." She told me to not believe everything, as if it was up to *me*, a ten year old, to decide what I would believe. My beliefs, she was saying, are between God and me.

Whether she realized it or not, by teaching me to question my faith with integrity and natural curiosity, my mother opened a door for me that could completely change my life. She gave me permission to change my spiritual life, and thereby radically affect every other aspect of my life.

I ended up choosing to pass through it. That began a twenty year journey that would cost me friends, a career, a marriage, pride, a great deal of money, lots of time, and much more. I grew to realize that if the soul is to be free, it will suffer. Yet that path of discovering who I am and what I believe was the only path that would feed my soul and bring me deep satisfaction. It was the only path that would draw me authentically to God.

The Price of Asking Questions

As my mother knew when she uttered those words to me in our kitchen, one of the great problems with going on your own spiritual journey when you are a Christian, or when you live in a Christian culture (as many would argue we still do in America), is that Christianity and questions don't quite mix.

Christianity owns God. Or at least it thinks and acts like it does. So, it doesn't take kindly to questions. God may love our questions, because eventually they do bring us closer to God. But Christianity has a very different take on questions and doubt.

Questions are disliked by organized religion for three reasons. First, the more questions are raised, the more theologians have to come up with answers. Eventually, the Christian "logic" becomes so convoluted that it is not only difficult to understand, but nearly impossible to teach and pass on to others, particularly without laughing at the sheer ridiculousness of it all. That is why Christian sermons often sound like absolute nonsense. That is also why religion usually prefers to say, "Just believe."

Using the prior issue of God and human debt as an example, what would the church's best response be to the question, "Why didn't God just write off human debt if we had so offended God and God was so desiring to show mercy?" If the church tries to answer the why, then it is accused of trying to know the mind of God. This is a bit presumptuous, even for the boldest of Christian leaders.

But some Christians will take a stab at it. Unfortunately, the response is bound to be more contrived than believable. The simplicity and believability of the logic for writing it off and sparing the son are almost too hard to overcome. Exasperated, the church simply says, "Don't ask questions. Just believe."

Second, questions challenge the authority of the leaders, tradition, and long-held beliefs. Questions and doubt steal control from those who are in charge. You can have questions, but you can only take them as far as the church's next pat answer. Doubt is a form of Satan. Doubt breeds division. To doubt means that our theology and thinking are no longer under control. It does not enhance the church, nor does it bring you closer to God, the thinking goes. Questions breed unrest, and unrest brings change, both of which are seen as bad for any institution.

In one of my years at a Catholic seminary, I was sitting in a class in which there was a discussion about doubt and faith. Most (but not all) of my classmates were fervently espousing the negative effect of doubt on faith and Christian community, as the instructor, a nun, quietly listened.

Unable to abide the discussion any longer one student insolently blurted out, "Doubt is not the enemy of faith, but the precursor to faith of strength and real-world applicability. Unless you have doubted, unless you have been shaken to the core, unless you have walked through 'the valley of the shadow of death,' unless you have known the 'Oh, Shit!' experience of what feels like the very absence of God, do not go into the pulpit! Do not step into church leadership and preaching unless you know what it means to lose God. For, if you have never known faith-shattering doubt, you will never be able to speak relevantly to the people in the pew. 'Cuz that is where they are, caught up in doubts and despair, aching to find God, and aching to have their questions answered. And your tired clichés of 'just have faith' ain't going to help them one bit until your faith has been tested, broken, and steeled by the fires of doubt and disbelief."

With the topic now well exhausted for the day, the professor wisely moved on to other topics. Later, as the future priests were leaving the classroom, the nun-professor pulled the insolent student aside and quietly said, "Thank you. You can say some things that I cannot."

This nun allowed the student to speak the brief defense of doubt as a strengthener of faith. She never could have spoken those words herself. It was clear that both she and the students lived, worked, and studied in an environment that was hostile to doubt and questioning.

Still, there is a third and far more interesting way that organized religion exhibits intolerance for questioning and doubt. It is not the leadership, alone, that dislikes queries and expressions of uncertainty. Often the most powerful resistance to questioning comes from the people in the pew.

My mother, now an old woman, enjoys telling the story of one particular student she had many years ago. Mom had been teaching a Bible study class for quite some time to a group of middle-age women at a large, conservative suburban church. After class one evening a woman in the class approached my mother and stated with exasperation, "We don't like you as a teacher. Your questions make us think too much!"

In the church those people who are "change agents" encounter great resistance and obstacles being thrown in their way. This resistance to change and unwillingness to think in new ways have led those who desire fresh answers and changes to leave the church in frustration. While such departures bring lessening of frustration, they also bring greater difficulty. Rather than being helped to find new growth and deeper understanding in a community of support and encouragement, the questioner must engage the spiritual journey alone. That is no small feat.

Granted, doubt can breed division of people who are supposed to think alike. But, in the long run doubt and questioning lead to an increased depth and richness of faith.

Further, as the seminary student in the nun's classroom clearly articulated, what we are seeing in America today is that the church's answers fail to resolve people's questions and meet people's needs. The result is that outside the church is a whole mass of people who are unified in their indifference (or even contempt) toward the church and its theology. Doubt and questions have bred a loose unity.

It is a remarkably similar mindset to that of the Peasant Revolt of the 1500s in central Europe. Fueled, in part, by a loathing of the church's oppressive practices and apathy toward the church's theology, the common people lived in a two-world tension between loving God and bearing great discontent with the church. Their contempt grew so great that they rose up against the political and religious structures of their day. Christianity fought them and the changes they sought with every weapon in its arsenal. However, on the backs of great thinkers and questioners like Martin Luther, John Calvin, and John Knox, to name a few, what emerged was a church and theology that were radically different from what had preceded them.

It is worth noting that the thinkers who have asked the most questions and expressed the greatest doubt over the last 2000 years are the very same people who have been the most instrumental in changing the face of Christianity and religion. Starting with Jesus' questioning of the religion of his day, questioners such Augustine, Aquinas, Copernicus, Luther, Calvin, Kant, Kierkegaard, Jung, Bonhoeffer, Bultmann, Rahner, Martin Luther King, Jr., and others have brought massive change to how the world thinks about and interacts with God. These questioners and doubters have brought new life to the faith by questioning the faith.

As further evidence of organized religion's contempt for questioning and doubt, nearly every one of the great questioners of faith paid a heavy price (to be discussed in Chapter Eleven). Even though it is the courageous questioners who change the face of religion, the full force of the institution often crushes those who question and attempt change. It cannot be forgotten that it is the courageous questioners who rework their own beliefs, and then help us grow and change ours.

Being reprimanded or censured by the church is the least of your worries. You will soon find that neglecting your questions only gives rise to long-term pain. Denying your questions will not fill your soul. If you have questions and you simply deny them by stuffing them away rather than exploring them, you will become spiritually constipated. You will rot from the inside out, falling farther and farther away from God and the peace, hope, love, power, and purpose God offers. Your life will become hollow and shallow.

This isn't some cheesy, ethereal spiritual mumbo-jumbo. It is truth born of experience. Denying your questions breeds all sorts of ugly stuff.

In the long run, questions do not take us away from God, but to God. They are our pursuit of God. They make life hard in the short term, but in the long term they increase understanding and appreciation. Deny the questions, and you are walking away from a richer and fuller understanding of God and the fruits that understanding brings.

The problem is that Christianity, the church, the Bible, and the whole Christian story naturally give rise to far more questions than answers. It all can take a lifetime to understand, not to mention believe, if you so choose. For God is a process in which to walk, not simply a destination at which to arrive.

The Bible encourages us to dive in and ask our questions. The Bible is filled with references to humanity being encouraged to seek God (1Chronicles 16: 11; 28: 09; Isaiah 55: 06; Jeremiah 29: 13; Matthew 6: 33) What does it mean to seek? If *to find* means to finally have the answers, then *to seek* means to have and to follow the questions. And we are encouraged to *seek* God. The Bible pushes us to ask our questions of God and about God, and to attempt to find answers to them. The Bible encourages questioning. We need only have the courage to go to the dark places where our questions lead.

Understanding Doubt

To better understand the spiritual journey, to better understand the movement from religious certainty through questioning and doubt to synthesis of faith and doubt, it helps to imagine an old village on the edge of a giant forest. The always-sunny village on the edge of the thick, dark forest represents a sort of easy, uncritical stage of spiritual existence. Here the believer follows the beliefs and patterns of behavior that are laid down by the church and by former generations. This non-questioning spirituality does not doubt, but simply believes, often using willpower.

Life in the village is characterized by a state of dependence, especially upon external authorities (institutions, sacred books, leaders, etc.). The dependence is similar to that of a child. The child's life is about absorption of information and following the behavior patterns prescribed by a parent or authority figure. This state is simultaneously seen as both naive and mighty in faith. It is not particularly worldly, but it is quite confident in its authorities, its beliefs, and its God.

This form of spirituality is most readily available in more conservative-leaning branches of Christianity where questioning is discouraged. It is not inherently bad or good. It is simply one form of spiritual-religious existence.

If the village is the sunny skies of clarity and dependence, then the forest next to the village represents the dark realm of spiritual questioning. The forest is anything that challenges faith and the peaceful life in the village. People of the village warn their children to never enter the forest. For others have entered and never returned. There are horrible stories of people getting lost in the forest of questions and dying there alone.

Yet for the person who feels drawn to the forest there is simply no avoiding it. The answers of the village are not enough to satisfy the questions welling up inside. And so, the restless soul enters the forest and becomes a spiritual seeker — one who doesn't just need easy answers, but needs answers to his or her specific questions. And the journey begins.

In Arthurian Legend it is said that as each knight of the Round Table commenced his quest for the Holy Grail he would leave the walled city and walk his horse along the edge of the forest, entering not where a path existed, but where he felt the impulse to go in. (The Grail, or chalice, was believed to be the very cup Jesus used in his last supper with his followers. It was the cup of life from which all good flowed. The grail quest was a metaphor for the spiritual journey toward God, who was and is the cup of life.) The knights considered it unbecoming of a knight to make their entry into their quest where a path already existed. Nobility for the knight was found in original experience, on his own path in the quest for the cup of life. At that never-before-used point of entry the journey began, just as it does for any spiritual seeker.

It is slow going in the forest. For the spiritual forest is about crushing sorrows, pains, losses, and fear-filled anxiety. It is also about the enormity of questions and doubts that faith and hardship give birth to. It is dark in the forest, where getting lost is inevitable. The sun seldom breaks through the thick canopy of trees and foliage. Certainty is gone. This region is highly spiritual, but hardly religious. For the deliberate seeker, this is a long phase of great growth and great loss, similar to the teens, the twenties, or even mid-life crisis.

It is very interesting to note that two of the highest grossing movies of all time include this forest metaphor as part of the spiritual journey of its protagonist. In both *Lion King* and *Star Wars: The Empire Strikes Back* the lead character actually enters a scary wood or thicket alone as climax to a period of growth and change. In the wood both characters, *Simba* and *Luke Skywalker*, encounter their great fears as well as a deeper understanding of themselves, which in both cases is symbolized by the image of their own father.

This theme is also magically portrayed in the wildly popular *Lord of the Rings* trilogy. Nearly the entire trilogy is one big spiritual forest scene. Facing fears, overcoming adversity, coping with loss, questioning beliefs, finding new understandings of self, being guided by a spirit or energy, being supported by a community of friends, and achieving a higher form of existence on the spiritual journey are the threads that hold these movies together and give them such depth and power.

It is in these woods of spiritual doubt that many Americans find themselves. Today, America is no longer in the village; no longer theologically conservative; no longer spiritually safe and sunny. Since the 1960s, driven by emptiness, rebellion, and spiritual longing, America has become spiritually independent, venturing out of the village and deep into the forest where the pat answers of the village no longer work. Americans are wandering in the massive forest, trying to understand themselves as well as their questions of the village's beliefs.

Here in the forest parts of the self and new understandings of God are found. For, God is very much alive, breathing, and moving in the life of the forest. Hidden deep in the forest are gems of wisdom waiting to be uncovered, glorious waterfalls of new thinking in which to be bathed, as well as dark beasts to trip us up, and old sages to provide guidance.

Many in America have found the courage to leave the security and convenience of organized religion to enter the spiritual forest. On this journey they have found not only great fear and disorientation, but also richness and newness of thinking. This phase of spiritual development is not bad, either. It simply is an excruciating, yet sublime part of the journey of spiritual growth and movement to things higher. It is the hard work of life with God toward God.

Yet for the rare seeker who is diligent, there is life on the other side. The forest does end. There is sunlight again. Years away, on the other side of the deep dark forest is the sunlight of spiritual re-birth. The answers of the village have been challenged and questioned, and new insights and depth have been found in the forest. Questions get answers, and faith and doubt become integrated into a new, more powerful whole. Some questions that don't get answered aren't so frightening, and are simply accepted as life questions to be lived with. On the other side of the wood synthesis is finally achieved.

This is where God and world come together and live as one. There is no God-world tension. There is only union and cooperation between the two (true co-operation, *to operate together*), as well as mutual love. God's kingdom is discovered right here on earth, rising up from within us, and being seen in everything around us.

Unfortunately, while most of America is in the forest, most of Christianity is still in the village. The people of the village cannot understand why their answers do not work for the forest people. They don't realize that it is a completely different world in the forest.

Yet there are a few segments of Christianity in America that are finding that they, as a whole, have wandered into the forest. This is a sign of progress and openness to the spiritual growth process. However, those caught in the forest (generally the moderate and liberal denominations) are no more adept at answering the questions of the forest than are the villagers. While these denominations have a worldliness that at least understands the depth and severity of the new questions, it is still a case of the proverbial blind leading the blind.

Thus, while the spiritual seeker may find some warmth and even kinship in these churches, he or she is unlikely to find in them a path through the forest. As a result, a spiritual seeker may maintain only a brief or passing relationship with such a community. Simply put, there is not enough spiritual leadership or guidance to provide release from the significant forest afflictions that tear at the seeker's soul.

Until leaders rise up who have found the other side, Christianity will largely continue to hold God trapped in the village of what-was. Christianity will continue to be completely unable to meet the spiritual demands of a country of people who are cold and shivering in the forest.

If Christianity is to be even remotely close to relevant today it must set God free to be the God of the village, the forest, and even the other side of the wood. It must change its understanding of God. It must allow for a God that is different things to different people. It must allow for the validity of the questions of spiritual seekers. More fundamentally, it must recognize (and you must recognize) the absolute necessity of doubt in drawing closer and deeper into relationship with God. Spiritually speaking, it must realize that it takes both a village *and a forest* to raise a child.

With God to God

Life with God — life with the Spirit of the Universe — is a simple proposition. As it says in Micah 6: 8, it is to "love mercy, do justice, and walk humbly with your God".... *your* God, the God you draw closer to because of your questions, your doubts, and your seeking.

The role of Christianity and the church, therefore, is to facilitate your walk by:

1) Helping you hear God's voice inside you and in your life, thereby helping you to grow closer to the spirit of God in the universe;

2) Leading you through the forest of questions and doubt, not by forcing answers on you in a sort of spiritual date rape, but by helping you find *your* beliefs and *your* answers to *your* questions;

3) Helping you find your God-given purpose.

If you are a spiritual seeker, until you can find some kind of spiritual community that does facilitate that walk and growth, you will continue to feel unrest in your soul. You will be forced by the need for answers to go through the forest on your own. It would be easier and far less painful to be led through the forest or to go with others. But if you have the courage, you can do it alone. In fact, if you are to truly feel alive, you must do it alone if there is no one to help you. For staying in the village will bleed the life out of you. Denying your questions is the most miserable of deaths.

So take God with you. Trust that God is there in the forest with new answers to meet your changing needs. At the same time, know that God is not there to "save" you, per se. God is there to let you fight for yourself, heal yourself, and become spiritually stronger. Life with God is no longer about dependence and desiring to have God take your troubles away and make everything better. Now it is about conversation, back and forth, question and answer. It is about peace and volatility. It is about love and anger. It is about suffering and release. It is about presence and absence. It is about finding and losing and finding again. It is about discovering, eventually, that you are a spiritual adult, and God trusts your decision-making.

This also means that part of the spiritual journey is not only questioning, but speculating answers. Just as God gives answers from external sources, God has given you the ability to create answers to your own pressing questions. God has given you the freedom to incorporate answers from whatever sources you may find. God has given you a mind and an ability to test your answers to see if they are strong enough to buoy you.

It is not just about getting your spiritual needs met by spiritual leaders, but about using the gifts God has given you to meet your own needs. Survival in the forest demands developing solutions that breathe life into you and resonate deep within you.

If you are already in the forest, keep questioning and creating solutions.

Perhaps ten years from now it will start to make a little bit of sense. Though, the more fervently you seek God, the harder the journey, but the shorter the likely duration of the pursuit. You will catch glimpses of sunlight from far ahead. Slowly you will emerge from your spiritual hard work and fatigue. Eventually, you will reach the other side and collapse. And one day you will scrape yourself up off the ground and you will stand upright in the sun while marveling at the growing new strength you feel. Then you will be ready for your return. For the journey does not end in the sun.

The heroic path demands a return to help others. Believe it or not, one day you may be back in the forest or even back in the village. You may find yourself leading people into or through the dark woods of doubt, questioning, seeking, and despair. Perhaps you will be throwing others onto your spiritual shoulders and carrying them out of the forest.

Whatever the case, the journey with God to God is a lifetime of challenges, growth, change, defeats, conquests, peace, power, and a whole lot of laughter. It is to walk courageously where your curiosity leads you. It is to lean on your questions as you once leaned on answers. This is the spiritual life: To discover ways to walk joyfully amid the sorrows and doubts of life, and to be an instrument of God in the world.

A Spiritual Exercise

The path to relationship with God is not easy. It is not easy to hear God's voice. It is not always easy to know what you believe and don't believe. It is not easy to know what your purpose in life is. For that matter, strange as it may sound, it is not always easy to even know who you are. This is why some people have trouble making decisions. They simply don't know themselves. Yet all of these elements, plus more, weave together on the spiritual journey.

Two highly effective methods for better discerning who you are, what you believe, and what your relationship with God is like are listed here. Neither was originally intended to be a spiritual exercise, but both are beneficial in that regard.

First, Joseph Campbell was fond of telling about a particular word in the Hindu language. The word is *neti*, which means *not this*. Campbell would say that sometimes in life you do not or cannot know what your exact path is. Sometimes the forest is so dark that vision is clouded. In times such as these, the only thing you can sometimes say is, "neti, neti, neti" — not this, not this, not this. Sometimes the right path reveals itself only by showing the wrong path. Sometimes we only know what we don't want.

With this in mind, as you struggle through this difficult period of your life, or through your difficult questions, to what can you say *neti*? To what beliefs, thoughts, and actions do you say *neti*? What are your *not this*-es? What is not-God for you? Often, while final answers and total understanding elude us, it is the *netis* that we know for sure. Write these out. What are the *netis* you know for sure?

The second exercise is taken from the thinking of Alexander Schmemann, a man most people in the Western Hemisphere have never heard of. Schmemann was a theologian in the Orthodox branch of Christianity. Specifically, he wrote about theology of liturgy, which means, loosely, Christian worship and all the components that go into it.

Schmemann's concept of *liturgical theology* was based on the premise that the way to determine what a given people believe is not to look at their writings of their beliefs or what they say they believe, but to look at what they do. Recognizing that behavior grows out of thinking and beliefs, actions are an excellent indicator of what people believe.

So, to determine what you believe, who you are, what you want, and what your relationship with God is presently — to determine what your coordinates are in the forest — simply look at what you do and have done. What do you do with regularity and consistency? What do you seldom do? What do you NEVER do? What do you often say you are going to do, but never really get around to doing? Actions and inactions indicate beliefs.

As an easy example, Jesus regularly extended love and kindness to all types of people. He brought love to social outcasts. He brought love to people on sacred holy days. He brought love to people who brought harm to him.

What do these actions indicate? By loving outcasts, we see that loving people was more important to him than his reputation and how people perceived him. By doing loving actions on holy days when inactivity was required by law, Jesus exhibits that love is more important to him than justice. Law is subservient to love. By bringing love to those who brought him harm, it can be inferred that his love ran deep, that retribution was not a big part of his character make up, and that at his core he's "a lover, not a fighter."

As another example, for years I had thought about starting my own church. I researched it, prayed about it, talked with people about it, and explored it. Four times I even took several steps toward doing it, including holding one or two services.

What I finally realized, only by looking back on my own actions and inaction, is that for as much as I really wanted to do pastor-type work, I did not, in fact, want to start a church by myself. I realized that I wanted help. I realized that I did not desire to do pastoral work badly enough to overcome my own fears and obstacles.

Such behavior could also indicate a person who simply has difficulty following through on intentions, but I had completed two academic degrees, several books and articles (and published some), and had worked for years at multiple jobs. Follow-through was not the issue. Follow-through on this one topic of starting a church *was* the issue.

By looking at my actions — repeated starts and stops in this one area of my life — I was able to see a piece of what I really believe, value, and desire. I realized that I desire to express what I believe, but not at the price of the enormous physical and mental energy necessary to sustain such an effort.[12] I also realized that an effective question for me to ask myself in my own spiritual journey is "What are the things I am *not* willing to exert energy for?" and to then ask myself what it is about that path that causes me to lose interest.

37

The challenge to these two spiritual exercises is to be reflective. It is to look on your own path and past with honesty and clarity. It is to find understanding of who you are and what you believe by going through the back door and side door. Still, it is questions that are the key to discovery and growth. You must be willing to face the questions.

So, why *did* Jesus die?

This brings us back to the original question from the beginning of the chapter, "Why did Jesus die? If it wasn't to satisfy some mythical angry judge, why did he die?"

The answer is simple. On a very human level, Jesus died because he was naive enough and had the courage enough to stand up to the religious institution of his day. He questioned authority and entrenchment, and spoke what he believed to be true. Religious institutions were just as intolerant then as now. That is why he died.

He questioned and challenged because the religious institution of the day was not succeeding in bringing people closer to God. In fact, like today, it was driving seekers away from God.

The religious institution of Jesus' day was power over people. Religious leaders were using their authority (which was both religious and political authority) to rob people of money and keep them entrenched in highly legalistic and judgmental theology. These facilitated a culture of oppression and fear.

Jesus died because he fought this theology and oppression. Jesus died because he also had answers to our questions. He tried to move people out of the village, through the forest, and into the light of a new understanding of God. More accurately, people were already discontent in the village and had entered the forest of questioning. Jesus sought to bring them into synthesis with the spirit of the religion that was on the other side of the forest. This would, in turn, bring people new hope, new joy, new life, new power, new purpose, and new peace.

People by nature, of course, hate change. Until the pain of staying the same gets bad enough, people won't change. So, it's far easier to get rid of the agent pushing for change, in this case Jesus.

Jesus did not die because God is an angry judge. You are not a wicked person in need of ransom to get you out of trouble. Jesus died because he had the courage to question that which was not right. He died because he brought questions to answers that no longer worked, and synthesis to doubts that had grown exhausting. He died because he had the courage to follow God's calling and enter his own spiritual forest, find the other side, and lead others to the new life he found. Jesus died because he desired to be nearer to God and to help others draw nearer to God. By having courage to question, Jesus gives us courage to do likewise.

May your questions and your courage lead you down such a noble and difficult path as Jesus walked. For, just as your questions exist to set you free and help you set others free, they exist to strip you of yourself, shake you to your soul, move you to God and the fruits God promises — joy, power, hope, purpose, love, and peace.

Chapter 4

[Separate Truths from "Facts" ... and Focus on Truths!]

"I think that to find meanings you have to look at things from different directions."

— Bev Doolittle, master painter of camouflage art

"Some problems are just too complicated for rational, logical solutions. They admit of insights, not answers."

— Jerome Wiesner

ALL ACROSS THE UNITED STATES, high-voltage power lines checker our cities, fields, mountains, and shorelines. They follow our highways, and enter our backyards. As they charge from power plants they are held up by giant steel scarecrows or peg after peg of old wooden poles.

These lines carry anywhere from 20,000 to 70,000 volts of electrical current, current that is quite unusable in a person's house, as is. Household appliances have little use for 20,000 volts. It is simply too much power. Instead, the average coffee maker, margarita-making blender, or Playstation 2 requires a mere 120-240 volts.

Therefore, the power companies must have ways to convert these massive amounts of energy coming from power plants into smaller and more functional energy for household use. This is the purpose of the transformer. The transformer

41

is that "box," roughly the size of a small trash can, that is attached to the top of power poles.

The transformer redirects energy from the poles into your home. Most interestingly, in this redirection it transforms the energy from very high levels to very low levels. By doing so, it makes energy and power far more functional, and much more accessible to the average person.

This is the role, too, of the spiritual leader: Transformer. It is the spiritual leader's job to take high-powered truths and ideas — culled from religious scripture, personal experience, the great thinkers, mystics, and a multitude of spiritual sources — and transform them into words, concepts, and simple truths that people can tap into, understand, implement, and be powered by.

Most people have neither the time nor the desire to dive into the many teachings passed down through history. Most people don't have the energy to engage significant reflection into their life experiences. Most people have too many other things going on to take time to re-wire their spiritual house.

Thus, the spiritual leader's job is to relieve people of having to do it all themselves. The spiritual leader's job is to be the transformer that makes the message so simple, yet so perfectly powerful as to be readily accessible and functional to anyone who needs it.

Getting Help on the Spiritual Journey

Whether you are considering leaving the village, just entering the forest, or have been in the forest for what seems an eternity, the need for timely and effective guidance and encouragement never leaves us. This is the reason religion and spiritual communities arise in the first place. No matter where they are on the journey, people tend to cluster around spiritual leaders who bring helpful and inspiring counsel. There is nothing wrong with that. In fact, in can be a very good thing.

However, as this book attempts to make clear, the most common spiritual clusters in America — i.e. Christian churches — are unappealing to non-Christians, and even many Christians, not only because of their bad image, but, far more importantly, because their spiritual counsel is ineffective in guiding people through the forest. At its root, it is not a methodological but a theological problem. Simply put, their theology doesn't work (and they just don't understand why).

Thus, many Americans seek spiritual guidance from a variety of sources. From Buddhism to Dr. Phil, from therapists to New Age, from Islam to self-help books, Americans overturn every rock in search of something — anything! — to help them in their quest. These are all terrific sources of spiritual guidance and can be a great comfort on any spiritual journey (discussed in detail in Chapter Eight).

However, it is the belief of this author that the God, the messenger, the sacred book, and the underlying stories of Christianity can be powerful, powerful instruments in navigating the forest. Not only are their stories and language familiar to many Americans, but the truths they can convey are absolutely life-changing.

It is important, however, to note that no path is the "best" or "only" path through the forest. To create authentic spirituality that genuinely enlivens you demands original experience born of traveling your own path. Thus, it is the task of the journeyer to find the way that is best for him or her.

It is the purpose of this book to show how the Bible, when read with fresh eyes and a fresh perspective, can be a highly effective spiritual guide, regardless of the path you have chosen. Just as it was the purpose of the preceding chapter to give you a "permission slip" to ask your questions and incorporate *your* answers into your personal faith, so it is the purpose of this chapter to help you find new truths and wisdom in the Bible. By considering the Bible here in ways traditional Christianity doesn't allow it is hoped that you will feel not only permission to rethink the Bible on your own, but excitement in uncovering the wisdom that goes well beyond the black-and-white and the literalness of standard Christianity.

It is the purpose of this book to transform the same Bible, the same Jesus, and the same stories that traditional Christianity reads into a powerful, new and relevant theology. It is the hope that people of the forest may then be fed and led by it, finding answers to their questions and new formulations that incorporate their doubts and questions.

To demonstrate this, we turn to the Bible and one of its most unbelievable stories.

Truth in Unlikely Places: The Story of Jonah and the Whale

The book of Jonah is one of the smallest books of the Bible. It is found in what is known as the Old Testament. The book of Jonah deals not with Jesus, nor what are considered any of the great men or women of the Christian faith. It is not a great story in the history of humanity, as the creation story and the story of the great flood are. It is so insignificant that theologians (people who spend their careers thinking and writing about God and religious matters) consider Jonah one of what are known as the "minor prophets" of the Bible. For these reasons, many Christians and Christian scholars consider the book of Jonah insignificant, if not irrelevant, to faith.

Yet, Jonah is one of the most well known stories of the Christian and Jewish Bibles. Even the most anti-religious and religiously indifferent non-Christians are familiar with this story. Despite its infamy, it is, in fact, the perfect example of one of the biggest problems currently afflicting Christianity.

Most Christian theology concerns itself with one primary question: What does the Bible really say? Implicit in this question is the belief that all we need to know as Christians and as human beings is contained within the Bible. Implicit in this question is the belief that Christian scripture is prose instead of poetry. It is the quest to determine all the denotations at the expense of the plentiful and powerful connotations. If we can fully know what is exactly in the Bible, we can fully know God's will, live what God wants us to be, and then be forever happy. Far from being just a jumping off point for faith, the Bible is for many the entire pool of Christian thinking.

This quest for perfect Biblical knowledge is what drives seminaries and churches to do their work. It is what drives most bickering between Christian denominations. This effort to always know exactly what God says through the Bible is what drives teachers and parents to have children memorize Bible verses. It is what drives the personal faith of many people. It is the quest to get as close to God as possible via the words of God. It is the quest for exactitude, which is based on the premise that there is one absolute truth, and our life mission is to find it and live it. This is perhaps the single greatest Christian theological mistake!

In the book of Jonah, the quest for exactitude means reading the text in the language in which it was first written (Hebrew), and then determining precisely what happened. And, as any Sunday School student knows, the story goes like this:

> A man, Jonah, was asked by God to go to the city of Ninevah and tell the people to stop their evil ways, or else God would punish them. Hating the Ninevites (because of their immoral living), and quite preferring they suffer God's wrath, Jonah boarded a ship sailing in the opposite direction. For this, God got mad at Jonah and brought up a big storm to thrash the boat. The sailors became afraid and, after Jonah admitted it was he who angered the Divine and caused the storm, threw Jonah overboard. Conveniently, Jonah was then swallowed by a whale, and lived in its belly for 3 days. Here he grew terrified and apologized to God. God, in his mercy, had the whale spit him onto shore. Jonah wiped himself off and went straightaway to Ninevah. There he preached the shortest sermon in the Bible — eight words, "Yet forty days, and Ninevah shall be overthrown" (Jonah 2: 4). Then, just as Jonah dreaded, the whole city did repent of their evil ways, and God forgave them.

That's the story of Jonah we all know. And most Christian theologians, if they give attention to this story at all, would say that is how it happened (likely substituting a "big fish" for the whale, as theologians want to respect modern science's explanation that whales really don't have the ability to do such a thing). They would also say that the main points of this story are:

1) God's mercy is great. God forgives the most wicked people (even entire cities); and

2) God is powerful. God commands the wind and the waves, and even the beasts of the sea. The will of humans is but a trifle compared to the awesomeness of God's might.

Per most of Christian theology, the reading of the Jonah story is quite plain, and the interpretation is quite obvious. However, despite its simplicity, most Christian theologians won't touch Jonah, but not because it's a small book or because he is a minor prophet. They won't go near Jonah because there's a big ol' fat whale sitting right in the middle of the story! And that just won't do, not for a self-respecting theologian or pastor.

It's too much. For if one chooses to sell the entire Jonah story as factually legitimate and entirely literally true, it means selling the second point (above) by saying: (a) God *spoke* to a man (not an easy sell when talking to people who have never heard God speak); (b) God caused a storm at sea because of one man, and biggest of all, (c) A whale swallowed a man (on God's command) and spit him out three days later, fully intact.

Yet, the Bible says these things happened exactly as told. And, if the average Christian's faith is based on what the Bible really says, then she must acknowledge that her faith is based on these whale facts. That, for many people, particularly well-educated theologians, is just too much to swallow. Though it may be difficult for Christianity to understand, these facts and the two points above are either too unbelievable or too trite to be comforting, inspiring, or guiding in the forest.

Interestingly, 300, 500, or 2000 years ago, such facts as these were seen as proof of God's power. In old days, though Jonah and God were the lead characters in the story, the whale stole the show. God frequently used men to accomplish God's aims. But to use a whale, now *that* was something! And it was something that really showed God's power.

In earlier days, when religions competed for the hearts of common people by comparing gods in a my-god-can-beat-up-your-god fashion, the more enormous or larger-than-life the act, the more powerful the god. The greater the story, the greater the god. Thus, stories of a subservient whale and the like were great testaments to the supremacy of God.

But, since the Enlightenment a few hundred years ago, things have slowly changed, and been turned on their heads. Now, such facts and stories are viewed by the public not as proof of a god's power, but as impediments to belief. So few people have ever seen fantastic or extraordinary events, and science casts great doubt on the possibility of such events happening. Hence, people find it very difficult to believe they ever did happen. Thus today, the bigger the story, the less believable the god. To publicly state today that one believes this whale story literally happened would bring only snickers and raised eyebrows.

The whale is such a hindrance to the story nowadays that many Christian denominations delete it altogether. At least three major Christian denominations (Roman Catholic, Lutheran, Episcopal) operate on a three-year cycle of Biblical readings, which they use in worship services on Sundays. This cycle is compiled in a book called *The Common Lectionary*. The cycle includes four readings each week: A reading from the Psalms, the Old Testament, the Gospels of the New Testament, and a reading from one of the "letters" of the New Testament, generally those written by the Apostle Paul.

Nowhere in the lectionary is Jonah's whale mentioned. Instead, when the book of Jonah is read, the lectionary only uses the part of the Jonah story that no Sunday School kid knows. That is the brief story of the vine in the closing six verses of the book of Jonah.

Here God appoints a vine to grow to full bloom so that Jonah might have shade from the hot sun after giving his sermon in Ninevah. God then kills the vine to teach Jonah a lesson. That story, while unusual, is far easier for self-

45

respecting theologians and pastors to sell to discerning religious consumers. It is a convenient distraction from the elephant in the living room.

Pastors and theologians know that if this whale story is what the Bible exactly says, and if the Bible is the primary basis of Christian faith, then preaching and teaching tall stories such as Jonah forces people to choose between believing larger-than-life Christian stories, and believing the reality of his or her own experience. It becomes embarrassing to tell people that in order to become a Christian they have to believe in stories that go completely against all of their sensibilities and what they know to be true about life. It has the effect of driving people away from more central truths.

As an aside, most pastors and theologians unofficially adopt an antidote to this problem. They take on what is called *canon within the canon* thinking.

If you look up the word *canon* in the dictionary, it will define it as something to the effect of "the Biblical books known as official Christian scripture." These are the 39 Old Testament books and the 27 New Testament books that many kids were made to memorize in Sunday School. The canon of scripture does not include such apocryphal (questionable) books, such as Tobit, Baruch, and Maccabees, which are recognized in some large Christian traditions as additional Biblical books. Nor does the canon of scripture include books such as the Gospel of Thomas, for example, which is considered an ancient Gnostic text that never made it into the officially recognized list of Biblical books.

With this in mind, to adopt *canon within the canon* thinking means to acknowledge that certain books and pieces of the official 39/27 Bible are more important than others. The Gospel of Mark, in this thinking, is infinitely more important and more central to Christian faith than Jonah, Habbakuk, or Jude, which are canonical but arguably less important.

Thus, what is often found is people claiming to be Bible-based or Bible-literalist, but, in fact, picking and choosing which parts they emphasize and which they quietly disregard, based on whether or not it makes them uncomfortable (A full discussion of uncomfortable Biblical verses is found in Chapter Twelve).

Picking and choosing is not a bad thing. In fact, it makes sense. Jesus himself did it (see Chapter Five). The crime is in claiming the Bible is almost God itself (as some Christian denominations come close to asserting), or at least infallible and inerrant, and then running from it when it gets uncomfortable. It perpetuates the notion of Christianity as hypocritical.

The Heart of the Problem

Back to the point, despite questions about the factuality of the Jonah story, and despite Christianity's uncertainty over what to do with a story such as this, the biggest problem is not the story, itself. The whale isn't the problem.

The biggest problem, as mentioned at the beginning of this chapter, is *why the story is read in the first place*. This is one of the single greatest reasons that God is in captivity today.

Christianity reads the Bible to determine exactly what the Bible really says, as if *that* is the essence of the Christian faith; as if that is possible 2000 years after the story; and as if that was Jesus' intent. Christianity stays hung-up on the literalness and the factuality of the story, oblivious to the deeper truths. The Christian must assent to facts rather than dig for truths. Thus, by focusing on what the Bible exactly says Christianity misses all the Bible says without saying.

This Christian hyper-focus on supposed facts is the source of embarrassment over the Jonah story. But it doesn't end there. Based on the notion of a 100% literal and factual Bible, Christian leaders must sell such notions as man-swallowing whales, flaming flying chariots (2Kings 2: 10-12), talking donkeys (Numbers 22: 28), talking snakes (Genesis 3), men walking unscathed through fiery furnaces (Daniel 3: 19-27), dead people coming back to life (Jesus in Mark 16; Lazarus in John 11: 43-44; 12:9), and people walking on water (Jesus in Matthew 14: 26; Peter in Matthew 14: 29), to name a few.

This leaves, for simplicity's sake, two types of Christians:

1) The literalist Christians: Those who actually believe every one of the stories of the Bible happened ... exactly as told. Because these stories are often viewed as ridiculous to outsiders, these Christians are viewed, by association, as ridiculous and irrelevant. While the strength of conviction of these Christians is admirable, their beliefs often repel rather than attract outsiders;

2) The "reasonable" Christians: These Christians pick some stories and omit others (The literalist Christians sometimes do so, too, but much more surreptitiously and with great gymnastics of justification.). They will condescendingly snub their noses at other Christians who literally believe in stories like Jonah and the whale or a talking donkey. But they themselves will then claim to believe in the factuality of people coming back to life after being dead for three days; or in Jesus' feeding of 5000+ people with five loaves of bread and two fish (John 6:5-13). And all the while they won't understand how outsiders can see them as just as ridiculous (and even more hypocritical) as they see those folks in group one.

To a large degree, these reasonable Christians aren't quite sure what they believe. They can't bring themselves to stand up and say, "I believe these stories are all literally and factually true," because they have so many doubts. Yet, they also can't bring themselves to say, "I don't believe. I don't believe in a few (or many) of these stories." Further, they know of no way to preach or understand Christianity if the Bible is not literally true. Yet, they can't bring themselves to preach literally about unbelievable stories. The confusion of beliefs is visible in their often lukewarm conviction, which in turn is reflected in declining numbers.[13]

I once had a conversation with an old woman from the second category of Christian. She claimed to be an absolute literalist, as in group one, but she admitted that she had one lone doubt. She couldn't believe the world was literally created in seven days (Genesis 1-2: 1). But, she was in a quandary, because if you start interpreting parts of the Bible non-literally then, in her words, "it all falls apart." Thus, denying her doubt, she clings to the belief that she is a true believer in God who takes the Bible as 100% true and factual, even though she admittedly isn't. For her to acknowledge doubt was equivalent to being an unbeliever. She believed that if you don't read the story literally you miss the point.[14]

Many Christians are in her same boat. They claim to be literalists (group one), but each has his or her doubts of this or that Bible story, just like the leaders who take on *canon within the canon* thinking. Further, what most don't realize is that, contrary to popular beliefs, no two Christians believe the exact same things. Everybody has his or her own spin on it. Few Christians believe every last detail of the Bible, though even fewer will ever admit it.

Considering all of these issues, it is far easier for many Christians to reside in the unquestioning world of group one literalism, even if it means denying one's doubts. For, to acknowledge and even affirm one's doubts creates far more problems than any one Christian desires to take on.

So where does all of this leave us?

Jesus Gives us Permission to Read the Bible and his Life as a Parable

Doubt is not the enemy. Doubt and unbelievable stories require work to rethink, but they can be powerful conveyors of truth. To find these truths requires detaching from factuality, literalness, and stock Biblical interpretations.

That is one thing Jesus kept trying to teach his followers. God's grace is bigger, God's plan is fuller, and God's depth is more complete than we humans have the ability to comprehend. We can never exhaust all the depth and meanings. Reading the Bible literally limits the breadth and depth of God's activity in life by boxing God into just facts, while the truths about God and life go way beyond the facts of a given story. When detached from the need for belief in superhuman stories and unbelievable miracles, God becomes much more real and accessible.

The truth is, Jesus regularly told made-up stories to make a deeper point. That is what his parables were. He constantly used this teaching method to get people to see below the surface of life, and thereby draw closer to God. Yet, Jesus was also known for scolding his disciples for not understanding what he was trying to say. He taught that there is far greater meaning and far greater activity of God under the surface of a story or event. The message was never the story itself, but the wisdom and truths the story conveyed about God and life.

The Bible is no different. The factuality of the stories isn't the point. The truths they attempt to convey are the point. Our job is to look below the surface.

Yet, Christianity has gotten hung up on reading the Bible in a literal way. That includes reading every story about Jesus as if you had to believe the story itself rather than the point(s) of the story. For instance, rooted in that my-God-can-beat-up-your-god thinking, Christianity insists you believe that Jesus literally fed 5,000 people with a few fish and bread, and there were twelve baskets of food left over. The point, Christianity says, is the miracle of Jesus feeding such a crowd. It's not about the much deeper truths that Jesus was always trying to get his disciples to see.

In this story, some examples of underlying truths are, first, that the bread and fish are Jesus' words. Also, Jesus' teachings are so powerfully deep that they fill up anyone seeking God, just as his teachings filled the 5,000. His teachings are the bread of life. When Jesus speaks of God and life it takes so little to be truly filled. On top of that, there is always more left over than we are ever fully able to take in.

As another example, Christianity insists that Jesus literally brought Lazarus, his friend, back to life from the dead. It chooses this literal path rather than preaching that these are beautiful metaphors for how following Jesus' teachings has the power to breathe life back into our tired lives.

Christianity insists that Jesus walked on water, rather than showing how Jesus' teachings can strengthen us and change us in great ways, making us capable of walking over many of life's deep waters that might otherwise sink us. Christianity insists that at the birth in the manger God became human, rather than helping us see that (a) God breaks into human experience and brings us new births of spirit, and (b) we, too, are a touch of God — embodiments of the will of the Divine.

The point of Jesus' life, like the point of Jesus' parables, isn't the story itself. Jesus' life was about delivering God. His very life was a parable, a story with deep underlying truths about God. It is these truths about God and life that have the power to bring us closer to God and improve our lives.

Our task is not to simply muster the will to believe a list of unbelievable stories and facts, as the church has too long been in the business of asking people to do. Our task is to read the parable of Jesus' life and the parable that is the Bible, and seek to understand God through them. Our task is to find God and God's truths about life. By doing so we will draw closer to God and the peace, hope, love, and compassion God offers.

Recently, I was doing some research on one of my favorite Bible verses when I stumbled across something that completely startled me and leapt off the pages of my Bible. In the Apostle Paul's first letter to the Christians at Corinth, when discussing his authority and his relationship to them, he brings out a verse from the laws of Moses in the Hebrew Bible (which is the same as the Christian Old Testament) to bolster his argument.

Before citing that verse, it is important to understand that, prior to becoming a follower of Jesus' teachings, Paul had been a persecutor of Christians. In fact, the book of Acts (7: 58) documents that Paul was witness to, if not directly involved in, the death by stoning of one Christian, named Stephen.

Paul's occupation was that of Pharisee. He was a Jewish religious leader. The job of the Pharisees was to constantly obey, interpret, and administer the 613 laws that God gave to Moses (of which the Ten Commandments are a part), and to insure that the people obeyed them, too. These laws were (and still are) believed to be the direct link to God. Obey the laws and God would be good. Break the laws, any of them, and fall out of favor with God. It was that simple.

The Pharisees were the strictest of adherents to the law. For example, when the law of Moses says, "You shall not lend upon interest to your brother, interest on money, interest on food, interest on anything that is lent for interest"

49

(Deuteronomy 23: 19), it was the job of the Pharisee to insure this law was strictly kept by the Jewish people. So also was a Pharisee responsible for insuring everyone adhered to laws such as Leviticus 19:19, which said it was against the law to wear clothes that contained more than one type of thread.

For as silly as these laws can sound to modern ears, these laws were not loose guidelines to be occasionally followed. They were, and still are for many Jews today, the very word of God, from which there can be no deviance. Indeed, the entire life of a Pharisee was spent obeying and understanding the exact letter of the law.

It was the Pharisees who were constantly trying to trip up Jesus on his faithfulness to the laws of Moses. What made Jesus so dangerous and fascinating was that he fully kept the law and honored the law while simultaneously radically reinterpreting it and breathing new life into it. It was they who sought to kill Jesus because, in the end, they felt that he (1) threatened their authority as sole interpreters of the Hebrew Bible, and (2) he supposedly broke the law in the most offensive way — blasphemy.

So, it is in this context of the complete authority of the law of Moses as 100% literally and factually true that Paul writes these words in 1Corinthians 9: 9, "For it is written in the law of Moses, 'You shall not muzzle an ox when it is treading out the grain.' Is it for oxen that God is concerned? Does he not speak entirely for our sake? It was written for our sake, because the plowman should plow in hope and the thresher thresh in hope of a share in the crop."

Here Paul is quoting the Law of Moses (Deuteronomy 25: 4) about not muzzling an ox. The Pharisees and their people believed that this law, like all others, was to be followed exactly. You should never put a muzzle on an ox when he is treading out the grain. Instead, if you observe the law, you will let him eat of the grain, too, so that he can be strengthened to better accomplish his work.

But Paul veers in a completely different direction. He says the point of the law isn't the ox! He explicitly states that the story and the ox are a metaphor for how God treats people. In fact, he states, almost angrily, "Is it for oxen that God is concerned?" Paul is directly telling the people of Corinth that the law is not to be followed literally, but instead metaphorically. By doing so, Paul tells us to not *interpret* scripture literally, either. Instead, we are to read the Bible to discover what God is saying to us below the surface of the story. By his example, Paul (who is credited with writing more books of the Christian Bible than any other person) teaches us proper reading of the Bible. The Bible, Paul explicitly teaches, is to be read as metaphor.

Both Jesus and Paul teach that there is not one absolute truth to be learned. It is critical that we understand this. There are, in fact, many truths that weave together. Life with God is about the interplay of many, many truths, not the overarching dominance of just one truth. For, all truth is God's truth.

The Nuts and Bolts of Seeing God's Many Truths

If we are to work through our doubts, if we are to find some way to make these sometimes-crazy Christian stories functional on the spiritual journey, the question we must answer is: How? How do we extract the truths about God and life from the supposed facts in which God has been bound? How do we read the Bible for what is beneath the story? How does the Bible bring us closer to God without binding us to a laundry list of beliefs?

It is quite simple, really. Anyone can do it. It starts by recognizing that, to quote Goethe, "Everything is a metaphor," not just everything in the Bible, but everything in life. Everything speaks of something else or of several other things, and all things speak of God. Call it symbolism, call it metaphor, call it parable: It is one thing saying something else. Something may look like "A," but it is really "B."

Because God has created all things and is in all things, there are no wrong answers. There are only answers that speak louder to you than others. Further, there is not a one-to-one correlation. Each "fact" can speak many truths (as we shall see shortly). Yet again, the goal is to find the truths in the story that speak to you of God. All it requires to get started is asking a few basic questions:

1) Does the point of the story transcend the literal "facts?" In other words, are the facts what the story is really about, or is there something deeper going on? The answer to this is that there is always something deeper going on? Thus, the most important element is just having permission to look beyond the facts. Jesus' and Paul's teachings grant you that permission. Also, the way God has constructed life itself (in that there is always far more going on beneath the surface) grants you permission. And lastly, the need to find truth that resonates inside you grants you permission.

2) What is that point? What are the deeper truths? These questions are best answered by first asking a few other questions: A) Where and how is God present and active in the story? How are God's actions in the story similar to our own experience of God? B) How is the Bible character like me or like us? How does this story parallel normal life today? In other words, what actions are the main characters doing that you and I do, as well?

By going through these simple steps it becomes very easy to see that God is about many, many truths. God is active in so many ways, types, languages, ideologies, thinking, actions, and words. It just takes a bit of digging beneath the surface.

For example, you don't have to read far into the Bible to see that nearly every single morally reprehensible action has been used by God or by God's people (on God's command) to "further the kingdom of God," as well. God has broken nearly all of God's own commandments, and so have God's people.

But even that is a metaphor. The point of God's reprehensible actions in the Bible is that God is active even in the bad things in life, and that God often uses bad things to accomplish greater good (see Chapter Seven).

Further, by looking for truths beneath the surface we no longer have to throw out or even question the really unbelievable parts of the story, such as the whale or a talking donkey. People can choose to believe the facts or not believe the facts. Factuality becomes irrelevant. Hence, believers and unbelievers can co-exist side-by-side, each drawing their own meanings. By looking at the stories as metaphors (using an ounce of the creativity God gave us) these larger-than-life events become poignant teachers for all people of how God works in life.

Again, what we are getting at here is that in any given story there are many truths about God and about life that jump right out at us. It is never about one lone truth. (And the truths are not always rosy and happy.) God's truths and activity are multi-faceted and many-hued. Our task is simply to pick up on the ones that jump out at us, and allow them to speak to us, comfort us, challenge us, and change our lives.

How the Whale Teaches Us

In my first book, *Spiritual But Not Religious*,[15] I offered an example of what an individual spiritual seeker or a preacher could do with even the Jonah story if he or she was reading the story as a metaphor or parable, instead of literally. It is helpful to consider that sermon at this juncture.

It is presented as a sermon only because that is a simple way of presenting any interpretation of scripture. Please do not think that because it is written in sermon style this is directed only toward ministers or church people. It is intended to help any person who wishes to read the Bible with fresh eyes for new insights. Sermon style is just a convenient and effective way to convey points.

As you read it, imagine sitting in a beautiful towering cathedral in Europe or, perhaps, a simple country church with towering steeple. Imagine lying outside at night under an amphitheater of stars, or sitting in a cozy seaside ale house warmed by a crackling fire. Use whatever thoughts create a more relaxed and open feel for you.

Sermon:

Let's assume that the whale did not really happen. Or, let's assume that it's impossible to know or prove that it did or did not happen. It was not only a very long time ago, but it requires an incredible bending of the mind in order to buy it. So, let's just set the whale aside for now, and come back to it later. We don't need to completely discard it, because we know that with God all things are possible. However, we'll set its literal factuality aside. We'll entrust that to God.

Whatever it was that factually happened to Jonah is unknown. What is known, however, is that in this story something happened to this man. Some experience so overwhelmed him — some whale-like experience — that it caused him to turn 180 degrees from his mad course, and go do what he knew he was called to do. Something rocked his world.

Jonah had life all figured out, and was going in his own direction, even though a calling — a calling of his heart — was nagging him to go to Ninevah. He was on his own, going the exact opposite direction of what God was calling him to do. He knew what he had to do, but he pretended he didn't have to do it.

He pretended like he could just do what he wanted.

And isn't that what happens to us, too? We have our lives and our plans all figured out. And we have every intention of running from what we know we must face, that which doesn't fit our plans. We do all we can to avoid that which we know we must do. But God has God's way with us.

See, Jonah is you. At some point in life, each one of us is called in our heart to do something big that we know we must do, but that we truly don't want to do. Maybe, like Jonah, we are called to speak a loving truth to someone or ones that we don't like. Or, perhaps we are called to speak a hard truth to someone we love. Perhaps we are called in our heart to do something we'd rather not do, like reconstruct a relationship or seek forgiveness for a long ago slight. Perhaps we are called to put to death a dying dream, or stand up for the justice of another, or be consistently firm in disciplining our children. Fact is, we cannot traverse life's paths without being called to do many things we'd rather not do.

I can still recall my mother saying to me as a child when I did not feel like doing the dishes on the day it was my turn, "Sweetheart, there are many things in life we don't want to do, but we just gotta do."

But we don't do 'em, do we? Unless there is a parent or authority figure looking over our shoulder, we run. Rather than do what we gotta do, we run. It is human nature to, at times, avoid new responsibility. Wherever the call comes from, we know those times in life when we are called. And just as Jonah ran in the 180-degree opposite direction from his calling, we run. We avoid. We hedge. We procrastinate. We deny. We downplay. We try to pass the buck to others. We follow our fear, our hatred, and our anger. And... we .... run from what we know we must do. We do anything to avoid the undesirable task.

But the storm only gets worse. As with Jonah, life gets more hairy as we avoid the task. Sure, Jonah got on the ship and fell asleep. And we sleep.... sometimes. We fool ourselves into thinking we have peace, but we still toss and turn. Like Jonah the waters of life rage around us, and the waters rage within us, until we are thrown into the storm. God lets us run, but God also lets the problem get worse and metastasize. God doesn't offer to do our dirty work. God doesn't swoop in with miracle cures. God didn't offer to go to Ninevah for Jonah. God offered Jonah strength to do the task, but Jonah was the one that had to do the legwork.

Eventually, we get thrown into the thick of it. God lets us follow our own designs. God lets the situation get so bad that it shakes our world. Like Jonah, we follow our plans. And our life goes down — *down* into the hull of the ship, *down* into a whale, *down* into the belly of the whale, *down* in the depths of the ocean. If it is a major situation that we are avoiding, a major calling we are running from, or a major pain we are denying, we soon find ourselves going *down* into sorrow, *down* into misery and an out-of-control life, and *down* into a maddening, anxiety-ridden neurosis.

Creative types know this all too well. When we deny or avoid that calling from within to create, when we deny our creative impulse, any of us, we begin to know a searing anguish. We begin to rot from the outside in. We let our outer world go to pot, because we've cut off our inner guidance system that is constantly trying to feed new life, new ideas, and new energy into our soul and minds. So, we overeat, overwork, overspend, over-travel, and over-indulge in any way possible. We do everything that might make us feel good, because we fear the responsibility looming before us, the responsibility of following the call.

Or maybe we keep up appearances on the outside, while we rot on the inside. When we cut ourselves off from following the calling of that voice — wherever it might lead — we go down! Our lives tank.

Sometimes at those major crossroads of life we are thrown into a very, very dark time. Maybe it is a darkness that falls over an individual, or maybe over a community or people. We become consumed by something so hideous that it eats us alive, just as Jonah was eaten alive by a whale in the story. It is a time when we know cataclysmic fear, aloneness, confusion, and sorrow.

Inherent in being human is having those experiences in life that absolutely shake us to the core. We go our own way, away from the true calling, and the fear becomes so searing and the aloneness so dark that it is nothing less than being swallowed by a whale in the darkest deep of the ocean.

But, like Jonah, we do not die. The whale experience does not kill us, usually. In fact, at some point, often long down the road, we find that our intentions have swung 180 degrees, back to what we were called. The torture and exhaustion of going our own way becomes so overwhelming that we gladly go the opposite direction. What it is that we experience outside ourselves, or whatever we see inside ourselves (whatever our whale experience may be), whatever tool is used, God makes his point. We are changed. And if God wants us to do something, we will do it. God will have God's way. We may have free will, but we also work for a God that has a plan for our lives.

If you don't believe in God, consider it simply as life. If life is calling us to do something, life will not let us run for long. And hasn't that been your experience? Life will force us to deal with it at some point. And it will transform us. In fact, we will often find that when viewed as a gift from God, or the universe, it is the darkest of times that most contribute to our growth, maturity, and joy as humans. That which challenges us transforms us. We emerge from the ocean's depths and from the belly of the whale changed, strengthened, and ready to follow the call.

Whatever takes us to rock bottom becomes the instrument of our return to new life. The alcoholic has to hit bottom. The abuser often has to be jailed. The widow needs to hit the depths of sorrow. Only then, when the whale has done its swallowing, does transformation take place in the individual or the community. We go down, down, down into the darkness of life, where we incubate until God pulls us out, somehow moved, somehow changed.

Or perhaps, like Jonah, we do the work, but are not fully changed inside until afterward. Maybe it is not the going down, but the simple carrying out of the mission that changes our hearts.

Whichever the case, this is not only the story of an individual named Jonah. It is the story of life. It is our collective story — our church's story, our communal story, our country's story. Jonah is you, and Jonah is us. We are called, often as a community, to do things that in our hearts we know we must do, but would rather not do. We are called to sacrifice our selves, our time, our possessions, our drives, and our indulgences in order to confront bad stuff, or to stand up for justice, or to work for something greater than ourselves. We are called to work, like Jonah did, for those who are in bondage — bondage to destructive ways, bondage to oppression, bondage to depression, bondage to suffering in its many forms. We are called to free the captives.

Like Jonah, we don't *want* to. We don't *want* to step out of our lives and help others. We don't *want* to pull ourselves out of the center of the universe. We don't *want* to give the time, the energy, or the love.

Yet, we must. We must turn 180 degrees, and go toward our calling.

So, the simple question is, to what is God calling you? From what responsibility or task are you running? Into what slumber have you been lulled? Into what sea are you falling? What is the whale that is swallowing you? Are you ready to do the work you have been put on this earth to do?

So, do it! Now is the time.

End of Sermon

Reading the Bible as parable or metaphor, as is done here with Jonah, is terribly exciting to the religious outsider (and even the religious insider seeking deeper and more powerful meaning). It opens up the book to many different ways of seeing God at work and experiencing God. There are many other truths in the Jonah story that could be the foundation for weeks of study and meditation that could go in completely different directions. For example,

1) Life changes us. Life spins us 180 degrees sometimes, shattering who we were, and creating someone new;

2) There is something about us that many times in life causes us to return to our responsibilities and our callings;

3) God's will will be done, period. God may be patient with us, but God will have God's way. *And* we get the rewards of conversion of heart and the joy of doing great things for God and humanity;

4) This is a classic story of death and resurrection, similar to Jesus' crucifixion and resurrection.[16] In the belly of the whale Jonah overcomes the dark energies inside himself, represented by the whale, and emerges a changed, or reborn, man. Now, having died to his lower form of existence, and having harnessed the conflicting forces inside himself, he now goes to meet the world with new power, new wisdom, and new depth. This is the hero story we all are challenged to live.

Any of these could also be the primary topic of a powerful personal meditation or sermon. None of them depend on the factuality of a man-swallowing whale, nor do any of them discount said whale.

A Spiritual Exercise

One excellent exercise that anyone who is interested in the Bible and spiritual discussion with God and life can do is to take a particular Bible story or verse and write a sermon about it! This is a powerful way to discover what you really do think and believe.

Someone once said that we never know what we truly think until we are forced to codify our thoughts. In other words, we all have thoughts tumbling around in our heads, but until we have to write or speak our thoughts, we never know exactly what we specifically believe.

That is partly why talk radio hosts are often so opinionated and passionate. From years of talking they know exactly what they believe and don't believe. This is why schooling can be good for people. Writing and talking about topics enables you to better understand yourself. Keeping a diary or journal has the same effect. It not only flushes out pain that is inside you, it helps you understand you by forcing you to put your thoughts and feelings into words.

Writing a sermon is journaling with a direction. It can help the spiritual journeyer grow to hear the voice of God speaking. I like to sit outdoors at any my favorite corner pizza joint, buy a large Mountain Dew (the extra caffeine really gets the energy and creative juices going), read the verses, and then just let my mind run free, while my pen forever tries to catch up. I draw in examples, snippets, learnings, and conversations from any source I can.

Sermonizing (writing your own sermons) for personal use is not about doing research and in-depth Biblical study. It is not about focusing on what other people have said and thought. It is about discovering what you believe and think, sometimes incorporating the thought of others as it comes to you.[17] The worst preachers are those that do plenty of research but offer no insight, no personal interface with the truths, and no force of character born of their own experience and strong sense of beliefs that might be offered up as spiritual food for consideration by the listener. As LBJ once said, "Conviction compels."

Don't get me wrong, I do recommend Biblical study, both formal and informal, for the journeyer. I recommend diving into anything you can to further educate you on what others might have said, studied, and thought before you. I also recommend picking up a Biblical commentary, or two. These are books of study and interpretation that have been done by great Biblical thinkers, living and dead. Read the authors that tickle you. Follow the bread crumbs of your own personal interest. See where they lead.

All of these sources will expand your thinking, and help you further understand what you think. But never forget that the goal is to forever answer the question, "Well, do I believe this?" If what you are reading does not gel with your own experience, if it does not resonate deep within you, then move on to the next source.

As mentioned earlier, when I write my sermons or use texts for personal meditation I am forever trying to answer three questions: (1) What is the point, in my opinion? (2) Where is God present/active in the story? And (3) How is this

Biblical character like me? Then I make my sermon about one primary point and I stick to it as I draw in other examples. Simpler is always better.

Try the exercise, and see where it takes you in understanding your beliefs.

The Christian Reaction to Truth in Metaphor

To most religious insiders, particularly the Christian leader, this is all terribly frightening for the same reason it is terribly exciting to the outsider. It opens the book to many different ways of experiencing God and seeing God at work. It opens up the text for anyone to read it and find truth in it that may not be laying right on the surface. That is terrifying, of course, because it takes control from those in charge. God, the thinking goes, is much better when controlled by the few and handed out to the many.

To the religious leader, interpreting as metaphor means the death of control of God, and the seeming loss of clarity and certainty. To the religious outsider (and even a few folks in the pew), interpreting as metaphor breathes life into tired old texts and thereby gives new meaning and richness to the Bible, to God, and to life itself.

If a shift to metaphorical interpretation is made, it will have the effect of freeing God (and freeing Jesus and Christianity, itself) from Christianity, so that they may become great spiritual movers in the world. If this is to happen, a distinction must be drawn between fact and truth. Second, people must be given permission to be Christians even if they don't believe the supposed facts of the Christian stories in the way the facts have been traditionally interpreted. People must be allowed to doubt the facts of the story, if they so choose, yet still be helped in their journey toward God.

The goal in all of this is to allow people to discover the hidden truths about God and life for which literal interpretation just doesn't allow. It is to help people have a real and original relationship with God, one that agrees with the individual temperament and characteristics God has given each person. It is to help each person create a life and a system of beliefs that he or she can embrace.

Now, whether the church takes these steps or not should not deter you from doing so. You can have a powerful, deep, and intimate relationship with God, the Bible and Jesus if you begin to read deeper and look for life-truths. You can begin to see how powerful the Judeo-Christian story really is and how rich a teacher it can be. Basically, your doubt becomes the very instrument of your growth and your realization of new truth.

For another example of a metaphor sermon and the uncovering of deeper truths in a Jesus miracle see Appendix A.

The Effect of Literal Thinking

But there is still one big problem with Christianity (and you) staying stuck in literal thinking. Besides the fact that whales and flying chariots are not easy to buy into as cold hard facts, there is an even greater problem. The problem is the *effect* of literal interpretation. It is one thing to believe that God is working and active in regular occurrences every single day. It is something completely different to believe that God, Jesus, and the Holy Spirit engage today in factual, nature-defying, larger-than-life miracles as they did in the stories of the Old and New Testaments.

Once we believe that God literally did major nature-defying miracles in Biblical times, then we believe that God does nature-defying miracles now. As a result, we start waiting for God to do some now. And it is the waiting and the expectation that are the curse.

Rather than doing all we can to improve the world now for those people in need, we keep waiting for God to instantly turn water into wine and turn a few fish into a 5,000-guest banquet. Rather than allowing God to unexpectedly work small, pivotal miracles at crucial times, we take on a "lottery" mentality. We keep hoping to hit the spiritual jackpot that is instantly going to make everything better.

We then become bitter when God doesn't save us or give us all that we want. We fail to be eternally grateful for the many gifts and little miracles God gives us everyday. We seldom thank God for renewed energy at a crucial point in the day. We seldom thank God for the food it took to restore that energy. We seldom give thanks for the farmers and distributors who sweat and worry under the hot sun to bring that midday energy-producing food. We seldom give thanks for the resurrection of the farmer's great faith and commitment after floods, tornadoes, and economic downturns yearly challenge him and try to break him. We seldom give thanks to God for providing the sun that comes back to life every morning to give us heat and energy, or for the delicate ecosystem that grows up and dies off because of that same sun. We miss all of these little resurrections every day.

Instead, we keep waiting for the larger-than-life miracle to save us from what we have let our lives become. We keep wishing and hoping that God will resurrect our lives from the misery they have slid into. And, when that seems hopeless, the literalist just bides time here until the big come-back-to-life day in the sky with Jesus.

Thus, in addition to denying greater truths, literalism has the potential to breed inactivity and spiritual desperation. That is nothing less than spiritual death.

A Bit More Metaphor

The point of theology is not to cling to 2,000 year-old facts. The point of theology is not to figure out exactly what the Bible says. The point of theology is not to hope for miracles.

The point of theology and spiritual growth is to discover all that the Bible (and the scriptures of other religions, not to mention poets and mystics) doesn't explicitly say. The point of reading a Bible and engaging in spiritual exploration is to bring us closer to God. The point is to recognize all the Bible can't help but say about God and life. The point is to uncover the truths that lay below the facts. For those life-truths have far greater healing power, inspirational power, and saving power than do the questionable facts.

Whether you actually believe that Balaam's donkey literally spoke God's words to him (Numbers 22: 28), you cannot deny that in life God sometimes uses total jackasses to speak truths that stop you in your tracks, forcing you to confront your own stuff. Whether or not you believe in the story of Noah's ark and the great flood, you cannot deny that sometimes in life God will drown out and kill off all that used to be, in order to make way for an entirely new life.

Another example of reading the Bible creatively to uncover greater truths are the words once spoken by the scholar of religions, Joseph Campbell. Riffing on Jesus' words "Love your enemies," Campbell added, "...for your enemies, far more than your friends, are the instruments of your destiny." Our enemies often shape us in far greater ways than do those we love. Now that's deep!

I can recall my father coming home one night from teaching his high school Bible class at church, and telling a most curious story. My father, the pastor of our large and rather conservative suburban church, decided that evening to make a startlingly graphic point to his students on a point very important to him. As his students were filing into class that evening, they were shocked to find their pastor in front of the room *standing on top of his Bible!*

This, to anyone born of a serious Christian background, whether conservative or liberal, is nearly sacrilege. Yet, there he was, the pastor, doing it in front of a class of kids. After their awe had abated, he spoke a very powerful message. His words to them still often ring in my head, "Always remember, the Bible is not God! This is a book. The book, the stories, and all of it exist to bring you closer to God. We do not worship the book. The book exists as a tool to bring us into greater relationship with the God it tells about, the God we worship. Do not ever, ever forget that!"

To set God free we must allow God to be so much more than just the words on the page of a book. We must allow God to be the limitless, complex, contradictory truths that God is. We must realize we can still have a rich, full, saving relationship with God (as many people before Jesus and since Jesus have had) without consenting to all the facts of the Bible. Many Christians do have this relationship with God today, but do not believe every Biblical jot and tittle.

The Bible is a human construction that exists to aid us in our journey toward God with God. We must begin to look beneath stories and beyond facts to find the depths of God. For God wants us to be with God, doubts and all. For only then can God bestow on us the rich and creative life God has intended for us. Only then can we know the peace, power, purpose, hope, love, and joys that are the abundant life Jesus promised.

Winning Hearts

What the Christian Church doesn't realize, strange as this may sound, is that the key to reaching people today is to tell them they don't have to believe anything! There are no rules here. It is to tell them, "God loves you precisely where you are today." We do not win God by becoming a Christian. We discover God's love by first realizing that it is already there for us. We then grow into further love by exploring a greater relationship with God.

The key to winning people's hearts and gaining their trust is to accept them precisely where they are at. It is not to tell them that they must become this, believe that, or do this and that. It is to tell the person that she is a beautiful child of God, and that she is doing just fine where she is at. It is to make change and growth optional, rather than mandatory. It is to offer new ways of thinking, rather than forcing them.

To many Christians, such a thought is just humanism, liberalism, pluralism, and every other –ism of bad religion. All of that may be true. But the point is that it works. People are far more apt to respond and open themselves when they know they do not have to. People are far more likely to trust when they are treated with respect and seen as beautiful and good. People are far more likely to desire a relationship with God when they are allowed to do it on their terms and at their speed.

A Brief Theological Digression (You may find this section boring. Feel free to skip ahead to *A Few Practical Matters*.)

In the book of Romans, the Apostle Paul makes a very strong argument; one that is widely accepted throughout Christianity, that there is nothing anyone can do to win God's love. God's love is unconditional in a way no human love can be. In fact, rich, fulfilling, and total relationship with God is a complete gift that we need only accept.

In Romans 11: 6 Paul says, "But if it is by grace, it is no longer on the basis of works; otherwise grace would no longer be grace." The love of God is a complete gift. There are no "works" we have to do to earn it, including even believing in the Bible. That is why God's love is so radical. There are no rules, just love. This is what Jesus was trying to get through to people.

You do not have to lose sleep trying really hard to be moral. You do not have to believe every story in the Bible. You do not have to believe that Jesus did miracles. You do not even have to believe that Jesus was the son of God or was resurrected from the dead. God's love is so mind-blowingly radical, so totally and 100% free that you do not have to *do* anything except accept it, no strings attached.

Even after you accept it, you are not required to do anything. Christians think after you accept God's full and complete love, you have to change your life. But technically you don't even have to do that, for that would be grace with a "works" clause tagged on to be fulfilled after the grace is granted. It would be a contract rather than a gift. In other words it would still be works that win God's love, and that ain't how it is. Dietrich Bonhoeffer can call this "cheap grace," but that's what God's "free" and "unconditional" love means. Bonhoeffer may not like it, and Christianity may not like it, but "unconditional" darn well means "unconditional."

You may choose to change your ways after you encounter the bounteous love of God. God's love may so overwhelm you that you want to live life completely differently. But, again, that is your choice, and it is fully optional. Further, it is between you and God. You are not to be judged by other people. As St. Augustine, one of the earliest fathers of Christianity said, "Love God, and do what you want." (Yes, a Christian saint said that!)[18] The point of life is simply to drink in and live in the love of God.

But Christians are hesitant to allow God's love to be as radical as God intends it to be. For if God's love is free to all people (as you would expect from the very Creator of love, from the one who loves more greatly than any human mind can imagine), then there really is no need for the church. Church can be a good thing in people's lives, but it is not mandatory.

If God's life-giving love is free to all, then no one gets to be in control of God. No one gets to judge anyone else. No one gets to impose his or her religious morality on the world. And that is just too much for some people. So Christianity tells the world that you have to do something (such as believe in the Bible, or be really nice and good, or "accept Jesus as your personal lord and savior") to win God's love.

However, Paul states plainly in Romans 4: 3-5, "For what does the scripture say? 'Abraham believed God, and it was reckoned to him as righteousness.' Now to one who works, his wages are not reckoned as a gift but as his due. And to one who does not work but trusts him who justifies the ungodly, his *faith* is reckoned as righteousness" [italics mine].

Paul continues this argument in his letter to the Galatians (3: 6-9), "So you see that it is men of faith who are the sons of Abraham. And the scripture, foreseeing that God would justify Gentiles by faith, preached the gospel beforehand to Abraham, saying, 'In you shall all the nations be blessed.' So then those who are men of faith are blessed with Abraham who had faith."

It's like God left a pretty basket on your doorstep. And after you take it inside you open it to find all of the things you truly, deep down wanted in life (things like love, hope, strength, peace, purpose, joy, laughter), and so much more. Your neighbors may tell you a story of how that basket arrived on your doorstep. It may be a beautiful story, but you don't have to believe it or even worry about it. The basket and the story of its arrival are two different things.

God just wants you to have the basket. God wants you to take the basket in, and enjoy the free cornucopia of gifts God has left for you. If you want to find out how the basket came, go ahead. But you don't have to. God just wants you to enjoy the gift and use the gift to help you in your life!

So, if we truly believe that God loves every one of us, no matter what we do, then church shouldn't be about just trying to do the right thing, believe the right thing, or say the right thing. Church should be about helping people at all points on the spiritual journey, and at all places of doubt, truth, faith, and development. Church should be the opportunity to share spiritual community without guilt or fear, but in love and joy. Church should be about helping people tap into that overflowing love that God has for each one of us, no matter who we are or what we do.

The Interpretation Asserted throughout this Book

It is the assertion of this author that the entire Bible can be interpreted literally and metaphorically. It is not the goal to reject one or the other, but to allow the individual spiritual seeker to choose that which suits him or her. The spiritual seeker must also choose for him- or herself if and when to mix literal and metaphorical interpretations.

It must be understood that in this book literal interpretation is generally used only in two circumstances: (1) When challenging other traditional literal interpretations, and (2) When asserting the powerful message of love within the Bible, particularly Jesus' teachings.

A Few Practical Matters

Bringing this back around to our discussion of interpreting the Bible, we can say this: Once we acknowledge that we don't have to believe every single thing the Bible says in order to have a full relationship with God; once we acknowledge that it is quite possible to have a fully saving relationship with God without the Bible, at all, we open up a barrel of monkeys that many people would rather not deal with. For, how do you decide which verses and stories to read literally and which to read as parable or metaphor? How do you choose your *canon within the canon*? Furthermore, by what authority does anyone presume to interpret scripture?

Let me start by saying this, God created you with a mind, a heart, a creativity, an ability to discern good from bad, an ability to think and learn, and likely an ability to read. That is all the authority you need.

Dive into the Bible and decide for yourself what you believe. Most Bibles, nowadays, are well researched and well written, but are still very much open to interpretive leeway. Different versions read differently. Pick up a few and compare. Find one you like. Any can be used for metaphorical interpretation. You don't have to know Greek and Hebrew to be able to interpret scripture. (For example, in the Roman Catholic Church the clergy are not required to be able to read the Bible in the original Greek or Hebrew — a fact unthinkable in many other denominations.) But if it helps or if it tickles you, then pick up a Greek dictionary, too. Get into the Bible. Decide which verses you believe to be factual, which you believe to be truthful, and which you believe to be both, or neither.

The whole point is that God is directly accessible by you. You don't need a pastor, a theologian, a Jesus, or even a Bible. These all exist to bring you closer to God, and can be very good things, if used well. But they are all optional.

You can go straight to God. An intermediary is not required. As already mentioned, Abraham of the Old Testament did. Read the book of Genesis (Chapters 11-25). Abraham had no pastor, theologian, Jesus, or Bible. He had none of these things. It was God and Abraham. And we are told in the Abraham story of how God loved Abraham and provided for Abraham, again and again.

God has given you the power to become a child of God, communing directly with the Almighty. Use the powers God has given you. If you make a mistake or change your mind over time, that is okay. It's part of the process of creating anything, in this case your own belief system and spirit-filled path through the forest of life.

Further, understand that those who write theology and interpret scripture (including professors, bishops, and pastors) within the church are human, just like you. They make mistakes. They misinterpret. Some use original languages, such as Greek, Hebrew and Aramaic. Some don't. Some claim the benefit of proper interpretation being handed down through generations. Some claim authority simply because their job title allows them to claim authority. Some claim that God speaks to them.

If a particular church, pastor, school, or writer aids you in the construction of your beliefs and in your walk with God, then use it. If not, don't. If someone speaks a truth that resonates deep within you, listen and follow until the truth runs dry. But be prepared to step off at anytime you may encounter higher truth or a stronger teacher who resonates deeper within you.

You need to get through the forest. You will only do that by finding resolution to your questions and by discovering and discerning what *you* believe and *why* you believe it. Clinging to someone else's beliefs because you feel you have to only keeps you stuck in the forest or the village.

Of course, Christianity will object to this. The church would like to keep you stuck in the forest or even the village, dependent upon the church and its leaders for your guidance and interpretation. The church and its leaders will tell you only they have the power, authority, and ability to interpret scripture and to take you to Jesus, who in turn takes you to God. But that is flat out wrong. You can go to God directly.

The church says that if you open up scripture for anyone to interpret as they see fit, you will have anarchy. People will use scripture to justify all sorts of actions. But, the truth is, people already do that. People have been doing that for centuries. The church itself has been doing that for centuries, as well. The church and/or church leaders, at one time or another in the church's history, have used the Bible to justify:

- The Crusades
- The forced colonization of countries
- Forced Christian baptism of non-Christian peoples
- The torture and killings of the Inquisition
- American slavery and racism
- The Holocaust
- Collusion with Hitler
- Nearly every war ever fought by a predominantly Christian country
- The oppression of women
- The oppression of the lower classes

- Homophobia
- Gross misconduct by TV evangelists
- Extreme sexual misconduct by clergy
- Economic oppression of other countries

Thus, for the church to condemn individual interpretation of scripture based on the fear of spiritual anarchy is nothing more than the pot calling the kettle black. Run from anyone or any organization that insists you cannot understand or interpret scripture without them. It is a lie, and an attempt to control you.

In this regard, as you go on your spiritual journey, always read the fine print. Many churches that claim to be non-denominational or simply "Christian," for example, are actually ultra-conservative and quite literal in their interpretation of scripture. (Note: Being non-denominational does not mean a church uses all religions. That would be "trans-religious" or "universal." Non-denominational definitely means Christian, just not connected to one exact branch of Christianity. Though, most non-denominational churches have roots in some mainline conservative Christian church.) There is a veneer of acceptance and tolerance. But, all you have to do is click on "Beliefs" and you will see that they are often not what they appear to be.

Many are aggressive literalists, craftily marketing to unsuspecting spiritual seekers. They'll lure you in with a relaxed feel, cool music, and a seeming acceptance of seekers. But, eventually they want you to be like them and think like them. Some shy away from preaching or speaking publicly about heaven, miracles, and other ideas that might be hard for a spiritual seeker/doubter to immediately accept. But, as you move farther into church involvement and Bible study you will be taught the "proper" things to believe on these topics. It is classic bait-and-switch. They want you to believe in their God their way (using willpower if you have to), not grow in *your* understanding of God. Big difference!

When exploring any church to see if it fits you, look for trigger words. If on their "Beliefs" page you read such words as "We interpret scripture literally," or that the Bible is "infallible" or "unerring," or if you find such phrases as "We believe in the resurrection of the dead," it is just old time religion gussied up real nice. They've changed technique, but the content is the same. They have no intention of interpreting scripture in fresh, new ways. It is still a church of the village, unable to speak to the questions and doubts of the forest. They lure you in with coolness, but eventually stick it to you with aggressive Christianity. Beware. Be ready to get off the train when the time seems right.

Bear in mind, these are not bad people. In fact, they are often delightful human beings. The point is that you likely will not find their literalism and rigid belief structure helpful if you are person who is in the forest. Love the person, but be wary of the beliefs.

Perhaps you will attend a church such as this (or any church) for its music, for a sense of spiritual community (which is often the very best part of Christianity), or for great preaching and teaching. Perhaps you will attend because the people are good looking, they serve great food between services, your wife dragged you along, or you lost a bet.

Perhaps you will even choose to be a part of a church for many years. If it feeds you spiritually, great! Just always know where the back door is, in case it comes time for you to move on. Remember, God is the point, not church. Church is a tool. Your goal is to get through the forest, and grow closer to God.

So, go find God.

Where do you start? Wherever your interest lies, wherever your doubts are greatest, and wherever your questions persist. No matter where or what it is, God is there, usually just below the surface. It's time to dig.

Chapter 5

[Change How You Think of Jesus]

"Therefore let us leave the elementary doctrine of Christ and go on to maturity..."

— Hebrews 9: 1

"Anything will give up its secrets if you love it long enough."

— George Washington Carver

IN THE YEAR 2000, *Fortune* magazine published its yearly list of *The 100 Best Companies to Work for in America*. Number one on the list was the medium-sized, Dallas-based company, The Container Store. Started in 1978, and today boasting approximately thirty stores nationwide, The Container Store has carved out a strong niche for itself by helping people organize their living spaces and their closets.

In 2001, The Container Store, once again, found itself atop *Fortune's* list. It sported a newly implemented maternity leave program that surpassed every other company in the country in amount of time off. It also had an untouchable starting wage and vacation program for its retail employees, and many other benefits on top of these.

At the core of this company's success, and seen on many company memoranda, is the little quote by one of its co-founders, Kip Tindell. It reads, "A funny thing happens when you take the time to educate your employees, pay them well, and treat them as equals. You end up with extremely motivated and enthusiastic people.

This philosophy of shared power between owner and worker landed The Container Store a remarkable third year near the top of *Fortune's 100 Best Companies* list. In 2002 it ranked 2nd in the country! Success, according to The Container Store, is founded upon the power of the people. Conversations with employees quickly yield the obvious facts that not only are people taken care of and listened to, they are incorporated into the company deliberations and decision-making. The Container Store's great success is based on the belief that shared power multiplies success and drastically increases people's happiness.

Power to the People

One of the most vexing pieces of the spiritual-religious equation in America is this issue of power. Who really has the power? How is the power being used?

In the opening years of the 21st Century, the power of the people, the power of the victim, the power of the purse, and the power of the law are being wielded in convincing ways in the spiritual-religious realm. For example, the Roman Catholic Church is being publicly humiliated and stripped of a great deal of its power and credibility. This is seen in the dethroning of its highest ranking officer in the United States in 2002, Cardinal Law of Boston.

Just as surely as hidden secrets are coming to the surface about the tragic misuse of power by the clergy, an even greater and far-reaching truth is also becoming visible. Christian leadership is being reminded of what has always known yet never admitted; and the people are seeing what they have never known: The people in the pew have the power. The true ownership of the church and the true power to create change reside not in the church hierarchy, but squarely in the laps of the lay people.

The greatest fear in the Church (other than fear of scandal) is that if the lay are given too much power, or allowed to see how much power they have, eventually they will begin to try to change theology. And, horrible as it sounds, it is a little known fact that church leaders are generally so arrogant as to believe that only they truly understand God, and only they can make determinations of theology. Rather than seeing themselves as the interpreters of the Christian story and their own experience of God, clergy generally see themselves as owners of one unchangeable truth. This truth they must guard from the ignorant masses. This is preached from pulpits and taught in seminaries.

Yet, the people have always had the power. The religious revolution that picked up steam in the 1960s only magnified this power, because it had one primary effect that has forever changed how spirituality and religion are carried out in America. Because of that revolution, America realized that going to church was voluntary, and no longer mandatory. America realized that religion was a choice, not a requirement of life. As a result, religion became a commodity . . . a thing . . . to be chosen or ignored, consumed or discarded. Church, worship services, and beliefs all became optional.

People realized they could cross Christian denominational boundaries (a taboo in some denominations even today), and even the boundaries of other religions, to find a message or way of living that suited their interests and needs. They realized they could speak and be heard. They began to realize they could apply pressure to their clergy and bishops, when necessary, and have that pressure result in change. And, quite recently, people have begun to more fully realize that the power of the spiritual consumer's purse could be a mighty weapon in combating the abuses of bad religion. In all, people have realized that religion is no longer defined for them, but by them.

With this metamorphosis came a growing shift in power. The power shifted from the producers, who formerly commanded the market, to the spiritual consumers, who could now pick and choose the purveyors and services that best suited their needs and wants. People were tasting and sampling everything at the spiritual-religious buffet, from other religions to New Age to agnosticism. What the consumers picked and chose over the next forty years determined which religious organizations lived and died. As a result, many, many churches that weren't providing relevant and compelling services and beliefs soon went out of business, literally.

Another result of this shift in power to the spiritual consumer is that people began to create their own commodity. People began to construct their own religion, or at least their own belief systems. It is quite common today to hear a non-religious person say, "Well, I have my own religion and beliefs. I call it Cheryl-ism (or Jeff-ism). It's a bit of this and a bit of that. It is what I believe. I don't like anyone telling me what to believe. So, I have made my own."

As a result of, literally, thousands upon thousands of conversations with these non-religious Americans, I have begun to see themes and patterns to this multitude of individual religions and belief systems out there. Upon further study, I began to see that many of these belief systems are not incompatible with Christian thinking and the Bible. In fact, when Christianity is re-thought, based on metaphor, it can include most of the truths and wisdom that are already embraced by a great many people outside Christianity's doors.

The intent of the following chapters is not to make you a Christian, but to give you the power and the permission to create ways of thinking about God and life that fit you and aid you in your journey. It is the intent to show you what many people around you already believe. Lastly, the intent is to provide you with new ways of thinking about classic Biblical concepts, so that you might be aided in the construction of your theology and in your walk through life.

All of the concepts in the following chapters are based on two fundamental premises. The first premise is that growing into relationship with God is the point and journey of life. The second premise is that reading the Bible metaphorically, rather than literally, opens up great and powerful truths for the spiritual person seeking God, truths that are not visible by the Christian religion's limited reading of the Bible.

Jesus, Classic Theology, and a New Understanding of the Trinity

"I am in the business of bringing people into relationship with God. And I believe the best way to do that is through Jesus Christ."

— Billy Graham, American Christian evangelist, as quoted on the back of Billy Graham Evangelistic Association fliers. Here Rev. Graham states that *relationship with God* is the point of his life's work. Going through Jesus is not the only way to get to God, but is simply *the way he chooses*.

Once we acknowledge that not everything in the Bible has to be factual, and once we acknowledge that we each have the power and the freedom to read and interpret the Bible on our own, and thereby find God's truths, our attention is naturally drawn to what Christianity has long said is the point of the Bible: Jesus.

What becomes of Jesus? What do we do with a guy who did all sorts of miracles, who died and came back to life, and who eventually floated up into the sky? What do we do with a guy who says in John 14:6, "I am the way, and the truth, and the life; no one comes to [God] but by me?"

These are tough questions, but the answer is simple. You must constantly ask yourself the question, "Do I believe it?" If you do, great. But if you don't, you don't.

The truth is that there are other ways to God. Plenty of people had a relationship with God before Jesus came along, and plenty have done so afterward. In fact, if there is credence in the Biblical passage of 1John 4:7-8, then all people have a relationship with God. For, it reads, "Beloved, let us love one another. For love is of God. And everyone that loves is born of God and knows God. He who loves not, knows not God. For God is love." To love is to know God.

I can recall sitting in a religion class in college, and hearing a student ask the instructor, "So, let's assume there are a billion people in China, and they're all Buddhist."

To which the professor responded, "Well, there isn't, and they're not."

"Work with me!" the student replied. "For ease, let's assume both the population and religious persuasion. Some have heard of Jesus and Christianity, and some have not. But none have bought into it. Are you telling me that they're all going straight to hell when they die?"

"Well, after the Judgment Day, yes . . . more than likely," he responded blithely just as the time arrived for class to end. Quite agitated, most of the students departed amidst a murmur of discussion and questions.

Several hours later, in a conversation over dinner, a fellow classmate, who was seemingly undisturbed by the whole goings-on, said quite plainly, "That is why my parents walked away from Christianity. That is why I, myself, walked away from Christianity. In part, the Christian concept of God just doesn't reflect what I believe. I just couldn't get into the idea of a parent — and God is supposedly *Our Father*, as the Lord's Prayer says — punishing his children forever! Punishment with a purpose is discipline (or *to make a disciple of*, or *to learn*). Punishment forever is just plain cruel. But what's worse is that Christian arrogance that believes they have all the answers! And, if you don't do God their way, you're screwed."

As it turns out, that student was right on all counts. God is bigger than that — both bigger hearted and bigger and harder to understand than the professor's simple solution allows.

Most of Christian theology agrees that God will judge each person who has not been introduced to Jesus according to the law of each person's conscience. But those who have encountered Jesus *must* believe in him and all he said and did.

This is another major way Christianity has entrapped God. It is one of the primary perils from which you must extract God, if you are to personalize God and make God your own.

Put plainly, Jesus is *not* the point of Christianity, the Bible, or the church. If you learn nothing else, you must learn this. One man who lived 2000 years ago is not the point. The God Jesus spoke about is the point. Jesus himself said, "He who believes in me does not believe in me, but in him who sent me" (John 12: 44). When Jesus was in the Garden of Gethsemane before his crucifixion he prayed to God, not to himself (Matthew 26: 39). God is the point! Communion with God is the beginning and the ending.

Jesus is a tool, a method, a way, a path, and a vehicle for communion with God. Many times, Jesus says, "I am the way, the truth, and the life. No one comes to the Father, but by me" (John 14: 6). Now, we've already seen that people can get to God apart from Jesus. Thus, Jesus may not be *the* way, but he sure is *a* way, and a highly effective way. There can be no doubt that Jesus is an absolutely brilliant teacher, one of the best the world has ever known. Plenty of people come to God via Jesus. Yet, plenty of people come to God without Jesus. Sadly, however, Christianity has so fallen in love with the messenger it has forgotten the message and the one who sent them both.

Again, understanding this lone point is one of the single biggest things you can do to set God free and set your spiritual life free: You do not have to believe that Jesus is the *only way* to God. God is the destination. Jesus is a vehicle.

Unfortunately, long ago, Christianity mistook the messenger for the God. It became dogma at the Council of Nicea in the 4th Century when the church crafted the idea of the Trinity — one God in three personas or faces (Father, Son, and Holy Spirit). No longer were Jesus and his teachings the path to God. He became God. And God has been playing second fiddle to Jesus ever since.

Now, to use several different images or concepts to better understand God is one thing. But to *require* belief in each of these concepts is an entirely different matter.

To rescue God from cookie-cutter Christianity is to recognize Jesus' life example and teachings as paths to grow closer to God. It is to see Jesus' teaching as a great way to become intimate with the mover of the universe, whatever you may believe that mover to be. You don't have to believe that this one man was God, or even that he is the only path to God. You need only understand the nobility and power of Jesus' path in deepening a relationship with God and in living in this world.

Hear me clearly on this one point, Christianity says believe in what Jesus says because Jesus is the Savior of the world. But, what I am asserting is that you ought to consider Jesus' teachings *not* because he is Jesus, but because his teachings are powerful and deep, and have stood the test of time. The teachings are not true because the teacher is great; the teacher is great because the teachings are powerful. While it is nothing short of heresy to say this, the bottom line is that it doesn't matter who spoke the truths; the point is that these teachings and truths are just ridiculously powerful, deep, wise, and challenging.

Though Christianity may not like this either, a new way to understand the notion of Christianity's Trinity is to think of God as a house with three doors. One door is marked "God." Another is marked "Jesus." And a third is marked "Spirit." To be in this house is another way of thinking of communion with God. In this house, in this relationship with God, there is the peace, hope, love, and so forth, despite the sorrows of the world.

Some people get closer to God by going through the Jesus door. Some, like Abraham, go through the God door. Yet still others get into the house of God through the Spirit door.[19] This Spirit door is a big old garage door that allows a great many to know God apart from traditional Christian means. As it says in Romans 8: 11, "If the Spirit of Him who raised Jesus from the dead dwells in you, He who raised Jesus Christ will give life to your mortal bodies also through his Spirit which dwells in you."

Recognizing, per official Christian doctrine, that the Holy Spirit is a legitimate and equal member of the godhead, it is also a legitimate path to full relationship with God. In fact, the Apostle Paul in the letter to the Romans (8: 26), accords the Spirit status equal to that of Jesus when he says, "Likewise the Spirit helps us in our weakness; for we do not know how to pray as we ought, but the Spirit itself intercedes for us with sighs too deep for words. [And]...the Spirit intercedes for the saints according to the will of God." Jesus is not the only one who goes to God for us, if we desire, and who takes us to God. The Spirit does so, as well. In fact, Paul solidifies the fact that full communion with God strictly via the Spirit is fully acceptable in Romans 8: 14, "For all who are led by the Spirit of God are sons of God."

Christianity can control and monitor Jesus, because some of his teachings are in print (in the Bible). Christianity takes the liberty of deciding what is and is not official Jesus. In the same way, Christianity strictly monitors what is and is not God. But the Spirit is a far more slippery notion. So much of life, if not all of it, pulses and sighs with the breath of the Spirit of God. Thus, putting a bouncer at the Spirit door is impossible. So Christianity keeps that door locked and boarded up.

Though the Holy Spirit is often spoken of in the Bible, the scary part for Christianity is that nowhere is the Spirit completely defined. No one can claim to know how the Spirit does or does not work. The old saying sung by U2 is so true, "The Spirit works in mysterious ways." No one can say, "Oh, the Spirit doesn't work *that* way" because nowhere does Christian scripture lay it all out.

This means it is fully possible that the Holy Spirit uses creation, itself, as a means to bring people to God and the fruits God offers. This means the Spirit may use unusual events or quite common events. This means the Spirit might use people to bring others to God. This means, also, that it is fully possible the Holy Spirit uses other religions and philosophies as different languages and paths for bringing people to God. This also means you are free to meet God in whatever way God meets you. No one can tell you your path is not a legitimate path to God.[20]

"Who are you to pass judgment on the servant of another? It is before his own master [God] that he stands or falls," the Apostle Paul says (Romans 14: 4).

Again, if you acknowledge the primacy of the Trinity, as all of Christianity does — or even if you don't acknowledge it — you cannot deny that communion with the Spirit of God is fully a right relationship with God. And you cannot deny that there are no clear boundaries on what is and is not the Spirit of God (if there are boundaries, at all). The Spirit allows for far more flexibility and creativity in relating with God than Christianity has ever let on.

So if God is the point of Christianity (not Jesus), if God is the both the destination and the one with whom we walk, and if Jesus is not the only way to God, then what do we do with Jesus?

To answer this, we each must answer this one critical question: What do you want to do with Jesus? As you answer this question, also consider this, a great many people have problems not with Jesus the man, nor even Jesus the teacher. Many people take issue solely with all the other Jesus stuff: The miracles, the dying and coming back to life, the savior of the world, the god incarnate assertion, and the idea of his coming again to judge people at the end of the world.

So, consider this suggestion: If you can't believe the whole son-of-God-miraclemaker-die-and-come-back-to-life thing, try setting all of the miracles and hard to believe "facts" to the side, just as we did with the whale in the last chapter. You don't have to buy them. Let God worry about the "facts." Try thinking of Jesus as simply the master teacher — one of the greatest teachers about life and God that the world has ever known. All of the world's major religions already think of Jesus this way. You may find it to be a good fit, too.

To this way of understanding Jesus, many traditional Christians respond, "Well, doesn't *Christian* mean *follower of the Christ*? And *Christ* means *anointed one* and *savior*. So, how can you be a Christian but not believe Jesus is the savior of the world and the son of God?" This is an excellent point.

However, we must never forget that God was the point of Jesus' ministry. People followed Jesus as a way *to God*. It is no different today. Thus, to be a *Christian* means to follow Jesus' teachings, most specifically his command to bring love to the world, as a way to get closer to God. Jesus is an *anointed one* (or *Christ*) in so far as his path is highly effective in bringing people to God. Jesus is still a *savior* (as will be discussed later) insofar as his path to God can lead us through life's hardships and into a life of peace and joy in God.

Christianity is not named after Jesus. Jesus' last name was not "Christ" as someone else's last name might be Harris or Cartes. Point of fact, no one knows Jesus' last name. More than likely, in his hometown he was simply referred to as

"Jesus bar Joseph" (Jesus son of Joseph). Outside his home region of Nazareth, he was known, as the Bible indicates, as "Jesus of Nazareth." The sign over his head on the cross said, "Jesus of Nazareth, King of the Jews." "Christ" was a title that was largely ascribed to him by humans after he died. Thus, Christianity is not named after him, but is named after the life-saving nature of Jesus' teachings, and about how God "saves" our lives.

Still, the larger point is that you can be a follower of Jesus without taking on the moniker *Christian*. *Christian* is a convenient, general term for one who follows Jesus. But, it is not necessary to claim that title in order to follow Jesus' path or to use the Bible as a vehicle to get closer to God. Jesus said, "A new commandment I give to you that you love one another; even as I have loved you, that you also love one another. By this all men will know that you are my disciples, if you have love for one another" (John 13: 34-35).

The point of life and following Jesus' path, if you choose, is not to become a Christian, per se, and ascribe to a list of beliefs that Christians supposedly are required to believe. The point is to be an instrument of love in the world. Thereby will you know God.

Jesus said, "If you abide in me, and my words abide in you, ask whatever you will, and it shall be done for you. By this my Father is glorified, that you bear much fruit, and so prove to be my disciples. As the Father has loved me, so have I loved you; abide in my love. If you keep my commandments, you will abide in my love, just as I have kept my Father's commandments and abide in his love. These things I have spoken to you, that my joy may be in you and that your joy may be full" (John 15: 7-11).

It is pretty hard to deny that this guy, Jesus, had some brilliant ways of thinking about life, God, and love. He had some radical and difficult ways for living in this world, too. So, try considering Jesus' parables and how he lived life as more than enough to help you discover a deep relationship with God and other humans by using metaphor. You will find that using Jesus as a teacher and tool will bring you to God, and will pull you through the anxieties, sorrow, and frequent aimlessness of life and the spiritual forest.

So, if Jesus was a great teacher, what did he teach?

"Jesus calls men, not to a new religion, but to life."

— Dietrich Bonhoeffer, Lutheran theologian and pastor imprisoned by Nazis for plotting assassination of Hitler; died in prison weeks before Allied liberation.

Jesus taught a lot. In the Biblical books known as the gospels — Matthew, Mark, Luke, and John — you have enough Jesus teachings to challenge you for a lifetime. However, it is possible to boil Jesus' teachings down. In fact, Jesus deliberately boiled it down for us, so that we might never stray from the simplicity of his message.

Jesus understood how easy it is to get confused. Jesus understood that once you start stacking up teachings, beliefs, and requirements, your faith becomes legalistic, oppressive, and suffocating. This was the very religious situation Jesus was railing against.

The gospel books of Matthew (22: 35-40), Mark (12: 28-31), and Luke (10: 25-28) tell the exact same story of Jesus being confronted by a lawyer. The lawyer says to Jesus, "Teacher, which is the greatest commandment?"

Jesus simply responded, "Love God with all your heart, mind, and soul. And love your neighbor as yourself. Everything depends on these two things."

That's it. That is all of Jesus' teachings condensed into one exquisite thought. Jesus boiled it down to make it as simple as possible. So perfect is that teaching that it is quoted or referenced no less than thirteen other times in the Bible. It is found in Deuteronomy, Leviticus, John (two more times), Romans, Galatians, Ephesians, 1Thessalonians, Hebrews, James, 1Peter, and 1John.

If you remember nothing else Jesus taught, if you can strive for nothing else in life, remember and strive for this simple challenge from Jesus. For above all else, Jesus taught love. His central message was not respect, acceptance, tolerance, or even doctrinal flawlessness. It was love. It is the love that takes oneself out of the center of the universe, and puts others first. It is the love that subjects itself to others, so that others might fully live. It is the love that comes from humility and servanthood. It is the love that loves not because it must, but because it can.

It is fascinating to consider Maslow's *Hierarchy of Human Needs* in reference to Jesus' teaching on loving your neighbor. For, they are teaching nearly the exact same thing. Maslow taught that the highest level of need-fulfillment and self-actualization is accomplished by transcending oneself. This is Jesus' point. Isn't it a great irony of life that to make myself happiest I must let go of my own happiness, and strive to bring joy and fulfillment to the lives of others?

Our highest human need is to live for something greater than ourselves. This is done by putting God and other humans at the center of the universe, and to receive the enormous joy that comes from doing so. It is to live compassionately — i.e. with the development of the character and life of others in mind. In short, the highest levels of self-actualization come from helping others on their spiritual journey while simultaneously connecting with the Unknown in our own lives. To put it in Jesus' terms, *living an abundant life comes only from loving God and loving neighbor.*

Jesus taught of love, and lived a life of love for the unloved and the unlovely. Jesus taught that to love people, particularly to love the outcasts, is to love God. This alone is far more challenge than any of us is ready for. Try living that for just one day.

For example, just as Jesus loved the unlovely, try extending love to for one day to people you dislike, or find unattractive and unappealing. There is plenty of scientific evidence that says humans tend to favor or be nice to people we find "attractive," and ignore people or children we find "ugly." Try setting your judgments aside for just one day, and find the beauty — FIND the beauty! — in every person you encounter. Shower love on every person you meet, indiscriminately, as the sun shines on every person.

Conservative yet refreshingly progressive Christian pastor and theologian Gregory A. Boyd, writes, "We have failed to understand and internalize the Biblical teaching that our fundamental sin is not our evil — as though the solution for sin was to become good — but our getting life from what we believe is our knowledge of good and evil. Our fundamental sin is that we place ourselves in the position of God and divide the world between what we judge to be good and what we judge to be evil. And this judgment is the primary thing that keeps us from doing the central thing God created and saved us to do, namely, love like he loves."[21]

Or, maybe it is not physical. Maybe you find someone's meanness, intolerance, or narrow-mindedness ugly. Challenge yourself to put love into action. Talk with them, perhaps. Force yourself to find the beauty in them. Find something you genuinely admire or appreciate about them, and tell them so. Find a way to love an enemy.

Or, bring love and kindness to those who can benefit you in no possible way. Now that is love! Bring the love of compassion, the love of service, the love of forgiveness, and the love of contrition to those who need it.

Or, what about orienting your life to a new life project? Rather than continuing to focus your energies on the acquisition of more things for you and yours, consider re-orienting your life to an entirely new endeavor to do something significant on behalf of some group of people, or some need that you sense. Consider giving love in a way that stretches and taxes you.

This is what Jesus taught: Giving love by putting others first. He taught that *the way to give love is to pull yourself out of the center of the universe,* and put God and the needs of others there. Then you will know joy and the highest levels of human fulfillment and self-actualization!

One of the great issues afflicting America, specifically spiritual seekers, is that of the meaning of life and your purpose in it. It is a common theme in the forest. In his teachings on love we find Jesus speaking directly to this purposelessness. When you find yourself struggling with your purpose in life or God's will for you life, begin to find resolution by asking these questions: "Who do I know that needs love?" and "How can I best bring it?" Jesus' teaching was so simple, yet so incredibly difficult: *Love God and love neighbor.* To be sure, there is more than this message in his teachings. Yet, all Jesus taught can be reduced to this one teaching. In fact, Jesus did reduce it to this. Our task is to live it.

One example of a regular guy living this life of love can be found in Alric, who was a very successful farmer during America's Great Depression and the World War that followed it. With five hard-working children and a wife completely dedicated to the farm, the family, and the community, Alric built a mini-empire in rural Minnesota, near the Canadian border. At the height of his success he owned and operated 1500 acres of land, a phenomenal amount in those days.

In addition to raising crops and animals, he spent the winter months developing new ideas for farming. At one point, he obtained a US Government

Patent for his creation of a Hood Duster, a tractor plow attachment used for crop-dusting potatoes. So productive were his farms and so important was his invention that he was granted an AAA-1 rationing status (a status identical to that of the military, itself) for steel during WWII, a time when most steel was being used to create ships and planes.

But, beyond concern for his own success, Alric was a huge giver to the community. He helped neighbors raise barns and was the driving force behind his community becoming one of the first rural areas in the state to be wired for electricity. He and his wife were philanthropic in support of their church, which was not only the spiritual but also the social center of the community. Alric showered gifts of furs, pearls, and diamonds upon his devoted wife, who regularly returned the gifts, and insisted the money be redirected to the farm, the church, missionary efforts, or the aid of neighbors.

Humble, hardworking, and generous in spirit, Alric and his wife lived a life of complete service to others. They loved their God, and they loved serving people. This life of service brought them more joy than their financial success ever did.

So noble was their example of serving others that their legacy long outlived them. One of their sons became a *de facto* spiritual leader of that rural community, recognized for his wisdom and hearty spirit. Their lone daughter went on to leave that community and serve the Christian church through music and as a manager of financial affairs, herself marrying a man who was a great financial giver to the church and other worthy causes.

On top of this, their three other sons all eschewed the wealth that was available to them, and went on to lives of sacrifice and service as ordained clergy. All of Alric's children went on to build lives dedicated to bringing love to others.

Alric and his family lived Jesus' calling to *love God and love neighbor*. They did so not because it was demanded or required of them, but because they sought only to return to God and neighbor at least a fraction of all that God had given them. In the voice of Alric's youngest son, "You can never out-give God."

But What about Jesus' Resurrection?

So, all of this discussion about Jesus raises the question "What becomes of Jesus' resurrection, which the church has long said is the central point of Christianity?"

The very cornerstone of the Christian faith has always been: (1) Jesus took our sin and died, (2) Jesus was dead for three days, and (3) Jesus came back to life, and eventually ascended into heaven. That is how we know that we are forgiven and that when we die we will come back to life, too. All we must do is say, "Jesus is my personal lord and savior" and believe in him, according to the church.

But reading Jesus' life, death, and resurrection as a parable or metaphor allows for a different interpretation: The cornerstone of the Christian faith is *not* Jesus' resurrection. The cornerstone of Christianity is Jesus' command to love, and is also something far heavier than one man dying 2000 years ago. Whether or not you

believe in Jesus' resurrection and in bodily resurrection for you and me after death, there can be no dispute that in life there is resurrection. God grants us the hope that comes from knowing that there is always new life on the other side:
- The other side of divorce;
- The other side of loss of a loved one;
- The other side of financial ruin;
- The other side of any loss, disappointment, or sorrow.

When in the throes of life's hardships, that knowledge is far more comforting than the flimsy hope for an after-death miracle. The hope for after-death heaven isn't nearly the solace that the guarantee of new life *in this lifetime* is. This is the deeper meaning of the resurrection story. This is the metaphor truth beneath the surface "facts." The very foundation of Christianity is the guarantee that life always brings resurrection.

The rock solid, time-proven certainty that there will be new life, if you can weather the storm, is far more comforting than the blind hope of coming back to life after physical death. "New life will come in my lifetime. And, I thank you for that, God" is a far more comforting thought than the desperate "Save me from all this, please, Jesus," or "Jesus, please make me come back to life and go to heaven when I die."

The point is that there is resurrection in life. Hardship and loss are not the final words, for they constantly give way to new life. God has created a world in which there is new growth and new life. "Behold, I make all things new" (Revelation 21:5). That is the point of life and death, loss and hope, suffering and joy. There is resurrection!

Baby Jesus as a Metaphor

If we view Jesus' life itself as a parable or metaphor, we see that the beginning of his life has great significance, too. It is not just the guarantee of resurrection that brings comfort in life. It is also the miracle of the incarnation that brings us closer to God.

As the story goes, God became man in the form of Jesus. God became incarnate (Latin *caro*=flesh) and broke into the life of humanity so that we might come to God again. Whether or not you buy the factuality of that event, you cannot deny the truth of the metaphor that God breaks into our lives every day. God becomes incarnate in our neighbor, in those in need, and in those who bring laughter and joy to our lives. Jesus said, "As surely as you have done unto the least of my brethren, you have done unto me" (Matthew 25:40). God breaks into our lives in the rising sun and in the beauty of creation; in the comfort of an animal, and in the harmonies of our favorite music. God is continually becoming incarnate in all that is around us.

God breaks into our lives in the morning sun that greets us as we walk to our car; in the nourishment our breakfast provides; or the comfort our morning coffee brings. God offers encouragement and new strength in the words of a co-worker, or in the exercise of a day-ending, head-clearing jog. God brings hope in the form of an unexpected raise or in a vacation waiting four months in the future. God breaks into our lives granting us a sense of purpose by showing an unmet need in the life of someone else.

It is for these daily incarnations that we must give thanks. It is on these daily and dependable actions of God that we must base our lives. These are the promises of God that require no assent to intellectual beliefs. These are the life-truths that underlie the facts.

Besides pointing to resurrections all around, the point of Jesus' teaching was to attune us to and teach us to live in gratitude for all the ways God breaks into our lives everyday. The spirit of Christianity should be one of constant awareness of God's blessings, and a life of constant thankfulness for those blessings. Further, the spirit of the God-follower can be one where God's breaking into our lives becomes the inspiration to do likewise. By God's example, we step into the lives of others as instruments of God, when invited. With us we bring humility, service and loving-kindness.

The effect of Christianity focusing on the literal resurrection as core, rather than daily resurrection and incarnation, is that we lose sight of God in the everyday. By literalizing both resurrection and incarnation we are constantly focused on what God did 2000 years ago and what God is going to do after we die. We live largely in the past or the future. The present is only to be endured.

This mentality is encapsulated well by the refrigerator door of an old friend of mine. The front of the refrigerator was completely bare, except for one item stuck near the top. It was a short, typed statement that read, "Other than heaven, nothing really matters!"

This other-life Christian focus stands in stark contrast to the mindset of today's spiritual seeker. The seeker says, "If your God can't help me *today*, then I don't want to hear about him." This is a mindset that can be more than sufficiently attended to when the God of Christianity is freed from literal interpretation. For, the God Jesus worshipped was the God of today. This God is certainly evident in the lives of many who have gone before us. This God also brings great promise for our future. But Jesus taught that God wants us to have abundant life today!

The point of Christianity is not to foist a belief system of incarnation and resurrection down people's throats, but to be a source of new life (resurrection) and God's blessings (incarnation) every day. The point of Christianity is not the letter of the law or standing on tired doctrine. The point is the spirit of the man who most embodied what humanity believes God to really be. The point is to live in the spirit of Jesus as one who brings resurrection and God to an aching and needy world every day.

It is interesting to note that Mohandas Gandhi, one of the greatest leaders of the 20th Century, often said that he considered himself a follower of Jesus, but not a Christian. To be a *follower of Jesus*, he said, meant to live by the principles of love, justice, and non-violence, which Jesus taught. Yet, to be a *Christian* meant to buy into a belief system that he just couldn't bring himself to believe. So great was this Hindu spiritual leader's respect for Jesus' teachings that they served as the very backbone of his non-violent overthrow of the British government in India. The nobility of Jesus' higher path calls to us, just as it moved in the heart of Gandhi.

The Salvation Jesus Brings

So, if not by bodily, after-death resurrection, then how does Jesus save us today? It took me thirty-plus years to finally understand that Jesus has saved me. I don't mean it in the mythical, difficult-to-understand beliefs that Christianity would have us choke down. Jesus has not saved me from some after-death fate. I mean it in a very real, simple way.

God is not some angry judge or king whom I've offended and from whom I need to be saved. For me to say, "Jesus is my personal lord and savior" is to say that his teachings 2000 years ago give my life purpose and direction today. His teachings were so radical and counter-cultural that Christianity today would be terrified if they really lived with the abandon he did. Yet, his teachings are so powerful that they have turned my life into far more than it would have ever been otherwise.

Martin Luther articulated this message of Jesus well, 500 years ago. At that time, the Roman Catholic Church more or less dominated the Western World. And this man, Martin Luther, is credited with standing up to it, and forever changing the face of religion.

Martin Luther was, among other things, an Old Testament scholar and professor. That meant much of his understanding of Jesus was within the context of the ancient wisdom of the Jewish religion. Luther taught that this religion is rooted, first and foremost, in the very first of the Ten Commandments. It reads, "I am the Lord, your God. You shall have no other Gods before me"....including yourself (Exodus 20: 2-3).

Thus, at the core of his beliefs, teachings, and understanding of Jesus was the rock-solid Bible-based belief that the greatest human error, or sin, (the one that leads to the greatest amount of suffering) is the human tendency to put ourselves at the center of the universe. Whether you buy into the whole Ten Commandments or not isn't the point. The point is that we all do it. We all get so absorbed in our own lives that we lose sight of others, particularly those outside our immediate circle.

Jesus' other-centered teaching is powerfully true, whether you're Christian, Jewish, or something different. Buddhism venerates the Bodhisattva, who finally upon entering Nirvana chooses to turn back; chooses to let go of his own salvation and heaven, if you will, to go back to serve and help others, so that they might know Nirvana.

It is that compassion . . . no, it is that other-centeredness that was at the very heart of Luther's message. But, far more importantly, it was the central point of Jesus' message. All of earth, heaven and hell are determined by your ability to take yourself out of the center of the universe, and place God and neighbor there. Your ascension to the highest levels of spiritual fulfillment is directly tied to your ability to love God and love neighbor.

In 1994, Mother Teresa was invited by President Clinton to speak at the National Prayer Breakfast in Washington, DC. This tiny woman peered over the podium, looking out at a room of highly influential leaders. "It is not enough for us to say, 'I love God.' But, I also have to love my neighbor. St. John says that you are a liar if you say you love God and you don't love your neighbor. How can you love God, whom you do not see, if you do not love your neighbor whom you see, whom you touch, with whom you live? It is also very important for us to realize that love, to be true, has to hurt. I must be willing to give whatever it takes not to harm other people and, in fact, to do good to them. This requires that I be willing to give until it hurts. Otherwise there is no true love in me, and I bring injustice, not peace, to those around me."

Mother Teresa spoke some hard and challenging words to the audience. She pointed the finger of prophetic justice, in love, at them. Yet, ironically, at the end of her talk, they gave her a standing ovation, even though she had just finished calling out their failings. Why did they do this? Because Mother Teresa preached what she had spent a lifetime living — Jesus' self-sacrificing love for neighbor and God.

This is how Jesus saved me! Jesus' teachings radically re-orient my life every day. They challenge and push me to yank myself out of the center of the universe, and give my life in service to others.

Jesus' teachings save us today by calling us out of a life of self-centeredness and consume, consume, consume. Jesus' teachings pull us through the sorrows of life that come when we experience loss — loss of a loved one, a dream, or a thing of great value — by showing us that if we focus on serving others and serving God we will know a God-sent peace that passes all understanding, and pulls us through the loss. We will know greater joy than that which was lost would have ever brought.

Jesus becomes a personal savior by simply having taught a very practical way out of the despair and unhappiness of self-centeredness, which is the most basic human flaw and the root of all human sin, failings, and atrocities. By living a life balanced between loving God and loving neighbor we find heaven today. It is in this balance that we find the joy, peace, power, purpose, aliveness, and hope that we seek.

A Brief Spiritual Exercise

Likely, you are somewhat familiar with Jesus and his story. Take out a paper and pen when you are completely alone, and write down the three things you can absolutely say you know, believe, think, don't believe, don't like, admire, enjoy, laugh about, don't care about, want, or cling to with regard to Jesus and his story. If you were to be totally honest, knowing no one ever has to see, read, or know what you write, write down the three things you honestly believe about Jesus . . . honestly.

Now do a Schmemann, as in the last chapter. Do your general actions indicate these three beliefs or stances? What do your actions indicate about your thoughts on Jesus?

Just for fun, do this same thing with the Bible and with Christianity. Write down three things you absolutely believe, think, don't like, etc. about each of them. If you are feeling strong negative emotions well up, challenge yourself to see if there are any strong positive beliefs you have about either of them. Or, if all you conjure are happy positives, challenge yourself to see if you have any strong negative beliefs. If you don't, that's okay. The point is to write down those things you absolutely believe or know inside you. And if you come up with more than three for any category, keep going.

With these answers you continue to build your foundation of who you are as a spiritual creature. Further you begin to get glimpses of what God is and is not to you. You begin to get rumors of what you need and don't need on your spiritual journey. Most importantly, you begin to more fully understand what you bring to life and how you can be an instrument of God's love in the world.

Reviving the Christian Brand (A brief note for the Christian Church. You may skip this section, if you desire.)

The Christian brand is not anywhere near what it used to be. The names *Christian* and *Christianity* evoked strong affirmative feelings and associations just fifty years ago. Today, Christianity is experiencing a severe shortage of brand strength and brand integrity. Its name and image not only lack punch, but are actually viewed adversely.

To become a player again in the spiritual-religious life of America, Christianity must revive its brand. This is one of the hardest things for any institution or corporation to do. Reversing the momentum of decreasing market share is next to impossible. For, it demands full understanding of the complexity of the market, full understanding and appreciation (if not love) for the organization itself, as well as the courageous objectivity that is unflinching in the face of truth and eager to make the changes needed. Brand revival demands the discipline to carry out strategic mission changes, and the broad shoulders to carry out short-term loss for long-term gain.

In the case of Christianity, brand revival means doing the one thing it absolutely cannot ever imagine itself doing — drastically changing (or re-focusing) its theology. The church had to do this once before, and it was excruciatingly painful. Radical theological change is precisely what happened 500 years ago when the Protestant Reformation completely upended and forever changed Christianity and Western civilization.

Again now, Christianity must re-define, or get back to, its core business. Changes in *how* it does business are not enough. Such changes are mere band-aids, akin to cosmetic tweaking, marketing gimmicks, and ineffective organizational reshuffling. Christianity must change *what its business is*. For it has strayed from its formula. Or, more accurately, its formula no longer works in this cynical and shrinking world.

To re-win the respect of a contemptuous nation Christianity must return to the business of self-sacrificial love. It must make the major shift from being heaven-centered, self-centered (or focused on the church as the essence of spirituality) and centered on Jesus as after-death savior. It must shift, first, to being centered on the self-sacrificial love of neighbor and God. Second, it must shift to radically reworking its understanding of God and the Bible.

Only then will Christianity stand a chance of, once again, being seen as a noble institution that is worthy of respect. It is only by returning to this core business of love at all costs that Christianity can become bigger than itself. Until these theological changes happen, the tide of anti-Christianity will only continue to swell.

Interestingly, just as finally reaching God only comes by relinquishing one's own happiness in order to bring joy and growth to others, so the church must lose itself to re-reach God. It must let go of its brand (and concern for brand strength) in order to gain its brand. This is a task it can only accomplish by sacrificing itself to live out Jesus' calling to *love God and love neighbor*.

To come alive, the church must relinquish all it thought it was, and become all it must be to serve the world. Jesus said, "He who finds his life will lose it, and he who loses his life for [the sake of what I have taught] will find it" [italics mine] (Matthew 10: 39). Jesus' words are just as true for the church as an organization as they are for the individuals who populate the church.

Jesus taught that there is no lasting joy or peace until you die to yourself. Whether speaking to an organization or the individual spiritual seeker, Jesus (like Maslow and the Buddha) said that you must give up all you hold dear if you are to ever taste the living water. The more you relinquish, the more your thirst will be quenched. To find God, you must let go of yourself. And, as self-obsessed, self-pleasuring Americans, this is the hardest thing we could ever be asked to do. Yet, there is no other way.

Chapter 6

[Change How You Think of God]

"Meister Eckhart [13th Century monk and mystic] *said, 'The ultimate and highest leave-taking is leaving God for God.' It is leaving your notion of God for an experience of that which transcends all notions. The mystery of life is beyond all human conceptions."*

— Joseph Campbell[22]

IN 2001, A DOCUMENTARY MOVIE WAS RELEASED that told the story of a handful of early-teenage outcast kids living near the ocean in southern California in the 1970s. This movie, *Dogtown and Z Boys*, shows how these kids of broken homes and modest financial means grew up dreaming of becoming professional surfers.

After telling of their surfing exploits and influences, the movie goes on to detail how, when not surfing, these boys (and one girl) would carve boards out of wood to resemble mini-surfboards. They would then buy old, metal roller skates at the thrift store, cut them in half, and screw the wheels onto the bottom of the board. After that, it was only a matter of finding and skating the nearest elementary school yards, whose lots had been newly paved.

Their thirst for new challenges quickly outgrew tame elementary yards. So, in the drought of the 1970s, when residents of Los Angeles were forbidden from filling their swimming pools with water, an opportunity was born in the minds of these boys and in the areas surrounding the *Dogtown* neighborhood.

These kids began driving through alleys of nearby neighborhoods, scoping out the many empty pools where residents were not home. They then spent the day, quite ingeniously, skateboarding the slopes, curves, and banks of empty pools, until the owners returned home. With time, their quest for fresh challenges became so fervent that they would bring along an old water pump and tubing in their car, and would drain residual water from promising pools.

This documentary, by director and former *Z Boy* Stacy Peralta, tells how, long before skateboarding's commercialization and move into the mainstream, these ten teens were daily honing their art, becoming masters of the craft. Then, by this odd, seminal act of mastering dry pool skateboarding, they single-handedly started the entire skateboard craze in America.

With that, a revolution started in the world of sports. This revolution would not only turn skateboarding into a sport, but would turn the very nature of sports on its head, literally and figuratively. With the impact of the *Z Boy*-style of skateboarding, American sports became upside-down, flipping, spinning, twisting demonstrations of flair that barely existed prior to then.

Hard to believe? Watch the video. Today, nearly the entire world of extreme sports (a billion dollar industry) traces its roots directly to skateboarding. The very language of these sports, for example, is original skateboarding language. One first generation descendant of skateboarding — snowboarding — is an Olympic winter sport! Ironically, today even surfing itself, which gave birth to modern skateboarding, uses moves and terminology taken directly from skateboarding.

So great was their impact that they also influenced the world of music and international commerce Skateboarding was a large reason for the spread and popularity of punk music, later directly influencing such enormously popular bands as *Pearl Jam*. On top of that, Tony Hawk, one of the original *Z Boys* and indisputably the world's greatest skater, has a line of video games that has been recognized as the very best in its genre in the world, yielding hundreds of millions of dollars for its namesake and its maker, Activision.

The direct and indirect effects of skateboarding — skateboarding of all things!! — are the perfect example of the odd, yet powerful work of the Spirit of the Universe. Those kids felt called to do what they did, called to express their energy and creativity. Thus, though far from a religious story, their story is a perfect example of beautiful spirituality — following one's inner calling, no matter how strange it seems.

Though God is never mentioned and cannot be read by an outsider back into the story, there can be zero doubt that by doing what they ached inside to do these 10 or so kids ended up becoming an inspiration for millions of others. Whether they intended to or not, these kids became vehicles for God's activity in the world — changing lives, generating new creations, and opening doors for God's spirit to act.

Now, 25 years later, their activity is still having an impact, to the point of having a movie made about them, being interviewed on everything from NPR to prime-time TV, and being included in a book on spirituality and religion in America. Go figure.

So, what does it mean to love God?

"Talents, large or small, are God-given. They are a sacred trust."

— Paul Robeson

In the last chapter, we saw that *love your neighbor* is straightforward in meaning. It is Jesus' challenge to each of us to become a servant of humanity. We are all called to stop making our own best interests, our own lives, and our own inner circle our whole reason for living. We are called to remove ourselves from the center of the universe, and place there those who are most in need.

That's the "what" we are supposed to do with our lives. But "how" we carry that out is unique to each one of us. And, it is this notion of *what* and *how* that offers insight into Jesus' teachings for creating an abundant life.

Jesus taught us *what* spirit is to dominate our lives — the spirit of other-centeredness. But the Bible never tells us exactly *how* we are each supposed to spend our lives. Your particular name is not mentioned in the Bible. So how can you know, specifically, *how* God wants you to use your life?

The answer is that God speaks an individual purpose to each one of us. That is the *how* of carrying out our mission of loving our neighbors. By loving God, listening to God, and heeding God we discover *how* God has planned for each of us to bring love to the world. You discover, specifically, *how* <u>you</u> are to bring love to your neighbor and humanity. By following God's will for our lives, we become co-creators with the Spirit of the Universe itself.

But what does that mean? What does it mean to love and listen to God?

Many of us spend countless frustrating years asking the question, "God, what is your will for my life?" Desperately, we read the Bible, read the self-help books, and look into the faces of those whom we trust, trying to discern God's will. And all that rises up to speak to us is a confusing and deafening silence. We discover that nowhere outside of us is God's will written for our individual lives. Nowhere in the Bible is your full name mentioned with God's exact will for your life delineated.

I have come to believe very strongly, after many years of wrestling with this, that Jesus did not speak mythically, esoterically, or in some heavenly, churchy, special God-talk. Christianity has so twisted what God is that we have lost the notion of God speaking to each one of us the calling of our lives. It is very, very Biblical that God speaks our mission directly to us. In fact, nearly every single major character in the Bible had God speak to him or her, at one time or another! If God's message doesn't come as a "voice" from the heavens, it is through some other means that is fully convincing to the hearer (convincing not by the standards of others, but by the standards, whatever they may be, of the hearer). Quite often this comes in very plain form of an inner knowing.

Jesus spoke in very tangible, very real, very everyday language and concepts. He spoke to plumbers, postal workers, anesthetists, farmers, landlords, lobstermen, waiters, administrative assistants, amusement park operators, hookers, customer service reps, social workers, and small business owners in their language. He spoke in concepts that were simple enough to be clear and appealing to regular people.

So when Jesus taught people to *love God*, and when Jesus spoke continually about letting God into your heart (Colossians 3: 15; Ephesians 3: 17, 6: 6; 1Timothy 1: 5; Revelation 3: 20), Jesus was teaching nothing grand or enormous, nothing more than simply listening to your gut, your own instincts, and that voice within that you know is your truth. To love God is to love and follow that voice inside you. In that voice is God's message for your life.

The spirit of God speaks a unique calling to each one of us. It is the *how* we are to live our lives. And it is the balance to the *what* of loving our neighbor and sacrificing ourselves for others. One is *what* the purpose of life is — to love God and neighbor. The other is *how* we carry out that loving of neighbor and God. It is the actions, projects, tasks, and dreams we do in service of humanity and God.

The voice inside is the only place you will find God speaking your specific name. Your calling speaks to you through your hunches, your own personal beliefs, and your views on life. Your calling speaks to you through the particular gifts and abilities you bring to life. Your calling speaks to you through the very simple things you are interested in and driven by. All of these things are indicators of your calling.

In Romans (14: 4), the Apostle Paul writes, "Who are you to pass judgment on the servant of another? It is before his own master that he stands or falls." God, the master, has a distinct relationship with each one of us. None of us can judge another's relationship with God. God speaks a unique message to each of us, and it is to this message, and only this message (in balance with Jesus' call to love), that we must answer with our lives. God's call to each of his servants, or children, is completely specific to that person. In the words of Rev. Greg Boyd, "We are thus to regard each person's relationship to God as *sui generic* (literally 'a unique genre,' or 'one of a kind'). It is as though each person has his or her own God before whom he or she stands."[23]

To live in service of God and neighbor is, for most people, not to go and be a monk in the mountains of Peru. Instead, it is to do something within the context of all the things you are already good at, have an interest in, and are driven by. It's as if when you were created God put a chip in you that encoded all of this. And it is within the context of all the encoding of your life that you are to fulfill your purpose. As mentioned, God doesn't speak in a terribly complicated language.

Just look at what you're good at and what you enjoy, and then dream of ways you can use that to be of service to humanity. It's that simple.

Those who are miserable, frustrated, depressed, or sorrowful have been trapped into not hearing or not following their own creative call from within. Those who are unhappy are so because they are not free to serve and love humanity in the way their hearts are calling them to serve.

In contrast, those who have the greatest joy are those who are not only creating what their spirit is calling them to create, but are doing so in the service of humanity. It is that notion of not only being happy (which is a residual effect of loving and expressing God's creative impulse inside you), but of giving back to the world in some significant way. These people are living the balance Jesus taught — *love God and love neighbor.*

However, such a life requires rescuing God from the Christian understanding of God as a being floating around somewhere in space. To live a bounteous life, to live the life Jesus taught demands seeing God not as a being, thing, or entity, but as a spirit, energy, force, power, the universe, or even as life itself.

In the book of John, Jesus says, "God is spirit, and those who worship him must worship in spirit and truth" (4: 24). It means thinking of God not as something or someone you may one day see, and not as a person. It means first understanding God to be a spirit, pulse, vibration, or energy you sense, feel, or know in you; something you have the power to tap into every day.

It also means taking God from being out there somewhere to being right here, right now, inside you and all around you. Whatever God is, God created nature and you. This is God's nature around you. You are a creature of the energy and matter of the universe. Just as the gazelles have been imprinted with an internal code to run fast and to eat; just as the gardenia has been imprinted with a code to grow, flower, and smell divine; so too have you been imprinted with a code by the creative energy of the universe for how you can best serve humanity using the gifts and passions you have been given.

A friend recently relayed how, as a child and teen, he used to spend hours reading comic books and trying to draw the characters in them. Deemed a waste of time by his teachers and parents, he kept hidden his desire to make his own comic books one day. Yet, he persisted in his reading and his drawing, because it made him very happy to do so.

Quite recently, he was hired as an intern by a reputable comic book company. Today, he is living his dream, spending his days making comic books to entertain and delight children. In this unique way he brings life and love to others, and his own soul is filled with joy. One can only speculate about the many ways he is not even aware of in which God is using his life to help and change the lives of others.

We rescue our own lives by rescuing God from Christianity's one way of thinking of God. By thinking of God as Spirit and energy, and as calling to us our purpose from within, we are set free to live the life-giving balance of *love God and love neighbor* that Jesus taught. We are not forced to choke down somebody else's version of God and somebody else's idea of what we should do with our lives. We know the *what* and the *how* of our existence.

We are given room to be a part of the creative process. We are freed to communicate with God ourselves. We are given a major say in what we do with our own lives, and what becomes of this world with which we have been entrusted. Free will and God's will become united and indistinguishable.

Love neighbor implies taking responsibility for others. *Love God* implies a freedom to live life and love neighbor as you believe God has called you to do. It enables you to carry that responsibility for neighbor joyfully, because you can create the fashion in which it is done. You have a say in how you live out your life purpose.

You must remember: Only you can hear the calling of your heart. While others may confirm your calling, only you have the liberty to know what God is calling you to do with your life. You have the freedom to craft *how* you live your life in love of others!

God Around Us

Yet, still, there is so much more to God and to loving God than just hearing and heeding the voice of the Spirit within you. There is also a real sense of God apart from ourselves and our neighbor.

As surely as God is the Spirit and energy of the universe, loving God means creating over a lifetime a sense of unity and peace with creation. It is a great respect for and communion with earth, creatures, trees, waters, fire, stars, and all with whom we share life.

Mahavira, the father of the Jain religion, said, "Harmlessness is the only true religion." Loving God is that great reverence for all of life, not just humanity and humanity's interests. It is living in connectedness with the Spirit of all that lives, moves, and breathes above us, under us, and around us. God is in all things.

This connecting to all of life is one area where Buddhism is so much more developed and effective than Christianity. Where Christian prayer too easily and too often is the degenerate wishing and asking for things un-had, Buddhist meditative techniques are a highly effective tool for quieting one's mind and life. They are great for letting go of the encumbrances that obstruct connection with all that lives and breathes around us. By letting go of the obstacles, one is able to better hear the voice of God within oneself *and* experience the presence of God all around oneself.

To see God as both within us and around us is to begin to understand the fullest nature of God. Just as anything you create (a business, a child, a house, or a piece of art) is a part of you, so also does each bit of creation throb with some part of the Divine. Ours is not a distant God. Ours is a very real and everyday God or Energy, constantly speaking to us in all we encounter. Every experience, every thing, and every person is a metaphor of God. Everything in some way bears a message to you from God. It may be simple or complex. You need only play with it and let it speak to you.

It is so easy to grow accelerated in the pace of life that we rush through it, moving and acquiring, quite oblivious to the pulse and heaving of life under and around us. As surely as we fail to feel that pulse in all we encounter, we fail to experience God. That pulse is the sure voice of God waiting to be heard.

If we step out of the consumerist loop that is continually shouting at us, we begin — just begin — to hear God's quiet voice. When we begin to follow that voice we feel a peace we've not felt before, even though upheaval maybe be all around us. Slowly our lives begin to lighten, and we know a new joy and laughter. Hope springs up for the great possibilities that can now happen. A new sense of brotherhood with our neighbor fills our lives. And, over time, as we follow our new sense of purpose, as we get used to hearing and trusting God's calling, we discover a new strength and power welling up within us.

As we begin to hear the voice and pulse of God, we also sense it teaching us of life and our calling. In fact, it is not until we can hear and feel the needs of this world in which we live that we can begin to know our purpose.

For, your life purpose is spoken to you inside you, but resonates with a need outside you. Until you can feel the needs and aches of this world, you cannot know how your gifts, talents, drives, and abilities can be of service. To live in joy is to walk in the balance of acting on the call from within as a response to the call of the world's needs around you. There has to be a perceived need in the world that hits you hard inside, inspiring you, calling you out of your little life of self-service into greatness of action.

To only follow your own voice at the expense of the world becomes self-centered shallowness. To only heed the call of the world's needs, at the expense of your own creative inner voice, leads to bitterness and misery. In contrast, for example, Mother Teresa gave her life for those in need, but she did so in a manner that complemented her character and brought her joy.

And this, most surely, is one of the sweetest fruits of knowing God. This is one very real and tangible human experience of relationship with God. This is what it means to be saved by God through Jesus. It is to have a sense of real purpose in meeting the needs of the world. It is to do so in a way that grows out of who I am, and is simply joy-filled, and even fun.

To know and love God is to be pulled from the frenetic madness of consumption and clinging to stuff and people; things that can never fill that longing and hunger inside. It is to discover a very real answer to the fundamentally spiritual question, "What is my purpose in life?" It is to be shown a new way of living that makes you a bearer of God's fruits to others. It is to rise to the top of the Hierarchy of Human Needs by letting-go of self-happiness and pursuing the building-up of others. And that sense of joyful service of humanity offers a greater sense of inspiration and aliveness than any other venture we may undertake.

A Bit More on God

Finally, to live in relationship with God, to be in the house of God, is to know not only purpose, but peace, power, hope, joy, and love. It is to know these even as life swirls about you, and as you pass through life's hardships and darkest storms. For, relationship with God has never meant being exempt from suffering or being rescued from life's sorrows. It is not a way out, but a way through. Relationship with God is living in these fruits, and bringing these fruits to others, even as life groans with sorrow around you.

You do not have to buy into the Christian notions of a "god." You do not have to believe in a being that is floating around in space. You don't have to buy into a higher power, an energy, or even an unknown force in the universe. You may simply see life as life, and what is seen is what is, and what is unseen is not. That is your choice. The spiritual quest is the same, however. It is that quest for the lasting fruits of peace, power, purpose, hope, community, joy, love, dance, and laughter.

This is the experience we all seek. This is the universal path and goal of the spiritual seeker — new life within *this* lifetime. It is a path only achieved by (1) Rescuing God from the sky and some Christian heaven; (2) Listening for the Spirit of the Universe and the Spirit of life within you and around you; and (3) Having the courage to follow the call of the Spirit, no matter where it leads.

Final Questions

Now, one may ask, what if your heart is calling you to "self-serving" things. Our hearts can be wrong, and can be motivated by selfish desires, some say. Is it really the voice of God if it is selfish? Shouldn't the hearts calling be rightly ordered? Shouldn't it be subservient to some higher good?

These questions raise an excellent and scary point. The answer is that if it's *not* somehow self-serving, it is probably *not* God's call.

Yes, that right. Read it again.

Remember: Life's greatest joy comes by living a balance between the *what* and the *how*. *What* Jesus encourages you to do is *love God and love neighbor*. That is your life mission. *How* you do that is up to you. You might as well choose some way that brings you joy — i.e. is self serving. In fact, if your fulfillment of the *what* is not self-serving, you will not long be able to carry it out. You will quite quickly become bitter. The difficult balance of life is finding a way to breathe life into others that simultaneously breathes life into you.

As mentioned earlier, the apostle Paul wrote, "For it is written in the Law of Moses, 'You shall not muzzle an ox when it is treading out the grain.' Is it for oxen that God is concerned? Does he not speak entirely for our sake? It was written for our sake, because the plowman should plow in hope and the thresher thresh in hope of a share of the crop" (1Corinthians 9: 9-10). Our "share of the crop" is that in bringing self-sacrificing love to the world we find joy, peace, and hope, ourselves.

Again, this is the balance of the *what* and the *how*. General Douglas MacArthur was quoted as saying, "Never tell a person how to do something. Tell them what to do, and they will surprise you with their ingenuity." *How* you carry out Jesus' command to love will grow out of your gifts, abilities, joys, and desires. That which you enjoy doing can be used to bring joy and growth of character to others. Even Mother Teresa and Jesus got joy, love, and peace in their self-sacrificial love. That is both the paradox and the balance of following Jesus' call to love and the God-calling in your heart.

By following the complementary calls of God and Jesus, by living the *what* and the *how*, and by boldly breathing life into those God has called you to touch, you insure that you will not be forgotten. The nobility of your actions will bring you the greatness of living on and inspiring those who have been moved by you. There is no higher goal to which you can aspire.

In whom will your spirit live on? What is it that you are doing in this lifetime that will live on as your spirit?

Yes, but. . . .

This still doesn't answer the question "What if your heart calls you to do something bad?"

The answer is simple. No matter what your heart calls you to do, it is always to be balanced with Jesus' call to love God and love neighbor (Remember the *what* you are to do with your life.). The intent, the context, and the goal of following your heart is to bring love to the world. Therefore, the ever-present check and balance to God's calling in your heart is the plain question, "Does this bring the maximum love possible to the world, or is there a higher path?"

A Little Spiritual Exercise

What do you know, deep inside, about you? Is there one gift, ability, thought, charm, reason, or talent about which you can honestly say, "I know this is a strong gift I have been given by God." Perhaps there are more. So, what are the three or four talents or abilities you have that you know you really have? What are the things you know you do well?

Next, there are likely many gifts that you have or will discover about yourself in your lifetime. But often they are unified by one primary purpose or drive, about which you can say, "This is the reason God put me on this earth." At your essence, what is the reason you have been given these gifts? More accurately, what is the drive that these gifts and talents work for? What unifies them?

Rev. Dr. Roland Martinson, a beloved Lutheran seminary professor, is an older gentleman widely known for his gifts of extreme vitality, innate sense of long-term vision, ability to win people's hearts, and a deep understanding of the complexities and problems of the church, among other things.

However, it is fascinating to hear Dr. Martinson describe his own reason for existence — that is to say, the unifying principle for his gifts and abilities. He says, "I am a star-thrower. I see my life as a long walk on an ocean beach. As I walk, I come across starfish that have washed up on shore. My job in life — the purpose of my life — is to throw the stars back into the ocean, so that they can live again. That's it. That's what I'm here for."

Beautiful, isn't it? By touching individual lives, by impacting the education of future leaders, and by changing flawed systems, Dr. Martinson gives life back to people. He uses his gifts and abilities toward the unifying loving purpose of throwing stars. Each hurting person is a star, in his eyes, just waiting to find its home, again.

What are your gifts? What is the specific message and call that God is speaking directly to you? Have you yet figured out for your life what the unifying principle is? What is the purpose to which all your gifts are applied?

And, Jesus might ask of you one more question, "Are your gifts and unifying principle being used to bring love to the world?"

"At age 7, Mozart wrote his first symphony.

At 12, Shane Gould won an Olympic Medal.

At 14, Leann Rimes topped the country music charts.

At 17, Joan of Arc led an army in defense of Europe.

At 57, Ray Kroc founded McDonald's.

At 71, Michelangelo painted the Sistine Chapel.

At 80, George Burns won his first Oscar.

At 104, Cal Evans wrote his first book on the American West."

— Gil Atkinson

Chapter 7

[Listen For God's Quiet Voice . . . So God Doesn't Have to Yell]

"Suffering, I . . . think, [is] essential to a good life, and as inextricable from such a life as blessings. It's a great enhancer . . . "[24]

— Lance Armstrong, 6-time *Tour de France* winner and cancer survivor

"My house is burned down, but I can see the sky."[25]

— Sally Reed, speaking of the role of cancer in her life

"Change will not occur until the pain of staying the same exceeds the pain of changing."

— Mark Ebner, Gen X bicycler

"Sometimes you have to lose major championships before you can win them. Losing is a learning experience that's worth a fortune."

— Tom Watson, golfing legend

IN THE 1950s AND 60s, America was consumed by the explosion of the Civil Rights Movement. Martin Luther King, Jr., Rosa Parks, Medgar Evers, Malcolm

X, and millions of others mobilized their power to bring equal rights to African Americans. As a result of their efforts, the chains of oppression were broken. Many people were given new life, and American culture was forever changed for the better, even though the need for further change continues today.

But what happened in that brief time was not something that had sprung up out of nowhere. The urgency expressed by those *millions* was the result of only *thousands* of people in the century leading up to it speaking against racial injustice in America. Prior to those *thousands* were *hundreds* of people trying to be heard. Preceding the *hundreds* were *mere pockets* of Americans, in the century prior to that, who realized that slavery and racial oppression were wrong, and who spoke out against them.

The lesson is that unfortunately in life, we seldom listen to the quiet voice. The truth is not always heard. Sometimes truth needs to gather momentum and be spoken louder before it is honored and heeded. Sometimes we only hear a message when it is shouted to us. This is what happened in the Civil Rights Movement. The quiet voices from centuries prior turned into the million shouting voices of the 60s. Then finally the message was heard.

The creative voice of God, speaking to you from within, is no different from the Civil Rights Movement in this regard. As mentioned in previous chapters, to love God is to listen to God's quiet voice inside, telling you what your calling is. It is to love and follow the destiny that life and God imprinted on you at a very young age. But, often we do not listen or follow. Instead, we ignore it, and tell ourselves that life isn't so bad, and that we don't need to change. However, as time goes on, God — or the voice of your own creative Spirit — uses louder and stronger means to get through to us and move us to higher ground.

The discomfort must increase. The pain must get worse. The disharmony between your inner life and the life outside you and around you must become so grating that you crave change. For oftentimes, as with Jonah in Chapter Four, until the pain becomes unbearable, you will not change your outer life to reflect who you are on the inside.

This chapter is about how God sometimes has to make life harder and more painful before we start listening to God's voice — opening ourselves to learn, grow, and experience more richness and fullness in life. This chapter is about creating a life where your inner and outer lives are integrated and seamless. It is about making your dreams materialize by learning to listen to the voice of God inside and learning to find meaning in suffering.

God Can be a Real S.O.B.

No matter what your religion or what your spirituality, the most politically incorrect (spiritually unacceptable) thing you could possibly say in America about God is that God is anything but loving. To assert that the Spirit of Life is angry, vengeful, or violent is heresy to Christians and non-Christians alike. Particularly in a terror-charged world, leaders of popular religion are quick to condemn anything violent, especially the notion of a destructive God. God, as popular thinking goes, is a force of love and goodness, and anything evil or suffering-related in life is the result of human depravity or sin, not God.

In the last century, Christianity has taken this to new heights, boxing God into not only goodness, but also niceness. God is love. God is happy. God is sweet. And Christianity has called Christians to be the same.

Yet, something about this nice-ifying of God and spirituality doesn't quite ring true to experience. For, where is the evidence of God being nice or only kind? If you accept Christian scripture as authoritative, you cannot possibly conclude that the God of Abraham, Moses, David, Jeremiah, Jesus, Paul, and John is non-violent. God may be loving and good, but God is also terrible, destructive, and at times mean.

For example, in the Old Testament saga of the Israelite people we read of God continually trying to enact good in their lives. We read how God had a plan, but how the Israelites continually strayed from what God wanted them to do, and what they had promised God they would do. They simply would not listen to God. Time and again, they turned a deaf ear.

Eventually, God laid down the law, or commandments, to tell the people exactly what was expected of them. But the people just couldn't bring themselves to get on God's agenda. They couldn't break themselves of their bad habits and broken paths.

So, on occasion, God used some very strong and unpleasant means to get God's voice heard and to move the Israelites to higher ground. Here is a snippet from their story:

"And God spoke all these words [to Moses], saying, 'I am the Lord your God, who brought you out of the land of Egypt, out of the house of bondage. [Here are my 10 commandments:] You shall have no other gods before me.... And you shall not kill . . .'

"When the people saw that Moses delayed to come down from the mountain, the people gathered themselves to Aaron....and he received the gold at their hand, and fashioned it with a graving tool, and made a molten calf; and they said, '[This] is your god, O Israel.' When Aaron saw this, he built an altar before it.

"And Moses turned, and went down from the mountain with the two tablets of [commandments] in his hands, tablets that were written on both sides.

"And as soon as he came near the camp and saw the calf and the dancing, Moses' anger burned hot, and he threw the tablets [of the Commandments] out of his hands, and broke them at the foot of the mountain. And he took the calf which they made, and burnt it.

". . . Then Moses stood in the gate of the camp, and said, 'Who is on the Lord's side? Come to me.' And all the Levites gathered themselves together to him. And he said to them, '*Thus says the Lord God of Israel*, "Every man should put his sword on his side, and go to and fro from gate to gate throughout the camp, and every man kill his brother and his friend, and his neighbor."' And the sons of Levi did according to the word of Moses; and there fell of the people that day about three thousand men.

"*Then the Lord sent [another] plague upon the people*, because they worshipped the calf which Aaron made" [italics mine] (Exodus 20, 32).

We learn in the story above that immediately after God gave Moses the Ten Commandments (including "Thou shalt not kill") it was *God's will* that Moses slaughter the Israelite men, three thousand of them. God is so angry that God breaks the law and destroys three thousand of God's chosen people.

But, as if that wasn't enough to quench God's rage, God also sent a plague upon the people! For the same offense! God was pissed!

We read in another part of the Bible that it was *God's will* that every living thing in the world, except for Noah and his family and two of every animal, be destroyed with a great flood (Genesis 6: 17-19). In the New Testament, it was *God's will* that Jesus, his own son, should be killed (Mark 14: 36b). Yes, according to Christian theology, God murdered his own son. This is an echo of another Old Testament story which begins with the words, "And God said [to Abraham], 'Take your son, your only son Isaac, whom you love, and go to the land of Moriah, and offer him there as a burnt offering upon one of the mountains of which I shall tell you" (Genesis 22: 2).

Now, the point here is not "Follow the 10 Commandments." In a way, the message has nothing to do with you. The message is that the God of Christianity is no nice god of simple happiness. This ferocious God also has a long history of violence, punishment, torture, and wrath. The God of Christianity cannot be whitewashed. God is what God is.

But, you don't even have to believe in God to see the violence of the Spirit of the Universe. Whether you believe nature is God's creation or simply just nature, whether you see God as spirit or as the force of the universe, you cannot deny that the forces of the world — the forces of nature — are both beautiful and terrible, warming and wicked, yin and yang. It would be just plain naive to think otherwise.

The lioness violently destroys the zebra. The quick kill of a thousand swarming bees becomes the food of life for other creatures. Fires rage with the fury of a thousand suns. Mudslides and avalanches kill in an instant what years have created. Floods wash away life upon life. The tornado laughs as it tears asunder whatever its random finger touches, smashing one creature while leaving the next unharmed. The tempestuous ocean crushes at will any that would presume superiority. Volcanoes erupt. Stars explode.

Yet, just as surely as the lioness crushes the skull of the zebra, new life is fed in the womb of the feline, and in all other creatures, great and small, that feed on that skull. Just as surely as fires ravage forests, new life breaks through the charred earth and continues the cycle. Just as surely as the ocean swallows the reckless, the creatures of the deep are given food for life and growth.

The nature God created is one where death begets life, violence births peace, suffering breeds strength, and chaos always, always precedes order. Things must die for things to live. Creation is always preceded by destruction.

Thus, conceiving of a God that is only nice, nonviolent, or happy is both difficult and ludicrous. Every religion of the world has as its creation story some tale of order being crafted out of chaos. Floods, fires, and voids are stirred to attention and sequence. And always there are stories of violence against violence in the destruction of evil or the nonfunctional. In every religion violence and destruction are characteristics of the divinity.

For example, the Japanese religion of Shinto tells of Izanagi, Izanami, and Amaterasu birthing a line of gods and emperors who tamed the chaos into heaven and ocean, and then conquered and consolidated the lands into the divine land of Japan.

One of Hinduism's three primary gods is Shiva, who is known as the god of creation and destruction, as well as god of the dance, god of preservation, unveiling of illusion, and liberation of the soul. In a classic icon, known as the Natraj, Shiva is in a dance Surrounding Shiva is a circle of fire (which destroys the universe), while one foot crushes the evil forces of spiritual ignorance and one hand beats the drum of creation. Just as Shiva destroys, he calls forth new life.

Jesus himself understood the dance of creation and destruction. He said, "Do not think I have come to bring peace on earth; I have not come to bring peace, but a sword. For I have come to set a man against his father, and a daughter against her mother, and a daughter-in-law against her mother-in-law; and a man's foes will be those of his own household. He who loves father or mother more than me is not worthy of me; and he who does not take his cross and follow me is not worthy of me. He who finds his life will lose it, and he who loses his life for my sake will find it" (Matthew 10: 34-39). A bit disturbing, don't you think?

Even more compelling than that is fact that the central story of all Christianity — the crucifixion and resurrection of Jesus — is also the most violent and terrifically gruesome, as well. God insisted that his son be not just killed (as with a quick-death-bringing heavy blow to the head or arrow through the heart), but violently and savagely brutalized and left to die the slow death of crucifixion — i.e. fatigue, blood loss, suffocation, and being eaten by creatures of the air. According to Christianity, the saving of the world absolutely required that God send his son to be killed. Yet, Christianity refuses to acknowledge that God uses bad to bring about good.

It's interesting to note that even the most peace-loving of all spiritual leaders alive today, the Dalai Lama, acknowledges that violence is sometimes necessary in life, even by the spiritual, as a way to destroy evil.[26]

The terrible side of spirituality and God scares much of Christianity. Certainly nothing bad can be related to God, the thinking goes. Further, if God is violent and seemingly fickle, then people will fear God, and fear seems so non-spiritual, so primitive, and so un-evolved. Surely we shouldn't fear God, Christians say.

But fear and death are just as much a part of life as love and laughter. They exist in a dance, quite inseparable.

A Bad God is a Good Thing

Ironically, this notion of a God who is both loving and destructive can be a great comfort to all who suffer. To know that it is an inevitable fact that order will follow chaos is a great comfort when in the throes of pain and hardship. To trust that death and destruction are parts of God's plan enables us to have confidence that suffering is neither random, nor pointless. Suffering is not punishment, but in fact holds the seeds of new life.

The ubiquitous bumper sticker of the early 1990s said, "Shit Happens!" This is a way some people explain the bad stuff that befalls them in life, stuff that seems to come out of nowhere. Shit just happens, people think. But that shit has an origin.

Horrible as it sounds, the "bad" stuff is a means God (or life, or the spirit of humanity) uses to speak to us and move us to higher ground. It is not that God simply turns life's bad stuff into good.[27] No, God knows that bad can be a great device for creating good. In fact, God sends bad, hard, challenging, and sometimes painful stuff. God uses it as a woodworker uses a tool, shaping us with it.

". . . For the creation was subjected to futility, not of its own will but by the will of him who subjected it in hope; because the creation itself will be set free from its bondage to decay and obtain the glorious liberty of children of God" (Romans 8: 20).

God has a dream and a plan for each of us, a life of purpose and creating. And when God can't seem to get through to us using quieter voices and methods, when God can't seem to nudge us onto our higher path, God lets our present path fall apart or sends some hardship to shake us up. Suffering becomes God's tool when other tools fail to move us to where we must go.

There are plenty of Biblical references to God using violence, punishment, suffering, anger, temptation, and death as tools to influence, change, and improve people. Proverbs 3: 12 states, "...the Lord chastises him whom he loves, as a father chastises the son in whom he delights." Matthew 18: 7 says, "...For it is necessary that temptations come..." Romans 5: 3-5 says, "...We rejoice in our sufferings, knowing that suffering produces endurance, and endurance produces character, and character produces hope, and hope does not disappoint us..."

Many Christians reject the notion of God using temptation, for instance, in dealing with humanity. They use Bible verses such as James 1: 13 as reference. It says, "Let no one say when he is tempted, 'I am tempted by God'; for God cannot be tempted with evil and he himself tempts no one . . .'" But this line of reasoning falls flat when put in the context of an all-powerful and all-creating God. For, by simply creating the possibility for temptation and evil, God tempts us and sees value in temptation and evil.

God has a plan for our lives. God takes us to this higher ground only by stripping us of that which we don't want to let go. The suffering we experience in life is the result of having a calling inside us that is not reflected in our outside world. Thus, God uses "bad" things. There is no growth, no integration of outer and inner life without suffering, hardship, and challenge.

This concept is heard in the words of many non-Biblical poets, writers, and scholars. The ancient philosopher, Seneca, said, "Wisdom has planted her foundation in the dung heap of life." The poet, Simone Weil, wrote, "Pain is the root of all knowledge." Theodore Roethke penned, "In a dark time, the eye begins to see." Martin Luther King, Jr., often said, "Unmerited suffering is redemptive." Many a coach has said in many a locker room, "There is no victory without defeat." The *Steve Miller Band* sang, "You know you got to go through hell before you get to heaven."

In fact, the entire story of Christianity has been founded upon the notion of God sending his own son to suffer and die. God sent suffering and death to enact good.

Long before Jesus was born, there was a traditional Israelite ritual of speaking the sins of the people and symbolically placing them onto a goat or a lamb, which was driven out into the wilderness. This was a ritual act of humanity making atonement with God. In fact, this is the origin of the word *scapegoat* — *one who takes the suffering of others*.

When Jesus came around it was his job to be the human scapegoat on which humanity placed its sins and mistakes, once and for all. Jesus' crucifixion was absolutely necessary for humanity to achieve proper relationship with God. Jesus' suffering and death are the essential elements of the story, according to Christianity.

The athlete understands this idea of suffering and growth. The athlete lifts weights in order to build muscles. But this is not an enjoyable process. Lifting weights is hard, sometimes painful, work. For, in order to get bigger muscles *the athlete must first tear down the muscles*. That is what weightlifting does — tear down muscles. It is, in part, the suffocation (or deliberately decreasing the supply of oxygen) of the muscle. It is, then, after the point of muscle fatigue and failure, during the period of rest, that the growth will occur. The athlete understands that growth first requires failure and destruction.

Similarly, the life of a dancer is spent destroying the body's tendency to be inert and common in movement. The dancer works hard to discipline (from the word *disciple*, which means *student* and *to be taught*) the muscles, the body, and the mind in ways outside of normal movement. Only by pushing and punishing the body are new heights of grace and new forms of movement achieved. Growth and creation demand suffering and discipline. The highest levels of dance and art demand the highest price and the greatest amount of hardship, pain, and focus.

This is the path of spirituality and life. It is after we are destroyed, beaten, and battered by life that we finally begin to grow. The greater the transformation and growth, the greater the necessary destruction.

God is always there, at every point in our spiritual growth. God inserts little "nudges" early in the process, hoping we will hear God's quiet voice, hoping our change and growth will not require force. Unfortunately, we often do not see or look for God until our lives are off course, well short of what we can be. Or, perhaps we do not see God until our self-destructive paths have completely run their course, we have hit bottom, and we are well in need of a total life makeover. Whatever the case, when God does step in, God isn't afraid to use extreme methods to help us grow.

Despite common belief in the cliché "God never gives us more than we can handle," God occasionally in life over-burdens us, over-pushes us, over-stretches us, and breaks us. For, it is often at the point of failure that growth occurs. Often, it is only when we are broken that we fully submit to God, acknowledging our need and dependence, and desiring (yes, desiring) change and growth. Essentially, it is at this point that we take ourselves out of the center of the universe and place God there.

Just eight months after the terrorist attack on the World Trade Center, *New York Times* columnist Adam Nagourney wrote an article which would have been unthinkable to even mention in the painful weeks and months immediately following 9/11. The opening sentence of his article stated, "For urban planners and elected officials, the destruction of the World Trade Center has provided an almost unfathomable opportunity to reconsider and reshape the future of one of the most distinctive neighborhoods in the world: 16 acres of land in the heart of downtown Manhattan."[28]

Once again in life, suffering gave birth to "opportunity" and new growth. This is not to say in any way that real estate is more important than human life. Instead, it highlights another example of destruction giving birth to creation. The hardship of dealing with loss gave way to the necessity of rebuilding after tragedy.

"... And the real question is what, if anything, New York might or should do to shape its future. 'This is the kind of thing that happened in Chicago in the 1870s when the fire burned it down: It gives you a chance to think afresh,' said John H. Mollenkopf, director of the City University of New York's Center for Urban Research."[29]

The central question at that time in New York and right now in your life is: What new life is this suffering and destruction you are experiencing (whatever the suffering may be) giving birth to? What opportunity for growth has God laid before you in your suffering? Further, in what ways do you need to trust God more fully? How is God at work in all of this?

The article concludes, "The question, though, is whether anyone in this still very shaken city is ready to seize the opportunity."[30] Oftentimes in life, seeing the opportunity is not nearly as tough as seizing the opportunity. So the other big question you must ask is: Do I have the guts to move forward boldly into this new opportunity that has broken into my life?

Reluctance to Seek Good in the Bad

As long as we continually search to find the hand of God at work, we will continually find the hand of God at work, metaphorically speaking. We will continually find God tearing down and destroying in our own lives so that new life might be created. It is not an easy pill to swallow, but it is more true than we can deny. And the opportunity is ours to seize the truths and act on God's leading.

Jim Collins, former Stanford University researcher, MBA professor, and author of bestsellers, *Built to Last* and *Good to Great*, states that one of the biggest differences between good companies and great companies is the refusal of great companies to settle for good enough. Good, he says, is the enemy of great.[31]

So too, in our walk with God, the great things we can accomplish are impeded only by the goodness we are willing to settle for. And so, God strips us of our comfort in the good, often using our discontent and sense of longing as compelling motivators. By doing so, God moves us to the greatness God planned for us when we were created.

All of this heaven-sent hardship, of course, usually happens against our own wishes. But, mediocrity is not good enough for God. God wants us to thrive. God wants us to live abundantly, and isn't afraid to destroy parts of life that we are clinging to or hold sacred in order to move us to higher ground.

The obvious downside of this for Christianity is that God can be neither controlled, nor fully understood, only trusted. One can only say that God's ways are greater than one's own ability to understand. God's plan is bigger than my plan. And, unfortunately, God is not always what I want God to be. "For my thoughts are not your thoughts, neither are your ways my ways, says the Lord" (Isaiah 55: 8).

We are left as mere mortals, dependent upon the Almighty; trying to make sense of God's ways; trying to find the learning and the growth amid the hardship and sorrows. We can only ask, "Spirit of the Universe, what would you have me learn? What would you have me become? What would you have me release? What am I not understanding about life and your call for my life?"

Then, often in the strangest of places, the answer comes. And, growth follows — painfully and slowly. With this growth we realize that a god who is only nice, happy, or kind cannot love us as fully, nor bring good nearly as effectively as a God who is freed to be kind and violent, destructive and loving, chaotic and ordered.

Though, quite frankly, we don't have much choice. We can fight the misery and suffering, complaining to God all the while. We can resist our fate. We can refuse to see any good in all that afflicts us. But that will not stop the suffering.

The only way through or past the suffering is to give it context. It is to infuse the situation with meaning. The only way to discover abatement of sorrow is to presume to guess the mind of God and what God might be trying to teach you. That demands seeing God as both creator and destroyer, yet still using all things for good.

As God is quoted as saying in Romans 9: 15, "I will have mercy on whom I will have mercy; and I will have compassion on whom I will have compassion." Matthew 5: 45b says, "...For God makes the sun rise on the evil and on the good, and sends rain on the just and on the unjust." God will be whatever God darn well feels like being. Or, if you prefer to think of God as nothing more than life, itself, you do not need to be told that life is quite fickle. Life bestows its blessings and its curses, its fortunes and its hardships with an unpredictability, a chaos, and a seeming unfairness that transcend human understanding.

To worship the fullness of God is to accept *all* that God is — all that the nature of life itself is — even if we don't understand or like it all. God is not just one absolute truth, but many truths....and they ain't all pretty. To walk with God is to trust amid our suffering that God is moving in it all, moving us to higher ground. To know God is to understand that though God is not always nice, God is most certainly always working for good!

It is to know that all suffering bears gems of wisdom and opportunities for growth. To quote the actor Susan Sarandon, "The point of life is to make mistakes

103

and learn from them. That's how we grow. When we keep making the same mistakes it is a sign we're stuck and not learning what life is trying to teach us." We need only be open to what is ahead, and do our very best to let go of what was (always the hardest part), giving thanks for this yin and yang that are the dance of God.

A Spiritual Exercise

This exercise is simple, just answer two questions. First, despite all that has been written about God in this chapter, do you personally prefer a God that only does "good," or one that uses both "bad" and "good" to help us in our lives?

Second, whichever you chose, what is the most disagreeable part for you about the other notion of God?

The Hardest Thing to Do in Life

As much as you may not want to accept this, and twisted as this may sound, I have grown in my lifetime to not only accept God's brutality to me, but to give thanks for it, extreme thanks. It is the severe suffering I have endured at the hand of God (at the hand of life, if you prefer) that has brought me to the place in life where I am actually proud of what I have become. I am proud of the spirit of kindness and strength God has forged in me.

Over the last twenty years, I clung feverishly to those things, those people, those dreams, and those goals which I wanted for my life. I knew what I wanted in order to make myself happy. Nothing could sway me.

But I was naïve. I was a child, an ass, hurtful, and just plain wrong. Because of this, I think, nothing that I wanted in life seemed to want me. The harder I chased my desires, the farther away they ran. As a result, I ached.

Friends and therapists used to tell me, "You must let go." Yet, I could not and would not let go of what I wanted. However, eventually the pain of holding on got bad enough that I did begin to consider what it would be like to let go. I found myself, to a small degree, wanting to let go. But, I had no idea how to do this. Little did I know that by even considering letting go, I had already begun the process.

With time, the writings of James Hillman and John Gray helped me to see that the only way to fully and finally let go is to fully hold on until your grip tires, and you naturally let go of that which you couldn't imagine living without. It is that suffering, that scorching deep-down pain (which I call the wrath of God) that comes from clinging tightly but not being able to have what I want that enabled me to do the one thing humans most hate to do: Let go.

See, we think we know what we want in life. Each and every one of us has it all figured out. We are convinced we know what will bring us joy.

But we have no idea of what can be. Our vision is limited. Unless we allow God to lead us, our future is bound by our past. We are only able to see as far as our past experiences make possible. One of the great truths of life is that what we thought we wanted is always exceeded by what we didn't expect.

Thus, at some point or another each of us needs the pain. Each of us needs a different level in order to feel the urge to move on. Unless the pain of life gets bad enough, we will not let go and allow new life to break in. As the old saying goes, "The ego, like the egg, is of no use until it is broken."

As I have aged and endured the misery of holding tightly to that which I desired, my unwillingness to change has diminished. My inability to envision and accept a different future from what I originally wanted has given way to an openness that does not fear an uncertain tomorrow. I am finally able to be led by God, rather than insisting I know best. I am finally able to get the gentle nudges God offers. And life blossoms much more easily.

I know quite clearly that it was the pain of life that brought me to this point of fluidity and acceptance. God did some serious pruning of branches with me. Now, each day, I give thanks to God for the great gift of suffering and pruning, in big and small ways, that enabled me and daily enables me to become a far better version of myself. For in so doing, God has enabled me to better love and serve those in need.

Six-time *Tour de France* winner Lance Armstrong, irrefutably one of the greatest athletes in the history of sports, has said on numerous occasions, ". . . Cancer was the best thing that ever happened to me."[32] The suffering it brought and his fighting through it forged him into the person he was meant to be, a man capable of winning 6 *Tours*. "[Suffering] might last a minute, or a month, but eventually it subsides, and when it does, something else takes its place, and maybe that thing is a greater space. For happiness. Each time I encountered suffering, I believed that I grew, and further defined my capacities — not just my physical ones, but my interior ones as well, for contentment, friendship, or any other human experience."[33]

Yet, not only has Armstrong achieved greatness on a bicycle in the mountains of France, his battle with cancer and the successes that followed have been the source of enormous inspiration and hope for others suffering with life-threatening disease and pain. Almost cruel as it sounds, his suffering has reaped great harvests for others, as well as himself. And, judging by the way he looks at life, he would have it no other way.

For the sake of our discussion of suffering here, Armstrong's belief in suffering as gift offers a stark counterpoint to standard Christian theology which sees suffering as bad, and therefore as something that could never be God-sent. Rather than being a blessing to be challenged by, grown through, strengthened by, and learned from, all suffering is evil and either Devil-sent or the result of the fallen nature of humanity, Christianity tells us.

Yet, once you are able to see the good in the evil and the good in the suffering it is possible to conceive that God is in it all, working in total love to transform you and transform the world. With this realization comes the opportunity to radically reinterpret the Bible. No longer is good from God and bad from the Devil or humanity's broken nature. Instead, all of life — all of life! — is some form of God's abundant love. It may be confusing and hard to understand, but the great challenge is to find the good in it all, even as we simultaneously work to bring love and reduce suffering in the lives of others.

Christian Violence

The downside of this for the rest of the world (the non-Christians as well as the closet and Christmas Christians) is that if God is violent and the bringer of hardship and suffering, then the Christians now have permission to be violent like their God. This, as we all know, is not a good thing to entrust to Christians. For unfortunately, in the past, the Christians have used the violent nature of God as a model for human behavior, underwriting great atrocities in the name of God and Jesus.

But there is the problem. We are not called to bring judgment and violence to the world. While it is God's prerogative to do so, we are called to rise above our desire to do so, and be instruments of peace. Paul says in the book of Romans, "Beloved, never avenge yourselves, but leave it to the wrath of God; for it is written, 'Vengeance is mine. I will repay, says the Lord'" (12: 19).

Jesus said, "Judge not, that you be not judged. For with the judgment you pronounce will you be judged, and the measure you give will be the measure you get. Why do you see the speck that is in your neighbor's eye, but do not notice the log in your own eye? You hypocrite, first take the log out of your own eye, and then you will see clearly to take the speck out of your brother's eye" (Matthew 7: 1-3, 5).

In the book of John (8: 7), Jesus challenges the judgmental among us by saying, "You who is without sin, throw the first stone [at someone else]."

It is written in James 4: 12, "There is one lawgiver and judge, he who is able to save and to destroy. But who are you that you judge your neighbor?"

Granted, the Dalai Lama reluctantly said that there are rare times when chastisement and even violence are necessary in life. There are rare times in life when we must fight fire with fire. And Jesus' life example was one of fighting injustice on behalf of others.

Still, our challenge in life is to strive to be bearers of kindness, tolerance, peace and indiscriminate love. This we do while constantly trusting that God (or life) is teaching us and guiding by all the good that lifts us and all the ill that afflicts us. We must not bring harm to any one or any thing, but trust to God and the very forces of life those who do harm.

For, it is a quiet maxim of life that, while hardships befall every person who walks the earth, oddly, life has a way of sticking it to people who continually bring harm to others. Call it karma. Call it God's wrath. Call it life. Call it what you will. Though it may not happen on the timetable others might wish, it is a fact of life that every bully eventually gets his ass kicked. There is always someone bigger, tougher, or meaner. The ancient Greeks had a saying that related to this truism, "Those whom the gods would destroy, they first make proud."

Inflicting pain is not something only bullies and cheats do, though they usually do it with greater regularity and malice. We all create suffering for others, intentionally and unintentionally. Anything you do is evil for somebody. Our task is to minimize both the intentional and the unintentional suffering we cause.

It is so easy for each one of us to let our lives degenerate into constant condemning and critiquing of others. It is so easy to use judgment as an excuse for doing harm to others and their character. But, that is God's prerogative alone. Jesus, the master teacher challenges us simply to be instruments of love in this world, tempting as it might be to do otherwise.

Finally

Like the gods of all large and small religions, the God of the Bible is a god of creation and destruction, order and chaos, pain and peace. Our job is to try to understand where God is pushing us to go and what God is encouraging us to become. By doing so, we can begin to know the joy of fulfilling our purpose in life.

Our challenge is to sense God's gentle nudges in times of peace. We must hear God's quiet voice in our lives so that a louder voice is not necessary. But when that louder voice of suffering comes (and it will come), we must listen and find the message that promises to move us to higher ground. Finally, we must have the courage to follow the call. Only then will we know the peace, joy, hope, purpose, power, and love God promises.

"We know that in everything God works for good with those who love him..."

— Romans 8: 28

Chapter 8

[Create a Religious Hybrid to Increase Spiritual Profitability]

"We have to find ways of organizing ourselves with the rest of humanity. It has to be everybody or nobody."

— Buckminster Fuller

Science Fact: The great endeavor to map the human genome has uncovered the startling fact that humans have 99.5% of our genes in common with one another! That means there is only a one half of one percent difference, at most, between any two human beings.

"There is one God, though he is known by many names."

— Hindu proverb

"The mark of true wisdom is the ability to see truth in opposing sides of the same argument."

— unknown

IN JANUARY OF 1995, Barings Bank of England went bankrupt. Prior to that, Barings was the world's oldest investment bank, and one of England's most prestigious. Yet, Barings died not a long, slow death, as might befit such a titan, but a quick and decisive one.

This bank financed the Louisiana Purchase in 1803 for a newly born United States and was a bank of the House of Windsor. This bank whose assets funded the armies of Britain in the Napoleanic Wars was brought to its knees not by another banking behemoth, but by its own arrogance and a 28 year-old kid. In a few short weeks, this blue-blood investment house lost approximately $1.2 billion! In a few weeks!

In the latter part of 1994, a young futures trader employed by Barings, Nicholas William Leeson, was dealing in the Singapore Monetary Exchange in the still-uncertain field of financial exotica known as "derivatives." The derivatives market was relatively new, exceedingly risky, and at times so confusing that senior bank officers paid scant attention to it and the actions of this young trading addict. Too aristocratic, and displaying complete absence of sensibility, they condescendingly dismissed this new realm of trading and the work of this trader as unimportant, completely unaware of the impending doom. Both dismissals would prove fatal.

Only weeks after the Kobe earthquake rocked Japan, Mr. Leeson made what amounted to a series of legal bets (derivatives being an odd form of stock exchange roulette) on the post-earthquake stability of the Nikkei (the Japanese stock exchange). Basically, he made huge gambles that Barings, having only $615 million in capital, didn't have the money to back.

Unfortunately, the temporary instability of the Nikkei, as well as the extreme volatility and vampirish nature of the derivatives game, bled Barings before it knew the fangs had pierced its flesh. Barings lost everything on Mr. Leeson's $27 billion bet, a bet that was supposedly margined.

To wit, just two years before his bank's fall, CEO Peter Baring, sounding strikingly similar to out-of-touch religious leaders in America when they speak about present spiritual-religious trends, said in a speech, "Derivatives need to be well controlled and understood, but we believe we do that well here."[34]

In the last analysis, it was ignorance of and indifference to the ways of the present trading world that brought about Barings' demise. Yet, it was also caused by the entrenchment in old ways of doing business, and the refusal on the part of senior Barings officials to offer strong and relevant leadership. Too lazy, too arrogant, and too naïve, they perished. In the last analysis, they killed themselves.

Spirituality with a Real-world Sensibility

Jesus lived his life trying to reform and update the religion of his people. He lived and died to make religion compelling again and to bring people into more full relationship with God. The same is true of many Christian saints since his day. The giants of Christian history who are lionized (and often demonized) are usually the ones who fought entrenchment in old ways of thinking and doing business. They lived and died to make their religion and theology relevant to their present-day sensibilities.

One of the primary reasons many people in America want God but want nothing to do with the church is that Christianity has failed to become fluent in present-day sensibilities. Not only that, it has been stubbornly unwilling to change to meet those needs and sensibilities. Like Barings Bank, Christianity has arrogantly buried its head in the sand.

One of the biggest modern-day issues that Christianity is perceived as inadequately addressing is the beauty and truths of other religions. Christianity is still entrenched in the mentality of "We are the one true people of the one true religion of the one true book of the one true God." For many, it has lost its ability (or ignored its opportunity) to speak compellingly to a world of people who do see the beauty and wisdom in the spiritual paths of their neighbors. Fearing change, Christianity and yet another part of its theology have together slipped farther into irrelevance.

Religion and a Crowded America

Walt Disney was 100% right. It is a small world.... and it's only getting smaller. America has become so small that my parents, living in a Midwestern state whose population has a mere 10% minority rate,[35] have people from the other side of the world now living in a house across my suburban childhood backyard. Today, my nephews playing baseball where I once did are hitting homeruns into what is now a Muslim's garden.[36] This also means that any kid riding the school bus I once rode and sitting in the desk I once occupied will be sitting next to a Muslim or two. Muslims, Jews, Hindus, Buddhists, Mormons, atheists, and New Agers, to name a few, are in increasing numbers becoming part of the beauty of American mainstream culture.

At this point in America's history, you cannot go through life without encountering other cultures, other people, and other belief systems. Whether you realize it or not, every day you bump into people whose beliefs differ vastly from yours. Sometimes you meet people of other cultures or belief systems who so impress you with their character, their values, or their love that you begin to view their beliefs more sympathetically, more openly, and with more curiosity.

More basic than that, you have no doubt sampled and developed a taste for the food of other cultures. From Indian to Japanese, from Mexican to French, food is the greatest initiator of inter-cultural dialogue. With a love for the food often comes an increased interest in the culture. With interest often comes appreciation. Over time, in some small way, you may even find yourself incorporating some of the beliefs of those around you into your own beliefs.

This slow incorporation of learnings from new origins is what happens on the spiritual journey. As you ask your questions on your spiritual journey, you will eventually begin to find answers that suit *you*. You will find answers in all different places, from all different people, through all different sources. Your belief system — your understanding of God and your belief of what works in life — will become a hybrid of all the different ways and times *you* have encountered God. This hybridization is all but inevitable in America today. Though it be a cliché, the United States is still one of the few true melting pots of cultures in the world today.

Just 100 years ago in this country, in my Swedish-American family history, it was unthinkable that a Swedish-Lutheran would marry a Norwegian-Lutheran. Then, over time, that became acceptable, and the unthinkable was the idea of marrying a Catholic. That too passed, and it became marrying a Jew that was not allowed. Marrying a Muslim or Hindu was simply unheard of. Now, the only difficult part for Swedish-Lutherans seems to be not other denominations or even other religions, but the marriage of gays.

Marriage is one powerful way that people of different religions and cultures come to know and grow to appreciate each other. For love has no boundaries.

Call it hybridization, entropy, religious equilibrium, or just mixing the best of all worlds. This gel-ing of religions happens every day in the world in which we live. Families gel. Cultures gel. Religions gel. If humanity must live shoulder-to-shoulder, there will naturally be a rubbing-off of one onto another. If nothing else, it is a way of sanding down the rough edges that all religions have.

Hybridization is necessary. Rescuing God from Christianity so that you can make God your own and make God come alive for you, so to speak, means breaking free of the Christian (and largely American) mentality that there is only one way to think about God and all other ways are bad. To rescue God means to stop limiting God. It means to allow for the possibility, if not the fact, that God uses many languages and belief systems to speak with God's many and different people.[37] By allowing for this, you create for your spiritual life a much larger world of truths and wisdom that would not be available if you had a blanket disallowance of their value.

The most significant implication of this shrinking religious world is not economic or political, despite what the media and politicians might say. The biggest effect is the increasing necessity for inter-religious understanding and appreciation. For it is our underlying beliefs that craft how we interact in the world. Beliefs determine principles and thoughts; thoughts determine behaviors. Understand another person's root beliefs and you begin to understand and even appreciate their actions.

This means that in order to create a world of greater peace and harmony religions must begin to understand and see the beauty in other religions. The Christian church will find in those other religions many truths that fit with Jesus' teachings, which it can then carry to the world in helping people construct their beliefs in their walks with God. For this to happen, Christianity must shift from seeing religion as the intense clinging to one absolute truth to seeing religion as drawing people into relationship with a multi-lingual God in the context of an ever-shrinking world.

The old, dominant Christian theology regarding other religions no longer works. Indeed, it is downright dysfunctional. The arrogant and tired Christian thinking (based on a gross misinterpretation of the Bible) that Christians are the one true people of the one true religion has given rise to generation upon generation of hatred, intolerance, unnecessary fighting, and many horrible acts ... all in the name of God and Jesus.

Christianity has viewed the beliefs of other religions as nothing more than hurdles to getting those people to become Christians. In many Christian denominations this is still the dominant thinking. This is, of course, incredibly insulting as it implies "Your religion is not as good as ours and you need me and my God to make you better." Christianity has too often interacted with other religions with only this condescension and force. These two modes are no longer justifiable Christian positions toward other religions.

As an aside, this we-are-right-and-you-are-wrong thinking applies to dialogue between the Christian denominations themselves, as well. Christians beating on Christians in the name of better Christianity is no longer theologically defensible. Christian brotherhood and an attitude of love must supersede the quest for superiority of doctrine. The Christian inability to live Jesus' example of love when dealing with fellow Christians only serves to alienate outsiders who see Christians as unwilling to practice what they preach. Rather than creating brotherhood and theological affection, many Christian denominations lazily declare that brotherhood cannot be presumed where brotherhood does not exist.

But this must change. Or, more accurately, this will change. Hybridization of beliefs is inevitable, to some greater or lesser degree. The only question is whether people will go there willingly or kicking and screaming.

A Brief Note to Christians (Non-Christians may skip to *A Hard Jesus Lesson*)

If the Christian church is to be a creator of peace in the world, it must make the finding of beauty in the religions of its now very immediate neighbors one of its highest priorities. Christianity must rigorously engage in a bottom to top education of its people. This education must be based on a change in Christian theology. Specifically, Christianity must overhaul how it views other religions and views itself in relationship with these religions.

As children move into their teen years and move into the ability to think abstractly and question life, they must be taught about other ways of thinking and believing. They will, soon enough, encounter other belief systems in high school, college and the work world. So, it behooves Christianity to manage the world religions education process internally, shaping young Christians with an attitude of respect, co-existence, discovery and appreciation for people of other religions.

Further, it behooves Christian churches to not only actively encourage teens to explore other religions but also grant teens the freedom to decide for themselves what they choose to believe. These two steps create an atmosphere where teens and young adults feel respected because they are allowed to choose their own lives. And who would want to leave a setting wherein you are treated with respect and the freedom and responsibility to make your own life decisions?

Within this context children can be taught the marvel of Christianity in relation to other amazing religions, all without reducing the argument to claims of absolute superiority. Not only that, this preventative medicine means that as kids age they will not experience other religions as a forest of new spiritual questions and dilemmas. Bumping into other religions and their truths will not cause spiritual crisis that they must endure alone.

Instead, such encounters will seem quite natural and enjoyable, and far more likely to produce positive fruit. Through deliberate and non-condemning teaching of other religions, children will become worldly literate, spiritually unflappable, and genuinely appreciative of others.

This notion of being encouraged to explore the world outside one's borders is, at least in concept, mirrored in the Pennsylvania Dutch ritual in which Amish kids engage in *rumspringa*, or "wild running." When they turn 16 they are allowed to leave the cloistered life of the Amish people to drink in all the outside world has to offer, from clothing to alcohol and from cars to sex.

After doing so, they then have an informed perspective on which to base their individual decision of whether or not to return to the fold. It is interesting to note that, according to *Devil's Playground* (a 2002 documentary), 90% do return to the flock to be baptized into the Amish faith.

It is as if leaving the faith is far less attractive when it is encouraged than when it is demonized or seen as apostasy. Or, more accurately, when kids are forthrightly presented with all the options (in an unskewed form) and then given complete freedom to decide for themselves, the "faith of [their] fathers" takes on a transparency, honesty, and beauty that render leaving both unnecessary and unappealing.

By educating Christian teens in the majesty and wisdom of other religions, by encouraging cross-religious exploration, and by giving kids the respect that comes with the freedom to decide for themselves the church accomplishes a powerful one-two punch. First, it breeds children who are world-wise and capable of genuinely loving other religions and the people of them (as opposed to just tolerating them), and thereby better able to function with love in a shrinking world. Second, and quite ironically, children are more likely to fall in love with the wisdom of their own faith as it exhibits a love for the people of the world and an openness to discovering and engaging in the world.

Such an anticipatory education program, while insuring a generosity of spirit for future generations (a generosity that can only be considered Jesus-like), must be mirrored by a similar education for adults of all ages. Adults must be given a theological framework that is consistent with the shrinking world and their daily exposure to people of other religions, whom they encounter at work, at the market, at PTA meetings, and in line at the post office.

This, too, is a critical element in the revival of the Christian brand. It is widely understood in the world of commerce that one of the most difficult things to do is to revive a brand. To return to success a brand that has lost its luster or died off can be next to impossible. Often the great impediment to turnaround is the belief that what always was is what always should be. And, except in the faddish world of retro-fashion, what was is never enough for what must be.

To be viewed as real-world relevant and thereby appealing, the church must depart from its practice of denouncing other religions. To revive the brand, Christianity *must* engage the hybridization process. There is simply no way people outside the church will be swayed to old-time theology that is condescending and dismissive of other religions.

In fact, simple tolerance of other religions is not enough for many outside Christianity's doors. For the brand to be appealing, for non-Christians to buy into what Christianity is selling, absolutely requires that Christianity include the many truths found outside its own borders.

A Hard Jesus Lesson

Consider this exercise: Name the people in your life whom you love. Is it mom, dad, siblings, spouse, children, dear friends, and maybe a few heroes? Now, is it an adequate representation of that love to say you simply like them, tolerate them, or respect them? Or is what you feel far more deep, rounded, and rich than that?

You feel differently and act differently towards them than how you feel and act towards mere acquaintances, co-workers, and everyday people you know. And then Jesus comes along and says, "Love your neighbor." In one verse he even says, "Love your neighbor as yourself" (Matthew 19: 19). As if that isn't radical enough, earlier in Matthew (5: 44) Jesus is quoted as saying, "But I say to you, Love your enemies and pray for those who persecute you." Jesus goes on to say (Luke 6: 27-32, 35), ". . . Love your enemies, do good to those who curse you, pray for those who abuse you. To him who strikes you on the cheek, offer the other also; and from him who takes away your coat, do not withhold even your shirt. Give to every one who begs from you; and of him who takes away your goods do not ask for them again. And as you wish that men would do to you, do so to them. If you love those who love you, what credit is that to you? For even sinners love those who love them. Love your enemies, and do good, and lend expecting nothing in return." Pretty strong stuff!

Jesus pushes you to *love* all people, including your religious neighbor. And *that* is hard for Christians caught in old ways of thinking. It is completely wrenching, because to love is so much more than just *get to know, like, tolerate,* or even *respect.*

Love is intimacy, fondness, sincere appreciation, trust, seeing the beauty in, respect, self-deprecation, service, kindness, fighting for (rather than fighting with), and laughter with another. This is love.

Guided by Jesus' exhortation to love God and love neighbor, and allowing for the possibility that the door marked *Holy Spirit* on the house of God is quite large and nowhere specifically defined, followers of Jesus' teachings have no other possible course of action than to treat people of other religions as fellow children of God who are worthy of every good accord granted the most revered of loved ones. For those seeking to live as Jesus taught (not as Christianity regularly teaches), and for those seeking a higher spiritual path, there must be a constant internal push to bring love to others and to the world. That is the goal.

And this is what makes Jesus' teachings so doggone difficult to follow. It is not about like; it's about love. It is not about the easy path; it's about the noble path. It is not about having love reciprocated, but about giving love anyway.

This means when interacting with people of other religions that the possibility exists for the Christian to not be as warmly received as he or she might like. Some Muslims may focus on Islam's veneration of Jesus as a prophet, but disallow for Jesus as Savior (a big problem for literalist Christians). They may then say that Christians and Muslims do not worship the same God. Or, some Jews may say the Savior of the world has not yet come — in other words, Jesus is not the Savior — thereby making brotherhood difficult in their eyes. Though it is likely that love will be met with respect and grace by people of other religions, the possibility does exist for other responses.

The person who strives to follow Jesus' teachings should not be thwarted by love that goes unreciprocated. Jesus calls us to self-sacrificial love that turns the other cheek when struck and forgives seventy-seven times (Matthew 18: 22). It is the love for neighbor that loves even when there is no love in return.

One of the wisest things you can do on your spiritual journey to God is to fall in love with the truths that come from all corners of the world. It is to find the truths that speak loudest to you, no matter their source, and begin to incorporate them into your spiritual-religious foundation. For, just as genetic in-breeding and the quest for purity give rise to deformity and disease, hybridization and cross-pollination generate strength, rich variety, and longevity.

On the spiritual journey this hybridization is the only path that will bring long term peace. It is to become one with one's neighbor. It is the noblest path one can endeavor when our religious neighbors have planted their garden at the edge of our baseball field.

Chapter 9

[Build Heaven Today]

"You don't have to be an angel in order to be a saint."

— Albert Schweitzer

GEORGE SOROS IS A HIGHLY PHILANTHROPIC, sometimes controversial, yet surprisingly low-profile figure in America today. Many people, perhaps including you, have never heard of him. *Forbes* magazine lists Mr. Soros as the 28th wealthiest person in America, worth $7 billion!

Yet, according to a *USA Today* article, "Soros spends more on politics than on himself. Although his family has many homes, including an apartment, a beach house, and a country house in the New York area, Soros is no Donald Trump. He has neither jet nor yacht, neither art collection nor retinue. Nor is he after the kind of access that political contributions usually buy. [Yet,] Soros has been called the only man with his own foreign policy and the ability to implement it. The joke goes that he merely does what the government would do if it had the money"[38]

Mr. Soros has given away nearly $5 billion in philanthropic ventures throughout the world. So remarkable is his philanthropy that a lengthy list from the previously mentioned *USA Today* article is quoted here:

- "$18 million to support campaign-finance reform.
- $115 million after the fall of the Soviet Union to support Russian science . . .
- $250 million in 2001 to found and endow Central European University; its main campus is in Budapest, Hungary.
- $100 million to free education in the former Soviet Union from Marxist-

117

Leninist dogma by buying new textbooks, training teachers and operating libraries.

- $12 million to promote high school debate programs in the USA ...
- $13 million (with an additional $37 million commitment) to finance affordable housing and building projects for poor South Africans, most of whom previously lived in shantytowns.
- $110 million over the past decade to Step by Step, an early childhood development program in 29 countries.
- $200 million to promote peace, tolerance, reconciliation, and democracy in southeastern Europe ...
- $50 million in 1992 for humanitarian aid to the besieged Bosnian city of Sarajevo ...
- $50 million to the Emma Lazarus Fund to combat unfair treatment of, and discrimination against, legal immigrants in the USA (1996-2000).
- $125 million to the After School Corporation for after school programs (1997-present) ...

"Leon Botstein, president of Bard College and a longtime Soros adviser [says], 'The average person asks, "What's in it for him?" They cannot imagine that if they were that rich, they would be that generous.'"39

Having survived both Nazi and Communist oppression in his childhood home in Hungary (for some time his Jewish family survived by posing as Christians), Mr. Soros understands hardship and suffering. Thus, one of Mr. Soros' missions in life is to use economic means to breathe life into those people and countries whose lack of economic means suffocates their very existence. His life is not about the continued acquisition of more wealth, but about using what he has to be a servant to those in need. By his efforts, a great many people have been rescued from the hardships that financial oppression can inflict.

The Christian Image

One of the single biggest reasons Christianity in America has such a difficult time connecting with the un-churched and the de-churched and drawing them into Christianity's fold is because Christianity has such a bad image. Many, many Americans view Christians and Christianity with contempt and plain old dislike.

To many Americans, Christians are perceived as either overbearing and naive, or as spineless and outdated. It is almost a given in popular American culture. It is heard on radio and is seen in movies, television, MTV, newspapers, Internet, magazines, on stage, and in the literary world. Christians are held in very low esteem in America. Even the "good" ones who have achieved universal respect — e.g. Billy Graham, who has not become corrupted by greed when other evangelists built amusement parks and air-conditioned doghouses — are unavoidably hobbled by the cultural malaise of dislike for Christians.

This is due in part to a sordid Christian history, corrupt television evangelists, some morally bankrupt priests, the occasional philandering or embezzling minister, and sometimes bullheaded bishops, among other things. Further, Christians have been fed by preachers a way of living out Christianity that is abhorrent to modern sensibilities and quite incongruent with the Bible. As a result of all these factors, many Christians have become offensive and hypocritical rather than loving, kind, and respected.

It is not, as the Christians think, that Christians are seen as wet blankets because they hold to some supposedly higher moral standard. Discipline and self-denial are still admirable qualities, especially when they're not used as a platform for looking down on others. Instead, the problem people have with many Christians, and the reason many do not wish to become like the Christians, is the never-ending hypocrisy and holier-than-thou arrogance of the Christian way.

It is not enough for Christians to follow their high morality. Instead, many Christians have to rub it in the world's face, too, claiming to be more morally pure than others. Yet, they always seem to have their own skeletons that eventually come out (hypocrisy), and they're often the harshest critics of other people (arrogance).

Evangelists such as Jim Bakker and Jimmy Swaggart are two classic examples of personal malfeasances coming back to haunt highly judgmental and holier-than-thou Christians. More recently, Bernard Cardinal Law of the Roman Catholic Church in Boston was quite content to flush out pedophilic priests, but was quite unwilling to take responsibility for allowing said priests to continue in ministry after their crimes had become known. In the end, this arrogance cost him his job and a lifetime's worth of work. As Jane Ace once said, "Time wounds all heels."

This arrogant and hypocritical mode of behaving *in no way* reflects Jesus' example. Jesus fought oppressive and corrupt institutions. But, though he often challenged individuals in their spiritual lives, Jesus almost never condemned individuals. He treated individuals with deference and kindness, understanding that each of us suffers and each of us is fighting our own demons. For example, even as he fought the religious institution of the day, he treated respectfully and bonded with one of the religious leaders (Nicodemus) who came to him in private to learn more (John 3: 1-6).

Jesus brought God's love to humanity. Jesus walked through life with nothing but humility. Moral purity was not his goal. He ran with hookers, con artists, longshoremen, psychotics, the terminally ill, and the morally depraved. He never denied the charges of his being a drunk (Luke 7: 34; Matthew 11:19), and Jesus turned 180 gallons of water into wine at a party that had torn through many gallons already (John 2: 69).

He not only visited the despised and the corrupt, he loved them. He saw them for the beautiful children of God that they were. Jesus' life was about easing their suffering and pain, and simply loving them. Further, because of their simple and sincere love for God and trust in God, and because of their absence of moral hypocrisy, Jesus even said they were closer to God's heart than the supposedly religious people (Matthew 9: 12-13; Luke 15: 7; 25: 40).

Any person who has ever volunteered at a homeless shelter, a soup kitchen, a prison, or a rehab program has seen the truth of Jesus' words on this topic. Very often there is a realness, an absence of pretense, an earthiness, and a salty saintliness in downtrodden and forgotten people that is almost childlike in its purity and divine in its nobility.

Jesus' life and teachings clearly bear this out. But Christianity sells holiness as the highest virtue. Being good (or seeking personal moral purity), in Christian thinking, is more important that doing good.

The Problem with Heaven

At the heart of this problem with Christian living, and at the heart of the entire Christian image problem, is a mistaken theology. The specific culprit is the whole Christian concept of heaven.

For most Christians, the entire purpose of Christianity, church, and life on earth is to get into heaven after dying. For Christianity, it all boils down to this one issue. Libraries of writing have been amassed over the centuries which deal with the lone question, "How do I get into heaven?" Saving my own butt after death has been the Christian's sole reason for existence.

Is it good works that get us in? Is it simply God's grace that gets us in? Do I have to be baptized to get in? Do all of my screw-ups have to be confessed to a priest before I die? Will my family be there, too? What about some of my friends? Do people who have never been introduced to the teachings of Jesus get in? What about my stillborn baby? Or, my favorite: What if you get to heaven and God gives you a choice: you can either enter heaven or go to hell, your choice; but if you choose hell 1000 people who are otherwise damned to hell will get to enter heaven and be with God (You get the chance to make the ultimate sacrifice, just as Jesus did.)?

As if that isn't obsessive and confusing enough, Jehovah's Witnesses believe, quite literally, that only 144,000 people will get into heaven after death. Thus, it seems a bit odd that these convert-seeking Christians are out aggressively knocking on doors trying to bring more people into the fold. For, any new addition to the Witness family means that the person doing the knocking has just decreased his/her odds of getting inside the pearly gates.

The questions about getting into heaven are unceasing. They are questions that Christians have fought over for 2000 years, and fight hard over even today. They are arguments that have led to the death of countless numbers of people and the subjugation of whole cultures.

And it all seems to have started with Jesus. Jesus spoke of a heaven and a hell. Jesus called men and women to a difficult path in order to reach heaven. Jesus called us to make him our savior, so that we may enter the kingdom of heaven.

Again, every fourth grade Sunday School student knows that if you ask Jesus to be your personal lord and savior, and if you be good then you, too, get to go to heaven when you die. Good people go "up" and bad people go "down."

But, what if all the fourth grade Sunday Schoolers are wrong? What if the teachers that teach them are missing the point? What if the curriculum and catechism they use, and the theologically educated people who write the curriculum, and the professors who teach the theologically educated people are all missing the point? Or, what if they are at least fearful to admit what they really believe to be true about heaven, hell, and Jesus as savior?

It all seems a bit hard to believe. Could so many people be missing the point? Could Sunday School have been wrong? The answer is yes. It is not uncommon for lots of people to be misguided on a given topic. The names Copernicus, Columbus, Lincoln, Gandhi, and King spring to mind when we consider whole masses of people just not getting something. And this whole issue of heaven is one more, clear example of Christianity just not getting it.

Eternal Life

"The Gospel is not, properly, that which is contained in books and comprehended in the letter. It is rather an oral proclamation and living word. It proclaims to us the grace of God, bestowed freely, apart from any merit of our own."

— Martin Luther, in his commentary on the Biblical books of Peter and Jude

Before diving into this section it is helpful to remember four facts of Biblical history, which offer some sense of perspective when engaging in any Biblical interpretation. First, many Biblical scholars and historians agree that the books of the New Testament were written 30, 50, and 70 or more years after Jesus' death. Second, it is also a largely accepted notion (though still contested in more conservative circles) that the four primary books that outline Jesus' life and teachings (Matthew, Mark, Luke, and John) weren't written by actual apostles of Jesus, but by disciples of the disciples.

Third, until written, these books were passed on by word of mouth, because very few people knew how to read and write. Thus, to think we have exact quotes, exact timelines, and exact depictions of events in the Bible is somewhat presumptuous.

In fact, the famed *Jesus Seminar*, which started 20 years ago, was a gathering of 200+ Biblical scholars attempting to determine what was and was not authentically spoken by Jesus. In their determination, based on modern forms of scholarship, 80% of the words attributed to Jesus in the Christian Bible are fabrications by later people and communities. Jesus, according to this collective, said very little of what Sunday Schoolers have been taught for years. Yet, whether or not you buy into all of the findings of this one academic endeavor, it is difficult to deny, after being presented with the findings of modern scholarship, that many parts of Christian scripture are questionable, at best.[40]

Fourth, as the most up-to-date scholarship indicates, many of the books of the New Testament were written or compiled by competing Christian factions in different places of the Mediterranean region. In a constant political struggle, these factions fought for influence and control of the Jesus legacy and the growing number of converts. Each faction had its own agenda for spreading the Jesus movement, for how to portray Jesus, and for what to emphasize in Jesus' teachings. This is part of the reason we have four very different renderings of the Jesus tale in the four different gospel books. With these bits of perspective we proceed.

As we return to the whole Christian notion of heaven, we must ask, what do we do with all of the Biblical teachings on eternal life? For, heaven and eternal life have always been equated with each other. One generally implies the other. Certainly there are many references to them just in Jesus' teachings and in the first few books of the New Testament, to name a few:

1) "And this is eternal life, that they may know you, the one true God, and Jesus Christ whom you have sent" (John 17: 3);

2) "'Teacher, what good deed must I do to have eternal life?' And Jesus said to him, '...If you would enter eternal life, keep the commandments'" (Matthew 9: 16);

3) "'Truly, I say to you, as you did it not to one of the least of these people, you did it not to me.' And they will go away into eternal punishment, but the righteous into eternal life" (Matthew 25: 45-46);

4) "For God so loved the world that he gave his only Son, that whoever believes in him should not perish but have eternal life" (John 3: 16);

5) "...But whoever drinks of the water that I shall give him will never thirst; the water that I shall give him will become in him a spring of water welling up to eternal life" (John 4: 14);

6) Simon Peter answered Jesus, "Lord to whom shall we go? You have the words of eternal life" (6: 68);

7) "...And I give them eternal life, and they shall never perish, and no one shall snatch them out of my hand" (John 10: 28);

8) "For the wages of sin is death, but the free gift of God is eternal life in Christ Jesus our Lord" (Romans 6: 23).

The more I have re-read Christian scripture, read about Christian scripture, read scholars of Christian scripture, and read the history and context of Christian scripture, the more I have become convinced that Jesus never intended eternal life to mean life after death. Or, if he did, it was secondary to his belief in a very different understanding of eternal life.

This thinking was years ago opened up for me in the writings of world-renowned Scottish theologian, William Barclay. His writings forced me to reconsider the Biblical notion of eternal life as life after death. As I have done so, I have become more solidified in believing that Jesus meant eternal life to mean living in the fullness of life *today*.

Barclay explained it so succinctly in his commentary on eternal life in John 17: 3 (#1 in the list above). Barclay wrote:

"There is another important thought in this passage, for it contains the great New Testament definition of eternal life. It is eternal life to know God and to know Jesus Christ whom he has sent. Let us remind ourselves of what "eternal" means. In Greek it is *aionis*. This word has to do not so much with duration of life, for life which went on forever would not necessarily be a boon. Its main meaning is *quality* of life. There is only one person to whom the word *aionis* can properly be applied, and that is God. Eternal life is, therefore, nothing other than the life of God. To possess it, to enter into it, is to experience here and now something of the splendor, and the majesty, and the joy, and the peace, and the holiness which are characteristics of the life of God."[41]

It is well worth noting: Jesus said, "I have come that they may have life and have it abundantly" (John 10: 10). Jesus was selling a plan for maximizing your joy and your sense of purpose *today*, in this lifetime! Heaven and hell are not some far off mythical places for after-death parties and never-ending torture.[42] Heaven and hell are right now, today!

Jesus desired for us to have abundant life by loving neighbor and loving God, by living out our creative purpose and by doing so in service to humanity. Jesus knew, as do many of the world's great religions, that this compassion and creative expression are together the path to life's greatest joy and fulfillment. They constitute the apex of Maslow's Hierarchy of Human Needs. "Heaven" is possible today if we heed God's calling and Jesus' teachings and example.

200, 500, and 2,000 years ago, the notion of heaven as an after-death party with God was both popular and necessary. Life on this earth was, for most people, hell. People lived in slavery, severe persecution, or excessive hardship. People were powerless to change their earthly fates and create lasting joy in their lives. The only hope was that it would all be made right upon death. Believing in heaven was a survival mechanism.

Today, this powerlessness is still seen in many parts of the world, particularly in Third World countries south of the equator. Poverty and starvation, so foreign to the American consciousness, are commonplace in these regions. Not surprisingly, these countries are also the places where traditional forms of Christianity are still growing rapidly. The concept of heaven as a place that offers a better life — the perfect life — is widely appealing.

In America today, life is totally different. While it cannot be denied that hardship and poverty are present in America, they are nowhere near the level of basic survival and privation that exist in other countries. In America and in other developed parts of the world people have the power, freedom, and relative wealth to bring themselves both joy and hope. We are not powerless in the determination of our individual fates.

In fact, we have so much power that we have the ability to pull other people in other lands out of the hell of basic survival, oppression, and powerlessness. For a people of such power there is little need for anticipation of an after-death party in order to find joy. After-death heaven is almost superfluous. For, heaven — not as a place of perfection, but as a place of great joy and lasting peace — is possible today.[43]

We create our own heaven and hell by the choices we make, but more importantly by the foundation beliefs on which we construct our lives. We have so many people living in hell right now, today, because the Christian beliefs about life and God on which they base their lives do not save them today. (We also have many people living in hell in America, today, because the supposedly "non-Christian" beliefs they have about God are such that they have no spiritual community to share their beliefs and life with.) Their spirituality or their religion is not potent enough to buoy them. Their faith in their beliefs may be strong, but the beliefs, themselves, are flimsy, and not enough to give them new life today.

If you believe the essence of Jesus' message really kicks in after death, then you must die to know release from suffering. And today is simply about endurance and survival. All the faith in the world won't make today any more bearable, much less enjoyable and fulfilling.

Granted, death does bring release and peace for many who suffer, such as many who are terminally ill, emotionally troubled, or brokenhearted. It would be an insult to deny that human suffering can become so excessive and intolerable that death is no longer fought, but welcomed. But often this is not about desiring to go to a better life as to be released from the agony of this one. Death becomes the great reprieve from a suffering that never ends and is too much to shoulder.

Consider Jesus' life and death: He endured harsh spiritual and mental hazing at the hands of the religious authorities of his day, and at the hands of many people who did not want his teachings. Yet, in his final days he also suffered physical torture and scourging so gruesome as to easily be considered a fate worse than death. For Jesus the cross was a welcome friend at that point. It meant the beatings, the whips, the taunting, the blood, the caustic laughter, and the pain (the flesh pain and the soul pain) would end. Death meant rest.

It is as if the cross beckoned to Jesus, "Welcome old friend. Come and take refuge on me. Up here they can hurt you no more."

Jesus' notions of heaven and hell are about so much more than release from today. They are about engagement in and love for today. When you recognize that Jesus saves us today by giving us a purpose in this life, and that heaven is right now, then there is hope and there is new life without having to die. One of Jesus' major points was that the kingdom of God had already arrived, and this is it. Thus, God cares that we create clean water, affordable housing, proper health care, a loving home, and the basics of life for those who are powerless to experience this life as anything more than hell, itself.

So, Here's a Question for You

In your opinion, what is heaven? How would you define it? What do you believe? Write down five things that you honestly (!) believe heaven is or is not. Now that you have written them down, are you surprised at what you wrote?

Why or why not?

Christian Arguments for Traditional Heaven

I once had an eager and good-hearted 20-something Christian tell me that if there is no after-death heaven and hell, then there's no point to Jesus; and there's no point to following Jesus' teachings. "I might as well just go out and sleep with women, lie, cheat and steal, if there's no hell or heaven," he said. He insisted that he is good now so to be rewarded after he dies.

I tried to help this young man see otherwise. I said, "I strive to follow Jesus' teachings *not* because I have to, but because I want to; *not* out of fear, but out of love. I don't do it because I have hopes for some other-worldly reward. I strive (and regularly fail) to live Jesus' teachings, because they are the noblest, most challenging, and the most fulfilling life path I have found in all my searching. I do it simply because it is, for me, the highest path I can walk. The paths other people take with their lives are their business. But this is the noblest path I can see for my life. And I would really like to take a path I can be proud of today and at the end of my days. I want to die with my own sense of honor."

"What about heaven and hell?" he shot back.

"What about it? I don't worry about them. First off, I doubt they exist as after-death places. I'm quite okay with 'You die, you're dead.' But I leave open the possibility that I am wrong and they may exist. Still, I just don't worry about it. I trust in God's love. I say, 'Y'know what God, you worry about it. I'm just going to do the best I can to simply bring love here and ease people's suffering in this lifetime. I believe in Jesus' path. And I'm going to trust you with the whole heaven thing, should that some day be an issue.' And if I fry in hell some day for that belief, then I fry trusting God." And with that my young friend sputtered a bit and left in the certainty that either I was going to hell or that I might have had a good point, or both.

I'm not saying there are no after-death heaven and hell, or even that you shouldn't believe in them if you want to. I am saying that: (a) Believing in heaven, hell, and life after death is not required for being a follower of Jesus; (b) Getting yourself into a post-death heaven is not the purpose of following Jesus; (c) Being good so as to get into heaven is not the point of life.

This lifetime (not life after death) is the point of life. Heaven is today. You create heaven today by living out the tremendously difficult path that Jesus taught and lived. You create heaven by loving God and loving the people around you, especially the people you do not even know. Specifically, you create heaven today by alleviating the suffering of others, by bringing kindness to the world, and by walking humbly in the full awareness of your own failings and your own tendency to screw-up and cause suffering.

Jesus actually had a conversation on this very topic with a member of the religious establishment of his day. It was the dialogue in which Jesus says that the first commandment is to "love God with all your heart, mind, and soul" and the second is to "love your neighbor as yourself." After Jesus said this, the religious leader said to Jesus that he was right and that these two commandments are more important than all the other sacrifices we might make.

What happens next is where this little vignette relates to this chapter. The Bible says, "And when Jesus saw that he answered wisely, he said to him, 'You are not far from the kingdom of God'" (Mark 12: 28-34). This implies that knowing these two commandments and living these two commandments are what get us into the kingdom of God *right here and now*.

This notion of heaven being now rather than after death is furthered by other similar verses:

1) "Repent, for the kingdom of heaven is at hand" (Matthew 3: 2).

2) "Being asked by the Pharisees when the kingdom of God was coming, he answered them, 'The kingdom of God is not coming with signs to be observed; nor will they say, "Lo, here it is!" or "There!" for behold *the kingdom of heaven is in the midst of you*'" (Luke 17: 20-21) [emphasis mine]. Biblical scholars assert that there is also a second and equally valid reading of the italicized portion. It can be read *the kingdom of heaven is within you.*

But, whether the kingdom of heaven is *within* you or *in the midst of* you (plural) largely isn't the point. The point is the word that precedes both clauses — the word *is*. It's not that the kingdom of God *will be someday*. The point is that the kingdom of God *is* ... as in, right now! And where is it? It is in the midst of you. It is among you. And it is inside you.

3) "Heaven and earth will pass away, but my words will not pass away" (Matthew 24: 35). If, as Christians have always interpreted the Bible, heaven is a place we go to live forever after we die, then how can heaven pass away? Isn't it far more logical that heaven is now, in your lifetime — a state of being on this earth?

4) "For truly, I say to you, till heaven and earth pass away [nothing] will pass from the law..." (Matthew 5:18). Again, heaven is not some after-death party in the sky; heaven is here and now. When you pass away, your heaven passes away with you.

Conclusion

The purpose of your life is to do good (as much as possible), not to be good in hopes of a pat on the head. It is to bring love to the world. It is to create heaven, here and now simply because you can. The purpose of your life is not personal holiness, but servanthood of neighbor and global servanthood, so that others, too, may know heaven today.

Being good implies a self-consciousness and navel-gazing that indicate self-centeredness. In contrast, doing good (for the benefit of others) is not self-conscious. As President Harry Truman once said, "There is no limit to the good you can do, if you don't care who gets the credit." Doing good is other-centered and therefore inherently humble. It is going through life without concern for how

I appear to others or God, but only with concern for how I can serve others.

Jesus' life was an example of servanthood and self-sacrifice. And that path, even as it brought him hardship, also brought him joy and peace. And *that* is our reward for the living of life like Jesus did. Our reward is the peace, hope, joy, power, laughter, and sense of purpose that life on Jesus' path brings. This is the heaven that is created in our lives and the lives of others.

Once that shift from trying to be good to trying to do good happens in a person, there comes a renewed sense of vitality and vigor. There is a sense of purpose and being fully alive. There is a shift in countenance to a beautiful humility that humanity cannot help but admire.[44]

To reach this consciousness is the very summit of life. Heaven and the kingdom of God are created today for ourselves and others when we stop making self-love our goal and choose other-love, instead. Thereby, others are lifted to higher ground and in the process so are we.

Chapter 10

[Re-think God, Science, Resurrection, and Greatness]

"For it's not the light that is needed, but fire; it's not the gentle shower, but thunder. We need the storm, the whirlwind and the earthquake in our hearts."

— Frederick Douglass

"Everyone should carefully observe which way his heart draws him, and then choose that way with all his strength."

— Old Hasidic proverb

WE LIVE IN THE WORLD GOD CREATED. We live in God's nature. We mess it up a lot, and we often improve it, too. But it is the nature that God (or the universe or energy) created.

It was God who created gravity. It was God who created sound waves. It was God who created heat to rise and combine with condensation to create clouds. It was God who created atoms and sub-atomic particles. It was God who created the physical laws of how nature operates.

Thus, trying to better understand nature is really an attempt to better understand God's creation, and even God. Science is religion's twin sister. In fact, many of the great scientists of the past and present were/are very religious or spiritual people seeking to understand God better by understanding the magnificent and complex world God created. Theirs is inherently a spiritual quest. As the great British theoretical physicist Stephen Hawking is fond of saying, "The point of science is to know the mind of God." In that vein, it is helpful to take lessons from science when thinking about life after death.

To begin, you are made up of trillions upon trillions of little molecules. When you die these molecules are not destroyed. They don't just disappear or go away. It may appear that way to a child, but, in fact, they change form. Physics and chemistry teach us that your molecules recombine with other molecules to change from you into other things (Law of Conservation of Energy).

A dead mouse is partly eaten by your cat, partly eaten by ants and maggots, and partly decomposes and fertilizes the soil where it lies. Nothing is destroyed. The matter that was the mouse just becomes nourishment for the cat, the ant, and the dirt. It, in fact, becomes the cat, the ant, and the dirt by being digested and absorbed. All of these, in turn, become nourishment for other creatures and plants. Matter is not destroyed. It only changes form.

This, for humanity, contains the simple guarantee of bodily resurrection. Your body (at the molecular level) will find new life in many different forms. It's really not even a religious issue. It's just a fact of life — life in this nature God created. Every one of us is guaranteed bodily resurrection and new life, even Jesus. As surely as Jesus sweated, sloughed dead skin cells, lost hair, urinated, defecated, lost fingernails, vomited, blew his nose, and bled, his molecules — Jesus' molecules! — recombined with other molecules to make other new forms of life. That means that Jesus is, quite literally, still here . . . .on the molecular level.

As with the resurrection of Jesus' molecules, our bodily resurrection holds great promise as we more fully become one with many more elements and creatures of God's creation. We are not required to believe that our bodies are resurrected in some heaven (or hell) after we die. Bodily resurrection is the factual, provable guarantee that we will emerge into new life, just as we grew out of the resurrection of those who have died before us.

Jesus said, "And as for the resurrection of the dead, have you not read what was said to you by God, 'I am the God of Abraham, and the God of Isaac, and the God of Jacob'? He is not God of the dead, but of the living" (Matthew 22: 31-32).

The Resurrection of Your Spirit

Yet, though your cat will someday die and become nourishment for the soil and other creatures, today your cat brings you great joy and warmth. And it is *that*, that memory of your cat — i.e. your cat's spirit — that will live on in you and in your home. If the cat brought love to your life, you will warmly remember it. Whatever you loved most is the spirit that will likely live on.

It is interesting to note that the very word *inspire*, when broken down to its original roots, is *in-* and *-spirit*. It is to have the *spirit inside*. If you are *inspired* by your cat or a person, you have his or her *spirit inside* you. It is also interesting to note that the Latin meaning of the word *spirit* is *breath* (*wind* in Greek). To be inspired by someone is to have their very breath breathing life in you. That is spiritual resurrection.

Every American knows that John F. Kennedy was one of our great presidents, cut down in the prime of his life. Yet there can be no doubt that nearly every American, even today, knows and feels JFK's spirit, to some degree. So strong was the force of his character that he still provides inspiration and life to people today, despite the fact that he has long since decomposed and become food, air, and soil.

On a much larger scale, Jesus has been doing the same thing for 2000 years. Whether or not you like Christianity, you cannot deny that this man had such a powerful and loving character, and accomplished so much good in his brief stay on earth that he has breathed life into billions of people since. As it is written in 1Corinthians 15: 45, "The first Adam became a living being. The last Adam (AKA Jesus) became a life-giving spirit."

This is what death promises. Not only will your body die, decay, come apart, and change into other solids, liquids, and gases, but your spirit — the spirit of who you were when you were alive — will live on. And the degree to which you brought life, healing, and inspiration in your living determines the degree to which you are remembered with affection when you die, and the degree to which you will bring life to others long after you die.

If you brought pain and misery in your living, you will be remembered. But you will be viewed by future generations as an aberration and an example of what not to do in life.

The Human Quest for Greatness

Jesus understood people. Jesus understood the very strong human drive to be great. He also had a powerful understanding of human nature and how we reserve the highest honor and remember the longest those who abandon their own lives for a noble cause, usually for others.

In the most bittersweet of ironies Jesus said, "If any would be first, he must be last of all and servant of all" (Mark 9: 35). If you desire greatness, you need only forfeit your life in service of others. It is to give your life's energy and spirit as food for others.

To be a source of inspiration and life when you are alive and even after you die is the noblest goal for which a human can strive. It is the fullest expression of *loving God and loving neighbor*.

This, too, is heaven: To be remembered, and remembered with affection and reverence. Your judgment day is not some end-of-the-world day in the after-death future. It is today and everyday when you give more to life than you take, and give more to life than you were given. Thereby your spirit lives on in the hearts of others, enabling them to be sources of life for others. Thereby do you achieve the greatness for which your spirit longs.

You see, there *is* resurrection of both body and spirit! When you die your body is quite literally resurrected, just not in the form of you. Instead, your molecules become life in other new forms of creation, just as other forms of creation died and comprise you.

In that way, we truly are all one. And, in that same way you continue to be a part of God's ongoing process of creation. What sets you apart and causes your memory to live on are the love, vigor, goodness, purpose, and passion you bring to life. What sets you apart and causes the resurrection of your spirit is what you give back to life today.

"The ancient Greeks did not write obituaries. When a man died they asked one question, "Did he have passion?"

— from the movie *Serendipity*

So How Do You Insure Your Spirit Will Live On?

Since the nights my mother read Bible stories to me at my childhood bedside, I have always had two favorite parables told by Jesus. The first story is of a wealthy ruler who was leaving town for a long time:

He called his three most trusted servants to him. To the first he gave ten bags of money, and instructed him to tend the money while he was away. To the second he gave five bags of money with the same instruction. And to the third he gave one bag.

After being gone for quite some time, the ruler returned. He called his servants to him, the one with the ten bags first. "What have you done with the money I entrusted to you?" he asked.

The first servant said, "I invested and traded, bought and sold, and now have your ten bags to return to you, plus ten bags more."

"Well done," the master responded. "I now grant to you a large part of my kingdom to care for."

The second servant, to whom five bags had been entrusted, when called forth by the ruler, said, "I, too, invested and traded, and bought and sold. Now here are your original five bags of money, plus five more."

"Also, well done," the ruler replied. "To you I shall entrust part of my kingdom to tend."

When called forward, the third servant said, "I knew you are an angry man who would get mad if I lost the money or blew it. So I buried the money in a field. Here is your original single bag of money."

"Get away from me," the ruler shot back. "I entrusted this to you to use, not hide. You shall be entrusted with nothing further. Leave my presence" (Matthew 25: 14-30).

We all have abilities, interests, drives, and desires that are unique to each one of us. They are the bags of money God has entrusted to us. Our obligation and our joy are to use these to enact the greatest amount of good we can in the brief time we have to do so.

Our reward, as in the parable, is not some heavenly party, but is even greater responsibility. Our reward in this lifetime is that when we do good and prove that we are capable of using what we have, we are given trust. That is the ultimate pat on the back. It is to be appreciated for what we have done, and to be trusted with the chance to do even more good. Thereby, as mentioned above, our spirit lives on more fully in the broader circle of those whom we touch.

The second parable Jesus told is of a man who was walking down a road and fell among robbers:

> The robbers beat him, stripped him of what he had, and ran off, leaving him near-dead. Now, by chance, a pastor was walking down that same road, and passed to the other side of the road when he saw the man lying on the road. Next came a bishop who, too, moved to the other side of the road to avoid the beaten and dying man. Lastly, an "impure foreigner" whose people were despised, came by, saw the man, and immediately rushed to his aid. He bound up his wounds, treating them with balm and bandages. He then put the man on his donkey and brought him to an inn. There he took care of him.

The next day, when the foreigner had to depart, he left money for the innkeeper to use to tend to the beaten man in his recovery. He also told the innkeeper that when he returned this way he would reimburse the innkeeper for whatever it would cost for extended care.

Jesus then asked his disciples which of the three men on the road proved to be neighbor to the man who fell among robbers. They responded, "The third one, who showed mercy."

Jesus said, "Go and do likewise" (Luke 10: 29-37).

This parable shows, quite plainly, what we must do. We must do all we can to take away the suffering of those in need. To ease suffering is to bring what you bring in service of others. It is to bring medicine to those who lack. It is to bring financial assistance to those worn down by lack. To take away suffering is to hold the hand of the person who cannot stand alone. It is to go out of your way to assist even when you don't have to. It is to see another's need without them ever having to say it, and to offer help without them ever having to ask it.

To take away suffering is to dance for the world when it cannot move. It is to bring joy and even laughter where there is only sorrow. It is to bring peace where life has been torn by fighting. To ease suffering is to bring your gifts and your calling in service to life, so that others might know release from all that afflicts them. When freed from affliction they, then, have the opportunity to discover the abundant life of which Jesus spoke. Every gift God gives one of us becomes a gift to the world when we offer it in service.

Your own abilities, interests, drives, and talents are the bags of money God has given you. They are the key to your easing the suffering in others.

Use them. Follow them. They are the voice of God in your life, showing you how God has made you to best serve humanity. By following and investing the bags of money God has given you, you will find your way to eternal life today and your way to greatness tomorrow. For as surely as you invest yourself in the sufferings of others, you guarantee the resurrection of your spirit in the hearts and minds of those who come after you.

Chapter 11

[Beware: Following Jesus Equals Suffering]

"This is why forgiveness is so important: Forgiveness frees us from continuing to hold on to our pain."

— John Gray, author of the *Mars/Venus* book series

"Wanna fly, you gotta rise above the shit that ways you down."

— Toni Morrison

HAVING BEEN RAISED IN A VERY CHRISTIAN HOME, forgiveness has always been a part of my personal make up. It was never required or demanded, but was always modeled for my siblings and me by our parents. Mom and dad lived a noble, humble life of contrition, kindness, and the constant seeking of forgiveness. They did so not in some shrinking violet way. Instead, they had a strength that is constantly aware of how one might be hurting someone else and isn't afraid to admit it and apologize.

Because I constantly saw it in my parents, I constantly apologized and sought forgiveness when I wronged someone. It became second nature to me. It didn't even require thought or willpower. I was just constantly conscious of when I had infringed on someone else, and sought atonement with whomever I had offended.

But as I aged and got well along into adulthood, I took on more and more of the pain and suffering of others. I was not only aware of when I had hurt someone, but I let others hurt me. I continued and continued to turn my other cheek. I continued and continued to forgive, whether forgiveness was sought or not.

Into my thirties I began to wrestle with whether or not we must forgive if the offender does not seek forgiveness. This, I realized, indicated that I was growing tired of forgiving and continuing to be harmed. I realized that seeking forgiveness was no longer a reflex. The same was true with granting forgiveness. I no longer did it automatically.

Instead, I began to withhold forgiveness, picking and choosing whom I forgave and when. I began to be selective in when and with whom I sought forgiveness. Some people, who continually hurt me, either thoughtlessly or heartlessly, were no longer forgiven. No longer did I seek forgiveness from them when I was the offender.

I realized that withholding apology and withholding forgiveness are not only self-protective, but they are ways of staying in control. For, to go before another person and seek forgiveness is to humble oneself. It is to put yourself lower than the other person. It is to be at his or her mercy. And that is a very uncomfortable position, because so many people use that superior position to spit back your offenses and release their venom.

In this world, many of us have become so calloused that we are no longer moved by another person's humbling him- or herself and seeking forgiveness. We no longer desire to pick that person up and say, "You don't have to humble yourself. It's okay. I understand. And, yes of course, you are forgiven."

To not grant forgiveness is to hold on to power. If someone comes seeking forgiveness, and I do not grant it, it is because I seek to maintain some power over that person. That person remains in my debt, so to speak. That person remains contrite and humbled, like a cowering dog. And I can use that to my advantage. I can feel superior. Like a child, I can get my own way.

But that only got worse for me. Soon, I was withholding my apologies and my forgiveness even from people who had not harmed me. Whether it was a boss, a co-worker, a mate, or a friend, it was just easier to not apologize. Or, it was a good way to keep from giving up energy, or it was a good way to keep from getting something vomited back in my face. It was a good way to keep the world under my thumb. "To hell with the world. I'm not Jesus. I don't have to forgive everybody. I'm just going to protect myself, because I'm tired of getting hurt," I thought.

Forgiveness had become a choice. It now took willpower, rather than simply being a reflex response. In effect, my spiritual reflexes had become deadened by my own pain.

Quite honestly, I have only begun to move past that stage. Now, in my late thirties, I am having to teach myself all over again how to forgive and how to seek forgiveness. I am having to break through my own anger and my own desire to withhold apology. I am having to become like Jesus. I am having to choose Jesus, where before it just came naturally.

Jesus' Path is Just Damn Hard

Following Jesus' teachings and example — I mean, *really* following Jesus — is one area I am reluctant to discuss, at all. It is neither a pretty thing, nor a strong selling point to the spiritual seeker. For, it holds a depth of truth so profound that it is terrifying. This is the stuff you won't get in church either. It is so complex, so powerful, and so sublime that it cannot be properly addressed in a 15-minute sermon. It is a lifetime's worth of teaching.

Jesus called humanity to a very difficult path, a path and a mindset that Christianity often forgets. Jesus called humanity to a life of total servanthood. As mentioned in previous chapters, the role that Jesus' teachings challenge us to willingly accept is that of servant of humanity, servant of our neighbor.

However, if there is one lesson that Jesus' life and teachings show us, and if there is one lesson that the history of Christianity teaches, it is that if you truly and fully live Jesus' example of serving others, you will suffer. Hear me again, if you follow Jesus, you will suffer.

In fact, you will suffer well beyond normal human suffering. Jesus' teachings on self-sacrifice, living in service of others, and speaking truth against oppression and injustice are not for the timid or the middle-of-the-road. When Jesus calls us to a life of self-sacrifice, it is just that — a life where you and your interests will be sacrificed.

Just as surely as you will come alive by following his teachings of *love God and love neighbor*, you will be struck down, ridiculed, beaten, and humiliated. Jesus' path (fully lived) is not for the weak, but for the strong to serve the weak, the hungry, and the oppressed.

But this is optional. No one, not even Jesus, requires you to give of your life. Jesus simply challenges you to do so. God will love you, no matter what you choose. It is not a religious demand. It is a spiritual opportunity. Jesus simply says that if you really want abundant joy, if you really want to feel alive and a sense of purpose, if you really want greatness, sacrifice yourself. Just don't expect it to be easy.

It was long ago documented that Indian braves riding into battle against American armies could be heard shouting this war cry: "What a wonderful way to die!" As surely as they knew they might die, they just as surely were truly alive. Many a war veteran, through time, has echoed this thought. Just as war is harrowing and dreadful, it is for some also the great deliverer of a sense of feeling alive. To live on the edge of life or on the edge of death, in service of some cause greater than yourself, can be sublime: The source of great aliveness, as well as great suffering.

Three Ways of Following, and Three Ways of Suffering

When trying to understand the cost of following Jesus' teachings, it is helpful to consider three general categories that Jesus-followers fit into. In fairness, there are many different ways that they can be categorized; and every follower of Jesus is unique. However, recognizable patterns do exist. Each category has its own mindset. Each has its own price.

For the purpose of better understanding suffering, followers of Jesus are categorized here as: The Classic Christian, The Christianity-kicked-my-butt Christian, and The Simple Follower of a Darn Good Way of Living.

1) *The Classic Christian.* This is the person most of us think of when we think of Christians. This person believes in Jesus as the one and only Savior of the world, lives Jesus' teachings, and attempts to bring others to Jesus by speaking his name, telling his story, and living a Christianity-centered life.

The most notable feature (for our purposes here) of this follower of Jesus is that faith is inextricably tied to speaking Jesus' name, using classic Christian jargon, and making Jesus himself the very center of faith. The mindset is quite clear. It is "Jesus, Jesus, Jesus." The most dominant character trait of the Classic Christian is the nobility of conviction. This person walks through life with the strength of an erect spine, which is made so by unwavering belief in Jesus Christ as savior of the world.

This mindset also takes on a somewhat negative view of the world outside Christian walls, and seeks to save the world from itself. This person's life goal is to bring liberation and salvation to the world through Jesus Christ.

The price of following Jesus in this way can be quite high. The history of Christianity, particularly early Christianity, bears this out. John the Baptist, Stephen, Paul, and each of the disciples suffered and/or died because they preached the name of Jesus. Further, under Roman Emperors such as Nero and Diocletian, followers of Jesus could quite easily be imprisoned or lose their lives by simply uttering the name, Jesus, to the wrong person. To claim to follow Jesus was certain death.

Over the centuries, as missionaries carried the name of Jesus into the far corners of the world, many discovered the same fate. Christian missionaries to Japan, South America, and Africa, to name a few, met with suffering and death as they tried to bring monotheism, Jesus, and baptism to an unwelcoming world. Missionaries have been beaten and killed, had their homes burned, their families killed, and their own bodies tortured (Rent the movie, *Mission*, for a powerful depiction of the life of the missionary.).[45] Even today in the 21st Century, we read of Christian missionaries being killed in the Middle East and other parts of the world.

Yet, one need not even look beyond our own borders to see the persecution of the Classic Christian in the world. The Christian can barely escape the church walls before being (1) harassed by an unforgiving media, (2) looked on condescendingly and distrustfully by secular people, and (3) consigned to a life of externally imposed self-loathing and guilt. The Christian still suffers ridicule and sideways glances upon the mere mention of the word *Jesus*.

Still, the suffering of the Classic Christian does not end there. It can mean death, even in America, even today. The April 2001 killing rampage at Columbine High School that so riveted this country brings to life a glowing example of Christian martyrdom. As the two young killers worked their way through the school, one of them came across a group of students and faculty in the library. There he encountered a 17 year-old, named Cassie Bernall. As the killer placed his weapon to her head he asked, "Do you believe in God?"

To this, she replied a simple, "Yes." With that, her blood was spilled at point-blank range. She died a Christian martyr.

While much bad has been said about Christianity's practices over the centuries, and while Christianity is subject to much justifiable critique, there can be no doubt that the life of the Classic Christian is one of hardship in this world today. For, even as we live in a culture of religious tolerance, that tolerance is not extended to Christians. The Classic Christian is a member of the in-group of Christianity and enjoys the strength that this group offers, but experiences suffering when he or she vocally steps out into the world. The Classic Christian knows the suffering of being unwanted for who you are.

2) *The Christianity-kicked-my-butt Christian.* This is the person who changes the world and often changes the church, both in very large ways. This is the person of perhaps the greatest faith. This is a person who is a follower of Jesus, and even considers him- or herself a member of Christianity, but who has stepped out into the world and developed an appreciation for all the good that is outside Christianity's walls.

No longer able to characterize nature and the world outside Christianity as bad, this Christian views the world and non-Christians often more sympathetically and gently than does the Classic Christian. This person is prone to compromise the hard-line Christian stances in favor of a more peaceful and tolerant church-world relationship.

Thus, the path for improving the world, the path for this person to be a follower of Jesus, involves not changing the world but changing Christianity and the church. This is the part that demands the great faith. For this Christian, by definition, is still a Christian, and therefore suspect in the eyes of the world. Yet, this Christian has the audacity and apparent disloyalty to question and change what is considered by insiders to be nearly perfect — Christianity. This person is a stranger in both the secular and the sacred worlds, bearing the support of no one. This person's faith rests on God alone, not the comfort of any group. Thus, this person is characterized by the nobility of courage.

However, if this person finds any sympathy it is likely on the outside. For, inside Christianity such a person will endure slings and arrows like no outsider ever has. This is true because the church has no patience for disbelief within its ranks. And to the church, to question and challenge is the same as disbelief.

The church will treat an unbeliever outside Christianity like a child who simply needs to be taught the right way of living. But the church will treat as a heretic, an apostate, and the devil an insider who appears to be a disbeliever of the one true truth. This is no exaggeration. Anyone who would claim to question the very church of God must be questioning, challenging, and defying God, himself. The thinking goes that it is our responsibility as Christians to defend the church and defend God (a rather odd notion!), and even kill if necessary. Sadly, hell hath no fury like the church chasing apostates . . . or supposed apostates.

Ostracism, torture, excommunication, and even death are hallmarks of this person's suffering. People who have taken this path in history have maintained their love for Jesus, for God, and for Christianity, itself. Many of these people loved Christianity enough, and saw so clearly what Christianity is capable of, that they were willing to suffer *at the hands of Christianity* for Christianity and humanity.

Many in history have traveled this path in great and small ways. Most notable among them are:

A) Galileo Galilei: Censured by the church for his outspoken support of the Copernican belief that the earth is not the center of the universe;

B) John Hus: Burned at the stake for supporting the translation of the Bible into the native languages of different countries in the 15th Century;

C) Martin Luther: Excommunicated for standing against church corruption and standing for radical changes in theology;

D) Pope John XXIII: Caustically slandered by conservative Roman Catholics for 40 years after convening the Second Vatican Council in the 1960s, a convention that brought radical changes to update Catholicism;

E) Martin Luther King, Jr.: Condemned by many religious leaders for seeking civil rights for African Americans;

F) Archbishop Romero: Killed in El Salvador because he challenged both the church and the state;

G) Jesus, himself: Killed because he attempted to revolutionize the theology of his religion . . . oh, and he claimed to be God.

It is a well-known fact of human existence that those who think way outside the box and challenge us are those who help us create brilliant new paths and forms of human existence. Yet, these are also the people who make us feel the most uncomfortable, and the ones we are quickest to dispose of because of that discomfort.

If I may be indulged to use a little bit of bad literary form, I will relay a research study that was told to a class of students in college, of which I was a member. It is bad literary form because I am unable to locate proper documentation of the study, even though I remember the professor reading it from a text book. Yet, I include it here, because it conveys a truth that we can all recognize yet still be startled by.

In this study, several groups of people were given a difficult problem to solve. Into some of the groups a "deviant" was included, unknown to the other group members. The deviant's purpose was to question, challenge, and turn upside-down the group's processes, direction, and solutions.

The study confirmed that in every group in which a deviant was present a solution was reached that was far more thorough, creative, and effective. The control groups, in which no deviant was present, simply couldn't compete.

Yet, the most fascinating part of the study is what comes next. When asked to vote for one member to be removed from the group, every group that contained a deviant voted to eject the deviant! The human aversion to conflict causes us to forego higher quality in favor of group harmony.

Back to the *Christianity-kicked-my-butt Christian*, everyday in this country people of this category are suffering. Try as they might to change and improve their little corner of Christianity, they suffer from frustration, fatigue, and the full force of an organization that believes it is beyond change, or simply fears change. These people — these prophetic people — who nobly step out from the security of the masses find that the sheer momentum of Christianity often crushes them. Day by day their spirit is broken, their life force is drained, and the color leaves their cheeks.

But, worst of all, these *Christianity-kicked-my-butt Christians* have no home. They never feel comfortable as long as the problems they seek to change exist. On top of that, once they have pushed beyond a certain point, they never can feel at home at church. They are never again treated as family. As Jesus said, "The prophet is not without honor, except in his own country" (Luke 4:24).

But they are not fully at home in the world either, as the world can never understand the mindset of one whose values go so counter to its. The world, while admiring the love the Christianity-kicked-my-butt Christian brings to life, always treats as an outsider a person who does not put herself at the center of the universe.

And so, while bearing a great love for both the world and Christianity, this person wanders, spiritually homeless. The Butt-Kicked Christian knows the suffering of loss; the suffering of having been stripped of his or her spiritual family. This person deeply understands Jesus' words (whether metaphorical or literal) in the tenth chapter of Matthew where he says, "Brother will deliver up brother to death, and the father the child, and the children will rise against parents and have them put to death; and you will be hated by all for following my path" (10: 21-22).

3) *The Simple-follower-of-a-darn-good-way-of-living*. This is the person who when asked in a Gallup Poll if he or she is a Christian, says yes (because he or she believes in God) but would seldom find him- or herself in church. This is the person who really likes Jesus and Jesus' teachings, and who really dislikes Christianity and all it has done to Jesus, God, and the world. Thus, this person considers himself more of a Jesus-guy or a Jesus-follower than a Christian, per se, but sometimes simply uses the word *Christian* for lack of a better word.

Yet, this person is also quite comfortable in the world — at home in it — far more so than he or she would ever be in a Classic Christian's church. As the Classic Christian looks down on the world and believes in the greatness of the fortress of Christianity, the *Simple-follower-of-a-darn-good-way-of-living* looks down on the church, and rather enjoys life in the world.

This person venerates Jesus' teachings and uses them as tools for living in the world and being a better person. But, for this person following Jesus is not about speaking Jesus' name or speaking Classic Christian language, or even bringing people to God and Jesus. This person might be reluctant to even mention the word *Jesus*.

Instead, following Jesus is about being good to people and bringing loving-kindness to an often unfriendly world. Jesus, to this person, is the master teacher (or one of several masters) of how to live in the world. This person has stripped Jesus' teachings of the religious language and symbols, and simply tries to live the lessons. Some Christians would say this is either least-common-denominator Christianity, or not even Christianity, at all, because it's not about the traditional religious concepts and language. Yet, this person is the epitome of nobility in simplicity.

But as with the others, this follower of Jesus suffers, as well. This person suffers in perhaps the most slow and painful of ways. While the suffering of the first two categories is more searing and sharp, the suffering of the Darn-good-way Follower is a dull pain that over the years simply eats away at one's insides. This person's spiritual beliefs are seldom brought to controversy or crisis stage, and therefore the suffering is never acute.

Instead, this follower experiences the growing hollowness that comes from seldom having a deep spiritual home, or seldom having spiritual brothers and sisters with whom to share the journey through the forest. So, family, children, and/or friends become the substitute for deep spiritual community, even though biological family often does not constitute our spiritual family, and even having friends is not the same as sharing spiritual community. Thus, when parents die, children grow up, and spouses leave the anguish is unimaginable. There is no spiritual home and no faith context to buoy one through the suffering.

There is one context in which this person does suffer more acutely for following Jesus' teachings: The political realm. Often in America, in the last forty years, the agents of social and political protest and change have been people who ascribe to Jesus' teachings (particularly those dealing with social justice), but who aren't necessarily religious. Often these people suffer in compassion. They vicariously feel the pain of those afflicted by injustice. Their *compassion* (which is, ironically, sometimes greater than that of Classic and Butt-Kicked Christians) is felt acutely, just as the word states: *com = with, passion=suffering . . . to suffer with*!

It is much more difficult to highlight people in history who have been followers of Jesus' teachings but not overtly Christian in any way. It is hard to know who these people might because they are not identified as members of any Jesus or Christian group. Though, one interesting example is Mohandas Gandhi. He was a great national and spiritual leader in India in the last century. He was also a self-proclaimed avid follower of the teachings of Jesus. He may not have suffered the absence of spiritual community, but, like others in this group, he believed very strongly in the depth and truth of Jesus' teachings.

More than just talk, however, his respect for Jesus' teachings was at the root of his justice-seeking, non-violent protest that was responsible for overthrowing the ruling government. Yet, Gandhi was a Hindu, and a Hindu leader on top of that. He was not a Christian, and saw no need to be a Christian in order to follow Jesus' teachings. He simply believed in the beauty, nobility, and effectiveness of Jesus' teachings.

And, if you ever want to understand what it means to suffer for your beliefs and your actions, just read a biography on Gandhi's life. His whole existence was about willingly sacrificing and suffering in order to improve the lot of the poor and oppressed.

And this is the final way the Simple Follower suffers. It is the way all followers of Jesus suffer. Whether you live to speak Jesus' name or never speak Jesus' name, if you live the principles Jesus' taught — self-sacrifice, servanthood, overcoming oppression in the world, tending to those in need, and the speaking of truth to injustice — you will know pain. For, who has ever sought to serve, and not been treated with entitlement, arrogance, and spirit-robbing indifference? Who has ever spoken truth against untruth or injustice, and not suffered for it? Who has ever sought to change entrenched ways of thinking so that others might be freed, and been warmly received? Who has ever sought to bring healing and immediately gotten a pat on the back?

Jesus' life was one of willingly suffering and willingly dying for what he believed in, in order to help others. He was the perfect example of the "suffering servant" talked about in Isaiah (53: 11), and a model of the scapegoat or "sacrificial lamb" to be slaughtered (1Corinthians 5: 7). Jesus' example for us is one of loss, hard work on behalf of others, disappointment, and pain, just as surely as it is one of hope, joy, laughter, power, and purpose.

Jesus calls us to follow the calling of our hearts and to do so in service of others. If we look at the history of humanity, we see that anyone who has ever followed their calling has known tribulations. That's why so many people don't follow their heart and their dreams and their calling. It can be very painful.

Noteworthy is the fact that the English word *passion* comes from the Greek word *pati*. *Pati* also happens to be the root of the words *pathology*. *Pati*, at its root, means *to suffer*. What this points to is the fact that that which is our passion is also our disease, or source of greatest suffering. That which moves us also destroys us. Those who stand up for who they are, what they feel called to do, or what they believe, are those who, by definition, will suffer.

Artists of all types know this. Most suffer ridicule and condemnation for their art or for the life they must live to pursue their art. And yet, their suffering infuses their art with life, relevance, and realness.

And that is the life Jesus calls us to. Jesus calls us to follow our truth, whatever it may be, knowing full well that it will come at a price.

Speaking truth will kill you. Jesus knew that. We teach our children to venerate and emulate Jesus. But it's as if we forget that Jesus was killed for speaking the truths he spoke, and living the principles he lived. Even if you believe he was the son of God, you must acknowledge that he wasn't killed by people because he was the son of God. He was killed because he *told* people he was the son of God — *he spoke his truth* — and that was blasphemy to their ears.

If you live his principles anywhere near the extreme that he did, you will suffer. If you speak truth against authority or against what is culturally acceptable, you will suffer. If you attempt to give of yourself to people and life, as Jesus did, you will suffer. If you attempt to bring healing, you will have the energy and life bled out of you.

Individuals will spill their careless fury and unwanted critique onto you. And Jesus will tell you to turn the other cheek for them to strike (Matthew 5: 39). Institutions will let their torturous momentum simply run over you, slander you, and tear you down as you attempt to bring about fairness and positive change. And Jesus will tell you to turn the other cheek. Keepers of ideology will rip you apart as you fight to create a better world by changing people's thinking. And Jesus will tell you to turn the other cheek. Friends, partners, and family will snipe at you and undermine your efforts. And Jesus will tell you to turn the other cheek.

Jesus will ring in your head. He'll tell you to not resist one who is evil, to offer the shirt off your back to anyone who simply asks for your overcoat to stay warm, to give to him who begs, to not refuse anyone who asks for a loan (and to not charge interest), to always say yes to someone who needs you, to take on the burdens of others, and to forgive seventy times seven. None of this is the recipe for a pain-free life. As it says in 1Peter 1: 6, "...You may have to suffer various trials..."

Despite what many Christian churches teach, Jesus' path is not one of prosperity. Jesus' path is not sunny or rosy. Jesus' path is one of sweat, toil, sacrifice, discipline, hardship, sorrow, and loss. Jesus' path is not a quest for a heaven-sent payoff, but recognition of how good life already is, despite the suffering; and it is a desire to help others find joy, purpose, and peace and life. The payoff is the joy of serving, the joy of sacrificing for something great.

It is simply important that whatever you choose, you be conscious of what you're getting into. Jesus' life is a radical path. Jesus' example is one that will force you at some point to either take some form of beating for another, or turn your back on your neighbor and on the noble path Jesus taught. It is unavoidable. In fact, most of us are faced with that very decision, on some level, every single day. The more you choose to walk the path of Jesus, the more suffering you will know; yet, ironically, the deeper your sense of life satisfaction will run.

So don't follow Jesus and don't let your children follow Jesus, unless you are prepared to carry a heavy burden, and unless you are prepared to see your children suffer. For Jesus' path is one of hardship and sorrow.

Jesus' *what* and God's *how* will bring peace, purpose, power, joy, hope, laughter, and love. But they will also bring great sorrow and great suffering. And the challenge, as Joseph Campbell so frequently and eloquently said, is "to live joyfully amid the sorrows of the world."

Christianity and Buddhism

But doesn't any path in life bring suffering? Is Jesus' path all that more suffering-laden?

Yes, all paths in life do bring suffering. That is what the First Noble Truth of Buddhism states (see Chapter Two). However, Jesus' path does, in fact, drastically increase your odds of experiencing suffering in this life.

Why? The best way to explain is to cite one of the fundamental differences between Buddhist teaching and Jesus' teaching. (Neither is better or worse than the other. They are simply two different approaches to life that can actually be lived together.) Buddhism teaches that life is suffering and that suffering is the result of clinging — clinging to stuff, to people, to ego, to anything and everything. The Third Noble Truth of Buddhism is that we eliminate sorrow by destroying desire.

It is because of these truths that the words "just let go" are so common nowadays. It is why the first step in 12-step Programs is to "Let Go and Let God." If you stop clinging, you will suffer less. Anyone who has ever known loss of any kind knows that a big burden is lifted from the heart when you just let go of it and accept that you will never have that person or thing again. Buddhism, like much of our culture today, is about reducing suffering.

In stark contrast to that are Jesus' teachings. Jesus is fundamentally about increasing joy, which, though a seemingly subtle difference, is actually categorically different from simply trying to hurt less. While letting go will bring less pain, holding on will often bring great joy. That is Jesus' point: Don't just live. . . . Be fully alive! Jesus teaches that "holding on to" others — giving your life in service and love to others — will bring a joy like you have never known before. Generally speaking, love is some form or another of holding on.

And, where there is a holding on suffering is sure to follow. If Jesus would have let go of his need to correct the religious institution of his day and if Jesus would have let go of his need to fight the injustices done against life's downtrodden people, he would have suffered less. He would likely not have known religious mockery and scorn, and might never have been crucified. But then, he might never have been remembered for changing the face of the world.

Buddhism teaches us to walk away from suffering. Jesus teaches us to walk directly into the suffering that will come when we try to make the world a better place, when we speak truth and fight injustice, and when we try to bring love to people. We walk into the suffering not for suffering's sake, but because we love and desire to express our love in acts and words. Jesus says that we will suffer, but the joy, love, peace and sense of purpose we experience when we do so will outweigh the suffering, and make it all worthwhile.[46]

Taking it one step farther, as taught in Chapter Seven, not only does suffering have to be endured, eliminated or fought past, but it can be learned from. Suffering can be the very instrument of your abundant life, bringing greater growth and joy.

The contrast between Buddhism and Jesus is similar to the contrast between psychology and Jesus. Like Buddhism, psychology is fundamentally in the business of alleviating people's suffering — bringing people back to a state of normal functioning.

But that is not Jesus' goal. He never sold normalcy. Jesus sold abundant life and eternal joy and peace. That is a far cry from just plain normal. That is not to say that psychology is bad. Just the opposite. Psychology is great for helping people return to normal functioning. But the question is: What do you do when you get there? What do you do with your life when there are no pressing personal problems that greatly afflict you? Normal does not equal joy, so how do you reach joy? It is at that point of desiring abundance that Jesus' teachings can re-orient and breathe life and vigor back into a person, despite the suffering such a life is sure to bring.

A Brief Digression on Christian Bitterness as it Relates to Suffering

Christians are generally very nice people. I love 'em. I do. However, Christians are often a short-fused people who can be rough, rude, and just plain mean.

While the same can be said of any person, Christian nastiness is doubly bad because it is invariably cast against the Christian mantra of "Love, love, love." Thus, the Christian comes off as not just rude, but hypocritical, which, in the eyes of non-Christians is the worse offense.

It's interesting to note, however, the root of this bitterness. Ironically, Christians become sour because their leader (Jesus) exhorts them to be loving. Jesus told his followers to love at all costs, to not fight back when you're being harmed, and to sacrifice yourself for others. The problem is that you cannot long walk that path without being beaten down and wearied, as mentioned above.

Even the broadest of shoulders cannot withstand a lifetime of bearing the burdens, as well as the slings and arrows, of others. And, even the biggest of gods, it seems, cannot provide enough buffer from daily torment. Thus, Christian bitterness is almost an inevitable outcome of the Christian calling. For how long can one endure the wrath of others without becoming bitter to giving, loving, and self-sacrifice?

Jesus got off lucky in that regard. He was martyred at a young age (33). He didn't have to actually live his values over a lifetime, which is a far more difficult task. Yet, he managed to stick Christians with a very rigorous calling.

And so what is the solution? How does one live self-sacrificially without falling into the pit of bitterness and anger?

I'd like to recommend a compromise of Jesus' values. But the very nobility and appeal of Jesus' teachings hinges, to some degree, upon their difficulty. The problem is not with the teaching itself. Rather, the need is to find another teaching to complement it.

So the solution is this: Add more of Jesus' truth. Heed Jesus' other teachings, particularly the one on forgiveness. Jesus' extreme path is not possible without forgiveness. It is not possible to allow yourself to be harmed by the world and long continue trying to serve the world, unless you are able to forgive the world. In the spirit of Jesus' final words on earth, you must be able to say (somehow, without being condescending), "Lord, forgive them. For they know not what they do."

Even when the offending party does not know they have hurt us (thoughtlessness), or even when they do know but either do not care or are unwilling to seek forgiveness (heartlessness), we must forgive. We must have some way of letting go of the infraction, or we will go through life carrying this big load of pain that people have heaped upon us. The load will grow until we are surrounded by mountains of our own pain. That pain will soon obscure our ability to see anything in life except our own pain. It will also obscure our ability to respond in life with anything but pain. Shake a cup that is full to the brim with coffee, and coffee will spill out. Whatever fills you spills out when you are shaken, under pressure, or in crisis.

Forgiveness was so central to Jesus' message because he realized that self-sacrifice and speaking truth against injustice are impossible without the ability, without some way, to lessen the suffering they bring. And so, our task is to continually be in the forgiveness mode. We must be continually willing and able to let go of the infractions that hurt us. Only then can we fully live out our calling to love.

On a Personal Note

To complete the thoughts I began discussing at the beginning of this chapter, I must say that I have learned four things in my own movement through anger and into forgiveness. (If I do end up being wrong about literal interpretation of the Bible and there is, in fact, a Judgment Day, then this first thing, more than anything else, is going to get me thrown into hell.) The first thing I have learned about forgiveness is that in order to bring the self-sacrificial love to people that Jesus taught, we must be able to forgive God for allowing hurts to befall us when God clearly has the power to stop such hurts.

It is only when we can forgive God that we can let go of past hurts and keep on overextending ourselves in love. Yes, it is pretentious to think the Divine errs and needs our forgiveness. I know it is arrogant to presume to question God's wrath and mercy. But there are Biblical precedents for God seeing the error of his ways and retracting his wrath (Exodus 32: 14).

It is not even that God needs our forgiveness. The point is that we need to forgive God. It is us who need to forgive. We need to have a way to let go of the hurt. We need some way to purge ourselves of the hurt of loving and being beaten down. For if we do not, only anger and bitterness will follow. Love will not flow, but will become clogged and jammed.

God is big and strong enough to handle it for us. God can handle our presuming to forgive God, if it will help us survive and keep on loving others. God lets us put our troubles and hurts in God's metaphorical lap, so that we might move forward and re-enter life.

The second lesson I've learned is the one fully discussed in Chapter Seven. God sends pain to move us to higher ground. God sends pain to shake us free of that which held us to a lower existence. God grants us suffering so that we may finally come alive.

Third, I have learned how to deal with apology and forgiveness when caught in the moment. We must stop ourselves and recognize when we are walking into an apology or forgiveness situation. We must have the wherewithal to recognize it. Then we must focus on quieting ourselves inside, and run a quick values assessment. We must be able to feel the other person's pain, and offer apology or forgiveness based on that need.

It is that quieting of oneself and choosing to feel another's pain that is the linchpin. If you have shut yourself off from the pain of others, forgiveness and apology are not possible. They are a mere trifle or a social inconvenience. But if you can feel what another feels, you can be moved to humble yourself or to pick up another person who is humbled.

This is one more reason that God bringing suffering to our own lives is such a bittersweet gift. It enables us to identify and feel the pain of others, thereby becoming instruments for their healing. This feeling of another person's pain is only possible when we have known our own pain. The most compassionate people in life are often those who have suffered the most, whether it is from loss, oppression, cruelty, or misfortune.

Who are the most collectively despised and rejected people in American society? Gays, African-Americans, Jews, women, Muslims? More than likely, those who are the greatest victims of suffering and oppression are also the people who exhibit the greatest compassion. Why? If they haven't become bitter, they know what real pain feels like, and it pains them to see others in pain. So, they do all they can to alleviate the suffering of others. Real compassion comes from knowing another's pain. It is the camaraderie and love that is born of shared experience.

The fourth lesson is one I started learning twenty years ago. It is one that weaved together my political and spiritual views.

After leaving high school I attended the US Air Force Academy. I was inspired by President Reagan, was a believer in the mission and nobility of the military, and wanted the biggest challenge I could get. I was so eager to be a fighter pilot that, when asked why I wanted to attend the Academy, I wrote on one of the infinite admission forms, "I want to fly fast and kill things." Violence, while undesirable, was a necessity of life, and I was not afraid to be an instrument of it.

Yet, after two years at the Academy with some of the highest caliber people I have ever met, I realized my heart, for many reasons, was not in it anymore. I left, and spent the next 12 years studying religions, spirituality, myth systems, and psychology. My feelings regarding military and force changed. I swung to the very liberal side, believing that force should never be used, either politically or personally. Based on Jesus' model of taking, taking, and taking the blows of others and of life, I became a good counselor and a very supportive friend.

But, over time, I realized that I couldn't do it anymore. I couldn't shoulder the burdens of everyone. Nor could I take it when I was treated unjustly. As my father often said, the pendulum always swings back and forth. I found that my views regarding the use of force and violence had begun to swing again, this time more toward center, as had my theology about Jesus.

Today, I believe a military is an unfortunate necessity. For, contrary to the popular bumper sticker, which says "War is not the answer," sometimes, unfortunately, war is the answer. This will frustrate my liberal friends, but sometimes the only path to long term peace is short term war, both in matters political and matters personal.

I believe that we are called to take the blows of others and take on the suffering of the world. The nobility of Jesus' calling, as well as the peace-bearing effect of such actions, is inescapable. Yet, I also believe that we are called to fight injustice, particularly when it is committed against others. Those with power and strength still have the responsibility to stick up for those who are weak and powerless. That means, unfortunately again, that sometimes the strong have to meddle in the affairs of the weak. It ain't pretty, but in rare cases it is necessary.

We are called to stick up for ourselves only when the harm done to us is deliberate and constant or frequent. Accidents and occasional hurts must be shouldered and dealt with using words. To think you will go through life without others hurting you is ridiculous. So you must be able to forgive and move on, even if forgiveness is not sought. Those who are stronger or more emotionally adept in any way have a responsibility to be more forgiving and understanding when hurt by another.

But then, there is also a point (a point only you can know) when enough is enough, and deliberate injustice must be fought. Sometimes in life, there is a point when a bully will not respond to anything except a punch in the nose. A person can only take so much before the spirit inside demands that they stand up and say, "This is just plain wrong, period. And I will no longer stand for it."

Forgiveness, force, pain, violence, justice, and kindness are all woven together. There is no simple solution, no absolute truth. The Bible does not offer one clear path. Jesus' teachings and example show multi-faceted truths. Even my own beliefs expressed here will continue to evolve with time.

Yet, each one of us is called to sort out for ourselves what we believe, and, as best we are able, not force our beliefs on others. May God go with you as you continue to evolve and grow in your understanding of life, God, and the nobility of self-sacrifice.

Another Spiritual Exercise

Into which, if any, of the above Jesus-categories do you fit, Classic, Butt-Kicked, or Darn-Good-Way? If none, what would be a better description of you?

In what way(s) have you suffered for your allegiance or non-allegiance to Jesus or what you believe?

Do you believe it is wise for parents to pass on to their children that which they believe? Do you believe it is possible to not, even tacitly, pass on to your children what you believe?

If, as Buddhist Principles state, all life is suffering, what are the things, people, or beliefs for which you are willing to suffer more (based on whatever it may be that you consider suffering)? Is there anything? Does there even have to be? Is your life geared toward reducing and eliminating your suffering, or toward embracing a goal and vision and enduring whatever suffering may come with that pursuit? Or is it something else altogether?

A Story of Impossible Forgiveness

Corrie ten Boom was a citizen of Harlem, in the Netherlands. She and her family hid Jews and helped them escape Nazi occupation during World War II. They were betrayed and sent to prison. All of her immediate family died in the concentration camps. Her sister, Betsy, died only a couple of days before the end of the war. But Corrie survived.

After the war she was often asked to tell her story to individuals and groups. Many years later, in her writings, she tells of speaking at a church in Munich. Her message at that church was about the love of Jesus, particularly evidenced in loving and forgiving our "neighbor." At the end of the service she saw a balding, heavyset man walking down the aisle toward her. Corrie instantly went cold. She remembered him as a ruthless guard at the Ravensbruck concentration camp years earlier. Suddenly, she was transported back to the horrors, fear, and murder of the camp.

Without time to slip away, Corrie found standing in front of her the very challenge she had just spoken about. Corrie wrote that she cried out in her heart, "How can I forgive this man? I know what he did during the war. I know how he treated other prisoners and me. How, Jesus, can I forgive him?" As the man stood before her he thrust out his hand. Corrie started to sweat. Although she had so often preached about forgiveness, her hand stayed firmly at her side. Angry, vengeful thoughts boiled up within her. She knew she couldn't forgive him, much less offer him love, not without God's help.

Corrie prayed, "God, I can't forgive him on my own. I need Jesus' spirit to help me forgive him. Give me your forgiveness, Lord." Corrie said that as soon as she prayed that prayer she could feel the "knot" letting loose in her.

She said to the man, "I know who you are. I was at Ravensbruck." The man turned white as a ghost. As she took his hand, a current rushed through her. Healing warmth flooded her being. "I forgive you, brother!" she cried, "With all my heart, I forgive you." They both wept.

"How grateful I am for your message, and for your forgiveness, Fraulein. I have been carrying these chains of guilt for years, and now to think that Jesus washed away my sin [through you]." This woman's action was the radical love Jesus taught.

A Final Note

The life lived trying to follow Jesus' teachings is a constant dance between suffering and release, hurt and forgiveness, sorrow and joy. We can never delude ourselves into thinking that "the yoke is easy and the burden is light." For it is neither. It was not for Jesus, and it is not for us.

But still, God calls. Hearing that call, we are left with a choice of whether to follow God's call and Jesus' example, or to walk away. And that is the decision we all must face as we walk the spiritual journey with God to God.

May God go with you as you choose the path that will breathe life into your soul, and enable you to be an instrument of God's love in the life of others.

Love

When love beckons to you, follow him, though his ways are hard and steep.

And when his wings enfold you, yield to him, though the sword hidden among his pinions may wound you.

And when he speaks to you, believe in him, though his voice may shatter your dreams as the north wind lays waste to the garden.

For even as love crowns you, so shall he crucify you. Even as he is for your growth, so is he for your pruning. Even as he ascends to your height and caresses your tenderest branches that quiver in the sun, so shall he descend to your roots and shake them in their clinging to the earth.

Like sheaves of corn, he gathers you unto himself. He threshes you to make you naked.

He sifts you to free you from your husks. He grinds you to whiteness.

He kneads you until you are pliant. And then he assigns you to his sacred fire, that you may become sacred bread for God's sacred feast.

All these things shall love do unto you that you may know the secrets of your heart,

And in that knowledge become a fragment of life's heart.

— Kahlil Gibran

Chapter 12

[Create Space for You to Get Close to God: Beat Christians at Their Own Game]

"The passion for setting people right is in itself an afflictive disease."

— Marianne Moore

I COULDN'T HAVE BEEN ANY MORE THAN TWELVE YEARS OLD in my 7th Grade year of junior high school. Though decades ago, I vividly recall that my first class of the day was down the hall and around the corner from my locker. It was the same corner that the 8th Grade tough guys hung out at every morning before school started. I, being one of the bigger boys in my class, might as well have had a target on my chest for these guys. Yet, because of the layout of our school, I simply could not avoid them. That hall was the only viable access to my first class.

To this day, I could not even count the number of times I was hit, shoved, sworn at, or put down by these thugs. Yet, there really wasn't a damn thing I could do about it. Complain to the Vice Principal and you risk not only looking like a sissy, but you quickly realize there was little he could do. The logistics of policing a large school, even with teachers standing outside their rooms, were just too much to ensure any child's full safety.

That left me with two choices: Either stand up to these 8th Graders and potentially end up fighting, or do my best to avoid them, knowing I would continue to be harassed. The first was suicide. They were a pack. Confront one and the others would gun for me. The second choice was just a slow death, which carried the daily dread of going to school on top of the actual taunting and hits.

I'd love to tell you I fought them each, one by one, but I can't. I just endured. I sweated out an entire year, as well as parts of an 8th Grade year that included attacks from some of those same boys. It wasn't until years later, in high school, that some of those guys became friendly, and bygones became bygones. In retrospect, those years of mild torture ended up making me both tougher and more compassionate. But it does not change the fact that at the time I wished there was some way to defend myself.

I raise this story simply to explain why this chapter, which is quite different from the rest, is included in the book. All too often today Christians are like those bullies — Goliaths, of sorts — getting in the face of unsuspecting non-Christians. Crazy as it sounds, there is much more Christian hooliganism going on in America than the church will ever admit. In fact, sometimes the church takes pride in it.

It's not physical taunting or abuse. It's just overly-aggressive salesmanship that has altogether too many negative effects on the person on the receiving end. More often than not, the victims of these encounters have no way to fight back. This chapter, to a very large degree, is intended to address that problem. It is included to give you the tools to defend yourself so that you do not have to suffer intimidation, upset, and humiliation. It is written to help you create spiritual space.

A Very Hard Bible Verse

"Any man who has had his testicles crushed or his penis severed from his body shall not enter the assembly of the LORD"

— Deuteronomy 23: 1

Did you know that verse was in the Bible? Look it up. It is actually 100% in the Bible. Deuteronomy 23: 1.[47] But you will never see a woman standing at the door of a church, unzipping men's pants seeking proper genitalia. And how would a church ever decide who gets that job? Is it an issue of seniority? Or is it more like cleaning the toilets, a job nobody wants?

Beyond that, you will never, never, never under any circumstances hear this verse brought up in church or in a preacher's sermons. Never. To quote that verse would seem to make the Bible a laughingstock. And so, it stays hidden in the Biblical backwaters.

That verse, at one point way back in history, might have served a very functional purpose, particularly for a culture which believed its survival depended upon legislating procreation and ethnic purity. Yet, today its very presence has a potentially disastrous effect on Christian image and scriptural credibility. Still, despite Christianity's efforts to create the flawless religion, that for-all-intents-

and-purposes ridiculous verse has stayed in the Bible.[48]

What is the point in highlighting this verse? The point in raising this, like one of the points of this chapter, is to illustrate that the Bible is not invincible and perfect. It is okay to not believe parts of it, and okay to even laugh at parts of it, yet still have a rich relationship with God grow out of your relationship with it. Weaknesses denied hinder authentic relationship. Weaknesses conceded engender endearment. The goal is to understand that Christian scripture has tremendous beauty and power, despite its deeply flawed nature.

Though God is infinitely more than just a book, to free the book from notions of perfection is to break Christianity's stronghold on God. Thereby, new ways of believing and growing closer to God may spring forth in America.

The second goal of this chapter is to dislodge from Christianity sole rights to interpret the God story. It is to grant to you permission to draw closer to God in ways that work for you.

In this regard, it is an often-overlooked part of the Christian story that when Jesus was crucified the veil in the temple that set apart the Holy of Holies from the common area was torn in two (Matthew 27: 51). The Holy of Holies was the section of the temple which housed the Ark of the Covenant, which in turn housed God's most sacred gift to humanity, the Ten Commandments.[49] It was also known as the place where the high priest could speak directly with God.

What is most interesting is that the Holy of Holies, per Jewish law, could only be accessed by the High Priest. Only he could commune directly with God. But when the curtain (or veil [of illusion]) is torn away, God becomes accessible by all people. The metaphor of the torn curtain is that Jesus came to give every person the right to go directly to God.[50] This chapter is intended to help you go straight to God without the need for an intermediary.

This chapter is a bit different from previous chapters. It is, on one hand, an auxiliary chapter; because it's primary focus is not to bring you closer to God, per se.

On the other hand, this chapter is the most necessary (and, in fact, the concept out of which this entire book grew), because its goal is to create the space in which a relationship with God can flourish.

As I have attempted to make clear from the beginning of this book, part of the problem non-Christians and non-practicing Christians have in attempting to get nearer to God is that Christians claim (or are perceived as claiming) to own God and the path to God. Some branches of Christianity go so far as to state, "There is no salvation outside the church." Compounded with that, in today's spiritual-religious climate there is open hostility on the part of Christians toward anyone or anything that differs from traditional Christian teaching.

Thus, for the person who dislikes Christianity, for whatever reason, the baby God is often thrown out with the Christian bathwater. The effect of this is millions of people in America have to struggle to find God on their own without significant and relevant spiritual leadership. Because of the difficulty of this journey, many abandon the God-quest altogether. A godless culture is created.

The great irony of this is that, ultimately, the very people who decry American godlessness are, in fact, the ones who create it. Rigorous Christian traditionalism and literalism become the chokepoints through which non-Christians, closet Christians, and Christmas Christians refuse to pass. Rather than being a bearer of good news to all people, Christianity becomes an exclusive club that fewer and fewer people wish to join.

Thus, the purpose of this chapter is to release Christianity's grip on God, the Bible, and theology so that you might have a way to begin or continue a relationship with God. The intent is to offer to every child in the neighborhood the knowledge of the sandbox toys, so that he or she can use it for his or her own defense when attacked. In fact, the hope is that each child will have his or her own toy so that he or she can know the joy of play in the sandbox of life.

Granted, Christianity may never let go of thinking it has or is the only way to God. Therefore, my goal is to help you understand *in your own head* that God, the Bible, and theology are not owned by Christianity, but are free for you to dive into and relate to in ways that make sense to you. My goal is to create space, unmolested space, for you to get acquainted with God. It is to give you permission to do it in your space and on your own time.

Just as surely as you bump into Muslims, Jews, Hindus, and atheists in your everyday life, you will bump into Christians who will disagree with your beliefs and tell you yours is not a real relationship with God. These Christians are potentially more harmful to your faith than people of other religions, because they are often people you know well and trust. People of other faiths will generally keep a respectful distance.

But aggressive Christians are often family, co-workers, and friends who have stuck with traditional Christianity and who know you well enough to feel free to comment on your personal faith life. Worse than that, however, as surely as death and taxes, you will encounter proselytizing Christians who will aggressively jump into your spiritual life and beliefs, often wreaking havoc, in an attempt to get you to join them.

Sadly, this Christian practice is all too common, even today. Whether it is the Mormons, Jehovah's Witnesses, Evangelicals, or just good old-fashioned Bible-banging and on-fire-for-the-Lord Christians, you likely already have and likely will again be approached by Christian sales representatives. And, if you're like most people, this is not a pleasant experience for you. But religious "outsiders" shouldn't have to take a beating every time they encounter a zealous religious "insider." For that is precisely the opposite of how Jesus treated outsiders.

Jesus did not pound outsiders into correct thinking. He beat on the hypocritical and oppressive religious institution and its leaders. He aggressively confronted anyone, especially the religious people, who would do harm to someone who didn't have the power to defend him- or herself. Jesus did not always "turn the other cheek." He got in the face of the Pharisees, and he went on a serious rampage against those (religiously sanctioned) people who were defiling the house of worship.

Yet, even as he challenged "insiders" he enveloped "outsiders" in love, period. In fact, his final dying act on this earth was to befriend and extend love to a condemned thief (Luke 23: 39-43). Zacchaeus, Mary Magdelene, and Matthew, to name a few, discovered from Jesus that transformation comes as a response to love. Yet, so often Christianity has forgotten this and resorted to coercion.

It is hoped that with this chapter you will be able to stand your ground when confronted with people who would do you spiritual harm. It is also hoped that by doing so you will create space in your life, in your mind, and in your heart to discover and choose the extraordinary love that Jesus taught, and to hear the still, small voice of God speaking to you.

Christians may not understand the need for this chapter. Many just do not understand how offensive, shaming, and debilitating these encounters with well-intentioned Christians can be. Christians may dislike this chapter because it seems inflammatory insofar as it exposes questionable verses and ideas that Christianity tries to keep hidden. Enclosed in this chapter are Bible verses most Christians don't know about, don't want to know about, or don't want to think too much about.

On the other hand, it is hoped that non-Christians, closet Christians, and Christmas Christians will delight in this chapter. First of all, this chapter is simply funny. There is a lot of just plain silliness in the Bible. Also, it is hoped that you will like this chapter because it exposes many of the flaws, incongruities, and weaknesses that can be found both in the Bible and in Christian thinking. By doing so, this chapter attempts to increase your endearment for the Bible and reduce your feeling of helplessness when confronted by both guerilla Christians and run-of-the-mill meddling Christians. This chapter gives you the tools not to do unnecessary harm to Christianity and Christians, but to defend yourself when Christianity begins doing harm unto you.

It must be emphasized here that not all Christians will attempt to beat you over the head with the Bible in order to convert you. In fact, most won't, even though it is hardwired into Christian theology. Most Christians are quite decent, non-intrusive, and generous human beings. But you never know when an unbeliever-basher is going to pop up. Though it is hoped you will never have to use it, this chapter is written so that you will not have to suffer at the hands of a basher.

It must be reiterated that it will seem to some that by including such a chapter the author hates Christianity and the Bible. But the opposite is true. I love Christianity when it is done well. I really do. Christian community and worship can be amazing! Also, I love Christianity's mission of trying to bring love and God to those who are hurting or in need.

Yet, I am keenly aware of the extreme level of contempt that non-Christians, closet Christians, and Christmas Christians have for Christianity. I am aware of the amount of space many people need to create their own sense of spirituality. I am also keenly aware of the amount of contrition, transparency, humility, and change that are necessary on the part of Christianity and Christians in order for non-Christians to even be open to conversation.

Thus, finally, this chapter is an attempt to show good faith by disarming Christianity and laying its "weapons" in the camp of those whom it has harmed so that all parties might be on equal footing.

Your New Christian Friend

Maybe it is at the beach, maybe it is on a plane, maybe it is at a convention, maybe it is in a doctor's office, maybe it is inside your own front door, or even at a bar; wherever it is, they will find you. It may start as the most innocuous of conversations, but somehow you can feel it coming.

You can feel it from the very beginning. It is not a normal, disengaged hey-how-are-you type of conversation. It is a conversation with an agenda. It's like when a girl can feel in a conversation — just sensing in advance — that a guy she is not really interested in is leading up to asking her out on a date. There is a knowing discomfort that only seems to grow.

And somehow, just as you thought, this person who has approached you brings the conversation rather quickly around to Jesus, God, church, or some other spiritual matter. It's stuff you barely discuss with your own husband or friends, but, quite uninvited, this person has made it his or her business.

For most people it ain't a fun spot. In fact, it is enormously uncomfortable. I have witnessed it happen so many times and heard so many second-hand accounts, that I know people *hate* — yes, hate — dealing with pushy Christians. It can be grating, annoying, confusing, frustrating, and often humiliating.

But there is nothing you can do, right? They trap you. Maybe it is a social or work setting that doesn't allow you to walk away. Maybe you are on a plane and there is nowhere to go.[51] Maybe you just don't like to be rude.[52] Whatever the case, you are stuck there, enduring another Christian zealot, cursing yourself for not leaving your cell phone on so that you might take a call — any call — and escape.[53]

Recognizing that this does happen, recognizing that they will find you, smell blood, and come after you, I have created a defense. This is a way for you to defend your spiritual home, so that you may have the space necessary to grow to God without the judgment and critique of others. Become familiar with it. You don't have to know all of it. Sometimes bits and pieces will be enough. But, also, I have included a trump card that will get you out of any jam (#2 below).

1) THE MOST IMPORTANT RULE: Don't ever fight a Christian at pick-a-verse Bible combat, unless you know a heckuva lot of Bible. Why? You'll probably lose. If they are bold enough to walk up to you and try to convert you, they are probably well-versed enough in the Bible to know how to accomplish it. In fact, many of them are actually trained, like car salesmen, in techniques for overcoming your objections and leading the conversation.

Now, you can do what you want, but I highly recommend that you don't listen. As kindly as you can, avoid answering their questions. Don't ask your own questions (Trust me, they have plenty of answers for you.). Don't get sucked into a conversation in any way, unless you are willing to risk being spun around and turned upside down. They will frustrate you and leave you asking yourself why you ever started talking with them in the first place.

There are several easy ways to accomplish this, but they must be done at the outset. Simply say, "I really do not wish to be rude. But, please accept my request when I state that my faith is my business, and I really do not want to talk about it." But then you must be firm, because they often won't be content with that and will continue to needle you. You can still have a lovely conversation about other things. Though, I don't recommend it, because it's risky. It could get back to spiritual matters. But, if you're just curious or if it's a long flight and you need conversation, go ahead. However, anytime the conversation even smells like it's going back to faith stuff, you must cut it short. They have every good intention, but they will slaughter you.

You must realize that you are under no social obligation to discuss matters of faith and belief. These are highly personal issues, more so than your sex life, your money, and your marriage. If you let a stranger walk in, you are inviting them to offer commentary on everything inside. And it is just plain foolish to allow someone you don't know to come into your spiritual home and start doing an extreme makeover — tearing up the floors and knocking down walls. So, don't do it.

2) MANY CHRISTIANS ARE PUSHY because they base not just their faith but their lives on what is commonly known as *The Great Commission*. These were supposedly Jesus' last words to his disciples before he floated up into heaven a few weeks after the Easter resurrection. He said, "All authority in heaven and on earth has been given to me. Go therefore and make disciples of all nations, baptizing them in the name of the Father and of the Son and of the Holy Spirit, teaching them to observe all that I have commanded you; and lo I am with you always, to the close of the age" (Matthew 28: 18-20).

These are the verses, more than any others, which push Christians to push you. In fact, they are known in Christian shorthand as simply "Go and make disciples!" These are the verses that cause Christians to get in your face, and do the most offensive of things. These are the exact verses that start the wars, drive the invasions, and craft aggressive political policy. In fact, nearly all of the really objectionable or awful stuff in Christian history started with these verses. For, this *Great Commission* is the Great Christian Job Description.

The problem is, nowhere does Jesus say, "This is your Great Commission." Calling these verses *The Great Commission* and placing major emphasis on them is a human thing, not a Jesus thing. To be sure, Jesus taught his disciples to bring his life-giving message to hurting people. But taking these verses as *The Great Commission* is just something people started doing a long time ago. In fact, this supposed "great commission" is stated only one other time in the Bible, and that time it is stated only vaguely (Luke 24: 47). It is then mentioned nowhere else in the entire Old or New Testaments.

The irony of it is that Jesus *does* say on many occasions about an entirely different verse, "This is *The Great and First Commandment* that I am now about to give you." In fact, he uses those exact words — Great and First Commandment. But he isn't talking about the "Go and make disciples" verses, which are stated above. He is talking about the words of Matthew 22: 37-40, "*You shall love the Lord your God with all your heart, and with all your soul, and with all your mind. This is the great and first commandment. And a second is like it, you shall love your neighbor as yourself.* On these two commandments depend all the law and all the prophets"[54] [italics mine]. No less than thirteen times this *Great and First Commandment* is mentioned in the Bible. 13 times!

Worthy of note, even within the supposed Great Commission of Matthew 28 is Jesus' instruction to his disciples to "...teach them all that I have commanded you..." (vs. 19). At the very least, this is an explicit and obvious reference to Jesus' *Great and First Commandment* of Matthew 22.

In truth, "Go and make disciples..." is not Jesus' Great Commission. That is nothing more than his last commission. His great commission is the one he lived, taught, and kept pushing, pushing, and pushing: *Love God and Love Neighbor*.[55]

This is your *Trump Card*. Should you ever find yourself engaged in a theological or faith discussion with a pushy Christian that you wish to abort (the conversation, not the Christian), you can always fall back on this. This is the one incontestable Jesus response.[56]

If you really want to win, get out of, or never get into a theological conversation, you must always fall back on this: "Jesus explicitly said that his *First and Great Commandment* is to love God; and his second commandment is to love neighbor. This is what I do. If it is good enough for Jesus, it is good enough for me. Jesus said many, many, many, many, many things. But he made it simple for simple people like me. Love God and love neighbor. These are the only things Jesus ever explicitly stated as his great commandments. He even said that everything depends upon these two commandments (Matthew 22: 40). So, I follow Jesus' teachings in a way that Jesus says is great. I love God and love neighbor, and you're in no position to tell me that I don't. Again, if it's good enough for Jesus, it is good enough for me. So, please, let me be."

But then you must constantly come back to and never flinch from that position. If your Christian does not have the social grace to back off, then the answer to every question must be, "I love God and love neighbor. It's good enough for Jesus. It's good enough for me. And, quite frankly, it is private and I would rather not get involved in a discussion about my private life."

Keep it simple. Keep it simple. Keep it simple. Simplicity sells! Do not try to go toe-to-toe on verse-picking from the Bible, because your combatant knows more than you do about verse-picking, if nothing else. If you constantly come back to *Love God and Love neighbor*, there can be no adequate rebuttal. For Jesus does explicitly say this is his *First and Great Commandment* on which all of faith hinges. This should always be your fall-back position.

3) AN EXCELLENT SUPPLEMENT to the fall-back position is to say this, "Nowhere in all of Christian scripture — nowhere in the Bible — does Jesus ever, ever, ever say that the Christian Bible (the New and Old Testaments) is the authoritative, inerrant, inspired, or infallible word of God. In fact, he never says the New Testament is the word of God, at all. Nowhere! Why? Jesus never wrote

the Bible. Jesus never wrote in the Bible. Jesus never read the New Testament portion of the Bible. Jesus never even heard of it, because *the New Testament did not even exist until AFTER Jesus died.*" This is indisputable, period.

The Christian Bible is made up of the Old and New Testaments. The Hebrew Bible — which is the original name of the Old Testament portion of the Christian Bible — had already been around for some time when Jesus came along. There are accounts of Jesus reading from it, and he clearly was fluent in it and a teacher of it. But the New Testament, which tells of Jesus' life and contains the stories of his disciples after Jesus died, was not written or compiled until long after Jesus' death, some scholars say parts of the Bible were not written until 70-100 years after Jesus' death.

Thus, Jesus never said that your faith has to depend on the Christian Bible. In fact, Jesus tried to break people free from literally interpreting even the Hebrew Bible. The spirit and underlying truths of the Bible were what scripture was about for him. Jesus never commanded anyone to read the Bible. Jesus *did* command people to love God and love neighbor, but he never, ever even spoke of the New Testament portion of the Bible.

Therefore, making the Bible the authoritative, inerrant, or only word of God is a human construction! It is not Jesus' command. Humans, not Jesus, are the Bible people and the Bible fanatics. Again, Jesus did not write, read, know of, endorse, or command you to read or use the Bible. Never forget that!

The Bible is meant to be a tool to aid in the development of faith. It is not an absolute requirement for relationship with God. It is an optional instrument intended to help. If it obstructs faith, ditch it and go straight to God. But never think that faith or beliefs must have a Bible. You can be a Jesus-follower and a Christian without believing that the Bible is the be-all-and-end-all.[57]

4) IF YOUR NEW FOUND CHRISTIAN FRIEND is throwing Bible verses at you incessantly, and you just can't bring yourself to walk away, and you forget the Trump Card fall-back, it is time to take the offensive. Again, this is the path only when no other polite method works.

Before considering the path of confrontation or aggressiveness that I am going to spell out below, please consider this: To live a life of genuine love, even when engaged in confrontation, is to be constantly aware of the fact that you are no better than anyone else. Life lived in overflowing love can only be done in the humility of knowing that we are all f———ed up, everyone has serious issues and problems, and no one — no one! — is any better than anyone else. Thus, confrontation must be engaged not in arrogance and not to do harm, but in self-defense or in the defense of someone else who is being harmed. It is knowing when to stop — when enough is enough. Call it compassionate confrontation.

With that in mind, unfortunately there are times in life when you must engage. Unfortunately, sometimes in life war is the answer. Should you find yourself in such a spot, what follows are the best tools I can offer for your defense.

When I taught junior and senior high religious education, my very first lesson was always the same. I would say to them, "You've spent the last 6-10 years in Sunday School learning about Jesus, God, Spirit, church and the Bible. Now it's time to learn the fun parts; the stuff no one wants you to know. Open your Bibles to Deuteronomy 23: 1, and read it aloud."

They would then read the verse about penises and testicles that started this chapter. Giggles and outright laughter would always follow. We would laugh together, because it is funny. And with that they knew this would be like no other religious education they had ever had.

Yet, the laughter was always followed by longing looks that seemed to say, "Well, what am I supposed to do with that? I thought the Bible was perfect."

My response to them is your response to your pushy new Christian friend, "Any faith that is based solely on the Bible is flimsy, because the Bible can get ugly. It was hand written by humans, and therefore is open to human error and culturally-specific thoughts. It is similar to how hundreds of years ago in Japan there were cultural expectations that if parents wanted their daughters to grow up to be beautiful they must at a very young age start compressing the girls' feet into tiny shoes, usually at great physical pain to the girl. When girls became marrying age small feet were a significant sign of beauty. To non-Japanese in America today such a thing might seem ridiculous. It would even be considered, by some, to be child abuse to do such a thing. But back then it was a given in that culture, and was even part of the Shinto religion. That is what culturally-specific means. Much of the Bible is the same way.

"Furthermore, it was hundreds of years before much of the Old Testament was actually written down, because it had been transferred through generations by word of mouth. Additionally, most Biblical scholars agree that it was 30-70 years after the Jesus event before much of the New Testament was written.

"In the last 2000 years the Bible has been re-written thousands upon thousands of times. It has been translated into thousands of languages and dialects. Translation creates so many opportunities for personal bias to determine what the text says. Anyone who has ever attempted to understand another language knows that there is seldom one meaning for any word.[58] It is read today by humans who can never know exactly what the authors fully intended. Your faith has to be stronger than just a book, because the book will mess up your head just as much as it will help your faith."

Then, as I did with my students, you can begin for your Christian friend the following litany of interesting Biblical verses, which, when properly administered, should serve as a bit of a brush back pitch, getting them out of your face. The basic premise is that you are using literalism against literalists — i.e. using their own weapon against them.

These are best delivered as a barrage. Don't come up for air. If you are going to take the offensive, you must be aggressive. Or, they will come after you.

"If you or I are to read the Bible in a literal or even partially-literal way, doesn't that mean we would have to believe":

A) "When men fight with one another, and the wife of the one draws near to rescue her husband from the hand of him who is beating him, and puts out her hand and seizes him by the genitals, then you shall cut off her hand; your eye shall have no pity" (Deuteronomy 25: 11-12).

B) "If a man has a stubborn and rebellious son, who will not obey the voice of his father or the voice of his mother, and though they chastise him, will not give heed to them, then his father and his mother shall take hold of him and bring him out to the elders of his city at the gate.... Then all the men of the city shall stone him to death with stones; so you shall purge the evil from your midst..." (Deuteronomy 21: 18-21).

C) "Happy shall be he who takes your [children] and smashes them against the rock" (Psalms 137: 9).

D) "No bastard shall enter the assembly of the Lord; even to the tenth generation none of his descendants shall enter the assembly" (Deuteronomy 23: 2).

E) And as [Elijah and Elisha] still went on and talked, behold, a chariot of fire and horse of fire separated the two of them. And Elijah went up by a whirlwind into heaven. And Elisha saw it and he cried, "My father, my father! The chariots of Israel and its horseman! And he saw him no more" (2Kings 2: 11-12).

F) "If a man is found lying with the wife of another man, both of them shall die..." (Deuteronomy 22: 22).

G) "And the Lord appointed a great fish to swallow up Jonah; and Jonah was in the belly of the fish three days and three nights" (Jonah 1: 17).

H) "When the ass saw the angel of the Lord, she lay down under Balaam; and Balaam's anger was kindled, and he struck the ass with his staff. The Lord opened the mouth of the ass, and she said to Balaam, 'What have I done to you, that you have struck me these three times?' And Balaam said to the ass, 'Because you have made sport of me. I wish I had a sword in my hand, for then I would kill you.' And the ass said to Balaam, 'Am I not your ass, upon which you have ridden all your life long to this day? Was I ever accustomed to do so to you?' And [Balaam] said, 'No'" (Numbers 22: 27-30).

I) "Now the serpent was more subtle than any other wild creature that the Lord God had made," and the third chapter of Genesis goes on to tell of the conversation between a woman (Eve) and a talking snake, a conversation we are all familiar with, in which the snake seduces the woman with an apple from a forbidden tree.

J) "Thus the heavens and the earth were finished, and all the host of them. And on the seventh day God finished his work which he had done, and he rested on the seventh day from all his work which he had done" (Genesis 2: 1-2). This verse is particularly fun, because many Christians don't believe God created the world in only seven days. It is ironic, because Christians think this God has the enormous power and intellect to create atoms, molds that cure infections, thousands upon thousands of different species of animals, nuclear fission, gravity, peacocks, recombinant DNA, love, the human cornea, and so much more, but God *does not* have the power to do it in 6 days. Evidently, God is powerful, but slow.

K) After Noah, his family, and the pairs of animals survived the great flood, God said, "This is the sign of the covenant which I make between me and you and every living creature that is with you, for all future generations; I set my [rain]bow in the cloud, and it shall be a sign of the covenant between me and the earth. When I bring clouds over the earth and the bow is seen in the clouds, I will remember my covenant which is between me and you ... and the waters shall never again become a flood to destroy all flesh" (Genesis 8: 12-15). This is quite funny, because rainbows are caused by the refraction of light through particles of water in the air. Thus, we can only conclude from this story that from the time God created the world to the time Noah survived the flood (at least 700 years, according to the Bible; physics puts it at millions of years) there was no such thing as the refraction of light through water particles in the air. It makes you wonder if God implemented other physical laws at other points in history as a reward for other good human behavior. Perhaps gravity was a parting gift as Adam and Eve left the Garden of Eden. Maybe the Second Law of Thermodynamics was a little extra something for Job after he survived all the challenges God let Satan put him through. Maybe if one of us is really good, God will grant us time travel or the ability to have Scottie energize us. Cool!

L) "[King Nebuchadnezzar] ordered the furnace heated seven times more than it had ever been heated. And he ordered ... men to bind Shadrach, Meshach, and Abednego, and to cast them into the burning fiery furnace. ...Because the king's order was strict and the furnace was very hot, the flame of the fire killed those men who [delivered] Shadrach, Meshach, and Abednego. ...Then [the king] was astonished ... He [said], 'I see four men loose, walking in the midst of the fire, and they are not hurt; and the appearance of the fourth is like a son of the gods.' ...[And when the men came out of the fire the king saw that] the fire had not had any power over the bodies of those men; the hair of their heads was not singed, their cloaks were not harmed, and no smell of fire had come upon them" (Daniel 3: 19-27).

M) Daniel was a faithful and profitable employee of the king, whom the king liked very much. But because Daniel would not worship the king instead of God, certain other men forced the king to punish Daniel. So they brought him before the king, and "[King Darius] commanded, and Daniel was brought and cast into the den of lions. The king said to Daniel, 'May your God, whom you serve continually, deliver you!' And a stone was brought and laid upon the mouth of the den ... and the king went to his palace. ...Then, at break of day, the king went in haste to the den where Daniel was ... and Daniel said to the king, '...My God sent his angel and shut the lions' mouths, and they have not hurt me...' Then the king was exceedingly glad, and commanded that Daniel be taken up out of the den ... and no kind of hurt was found upon him. ...And the king commanded, and those men who had accused Daniel were brought and cast into the den of lions — they, their children, and their wives; and before they reached the bottom of the den the lions overpowered them and broke all their bones in pieces" (Daniel 6: 16-24).

N) "The oracle of the word of the Lord to Israel by Malachi, '...And now, O priests, this command is for you. If you will not listen, if you will not lay it to heart to give glory to my name, says the Lord, then ... Behold, I will rebuke your offspring, and spread dung on your faces ... and put you out of my presence'" (Malachi 1: 1; 2: 1-3).

O) When Samson came to Lehi, the Philistines came shouting to meet him ... And he found a fresh jawbone of an ass, and put out his hand and seized it, and with it he killed a thousand men" (Judges 15: 14-15).

P) Perhaps the single greatest oddity of the Bible, yet the single most overlooked one, is the simple notion that God actually, physically, audibly spoke to people, especially considering how few (if any) people nowadays hear audible words from God.

• "Then the Lord said to Noah..." (Genesis 7: 1);

• "Then God said to Abraham..." (Genesis 22: 1);

• "Then the Lord said to Isaac..." (Genesis 26: 2);

• "And the Lord said to Joshua (Joshua 8: 1);

To Samuel (1Samuel 3: 11); To Job (Job 40: 1); To Jeremiah (Jeremiah 1: 7); To Ezekiel (Ezekiel 2: 1);" And to countless others.

Q) Then, if you really want to mess with your Christian friend, ask him, "Who was God talking to in Genesis 3: 22-23?" Bear in mind, the world has just been created. There are only two humans, Adam and Eve. Then these verses say, "Then the Lord God said, 'Behold, [Adam] has become *like one of us*, knowing good and evil; and now, lest he put forth his hand and take also of the tree of life, and eat, and live forever' — therefore the Lord God sent him forth from the garden of Eden" [italics mine].

Who was God talking to? Not Eve, as she was Adam's companion, not God's. God was talking *about* Adam and Eve, but who was God talking *to*? God could only have been talking to other gods, as only Adam and Eve took on god powers by eating of the fruit. Either that, or Yahweh is schizophrenic!

Your Christian friend may not like it, but historical studies teach us that in the Mediterranean region of the world, the Hebrew God (Yahweh) was originally one tribe's God in a world of many gods. The religious atmosphere of the day was essentially *henotheistic* — worshipping one God without denying the existence of other gods. The original writer of this Biblical text would have existed in and been influenced by that trans-cultural milieu.

Your Christian may have fits and get all worked into a lather, but it is indisputable. God, according to the text, was talking with other gods. So, if we interpret scripture literally there must be more than one god out there that has power equal to the God of Judaism, Christianity, and Islam.

R) Marriage shall not hinder a man's right to take prostitutes in addition to his wife or wives (2Samuel 5: 13; 1Kings 11: 3; 2Chronicles 11: 21).

S) A marriage shall only be considered valid if the wife is a virgin. If she is not a virgin, she shall be killed (Deuteronomy 22: 13-21).

T) If a married man dies without children, his brother must marry the widow. If he refuses to marry his brother's widow or chooses to not give her children and carry on his family line, he shall pay a fine of one shoe and his house shall be cursed (Deuteronomy 25: 5-10).

U) Marriage between a believer and an unbeliever shall not be allowed (Genesis 24: 3; Numbers 25: 1-9; Ezra 9: 12; Nehemiah 10: 30).

V) Finally, if you want to put a toe into the waters of the homosexuality debate, try on this thought form Nicholas D. Kristof. He writes: "What's [the Christian] basis for opposing lesbianism?

"Granted, the Bible denounces male homosexuality, although it strikes me as inconsistent not to execute people who work on the Sabbath (Exodus 35: 2) and not to crack down on those who get haircuts (Leviticus 19: 27) or wear clothes with more than one kind of thread (Leviticus 19: 19).

"But there's no clear objection in the Bible to lesbianism at all. And since some fundamentalists have argued that AIDS is God's punishment for gay men, it's worth noting that lesbians are at less risk of AIDS than straight women. So if God is smiting gay men for their sin, is he rewarding lesbians for their holiness?"[59]

Now, any Christian who is a good Bible fighter will respond to this entire list by saying, "Well, I believe and my church believes that the New Testament takes precedence over and fulfills the Old Testament," or some such words intended to invalidate your argument and hold up the New Testament as beyond critique. To this you should respond, "I see. So you actually literally believe these things":

A) "Behold, I have given you authority to tread upon serpents and scorpions, and ... nothing shall hurt you" (Jesus to some disciples; Luke 10:19).

B) "And these signs will accompany those who believe [in me]: in my name they will cast out demons; they will speak in new tongues; they will pick up serpents, and if they drink any deadly thing, it will not hurt them; they will lay the hands on the sick, and they will recover" (Mark 16: 17-18). At that point you may ask your Christian friend if he's feeling lucky. If so, take him to any local tavern, and invite him to drink a liter of Bacardi 151, which certainly qualifies as a "deadly thing." Heck, you can even offer to treat. Then watch him either wiggle out of literal interpretation or bring up some notion of it not being right to tempt another person or God.

C) "And suddenly a sound came from heaven like the rush of a mighty wind, and it filled all the house where they were sitting. And there appeared to them tongues as of fire, distributed and resting on each one of them" (Acts 2: 2-3).

D) "If anyone keeps my word he will never taste death" (Jesus; John 8: 52).

E) "Whoever lives and believes in me shall never die" (Jesus in John 11: 26). Have you ever known or heard of any person who has "never died?" Thus, is it safe to say that no one has ever believed in Jesus?

F) "Truly, I say to you, there are some standing here who will not taste death before they see [Jesus] coming in his kingdom" (Jesus in Matthew 16: 28; Mark 9: 1). It must be noted that Jesus has not come to earth a second time in his kingdom (at least not as Christians typically construe it), yet 100% of the people Jesus was speaking to are very dead.

G) "But Saul, still breathing threats and murder against the disciples of [Jesus] ... approached Damascus, and suddenly a light from heaven flashed about him. And he fell to the ground and heard a voice saying to him, 'Saul, Saul, why do you persecute me?' And he said, 'Who are you, Lord?' And he said, "I am Jesus, whom you are persecuting; but rise and enter the city, and you will be told what you are to do.' The men who were traveling with him stood speechless, hearing the voice but seeing no one. Saul arose from the ground and when his eyes were opened, he could see nothing; so they led him by the hand and brought him into Damascus. And for three days he was without sight..." (Acts 9: 1-9).

H) "Now at Lystra there was a man sitting, who could not use his feet; he was a cripple from birth, who had never walked. He listened to Paul speaking; and Paul, looking intently at him and seeing he had a faith to be made well, said in a loud voice, 'Stand upright on your feet.' And he sprang up and walked" (Acts 14: 8-10).

I) "Now when all the people were baptized, and when Jesus also had been baptized and was praying, the heaven was opened, and the Holy Spirit descended upon him in bodily form, as a dove, and a voice came from heaven, 'Thou art my beloved son; with thee I am well pleased" (Luke 3: 21-22).

J) "The revelation of Jesus Christ, which God gave him to show his servants what must *soon* take place; and he made it known by sending his angel to his servant John..." [emphasis mine] (Revelation 1: 1). This is the revelation that John said was going to *soon* take place: "And I saw a beast rising out of the sea, with ten horns and seven heads ... and the beast I saw was a leopard, its feet were like a bear's, and its mouth was like a lion's mouth. And to it the dragon gave its power and his throne and great authority" (Revelation 13: 1). "Then I saw an angel coming down from heaven, holding in his hand the key of the bottomless pit and a great chain. And he seized the dragon, that ancient serpent, who is the Devil and Satan, and bound him for a thousand years, and threw him into the pit..." (Revelation 20: 1-3). "And [Jesus] said to me, 'These words are trustworthy and true. And the Lord, the God of the spirits and the prophets, has sent his angel to show his servants what must soon take place. And behold, I am coming soon" (Revelation 22: 6-7). Soon? Ten horns and seven heads? Dragon?

K) "While [Jesus] blessed them, he parted from them, and was carried up into heaven"... alive (Luke 24: 51).

L) "So Peter got out of the boat and walked on water and came to Jesus" (Matthew 14: 29).

M) After Judas had betrayed Jesus, "One of [the disciples] struck the slave of the high priest and cut off his right ear. But Jesus said, 'No more of this!' And he touched his ear and healed him" (Luke 22: 50-51).

N) Matthew 16:18 tells of Jesus saying to his disciples, specifically Peter, "And I tell you, you are Peter (which means Rock), and on this rock I will build my church, and the powers of death shall not prevail against it." The Roman Catholic Church treats the lineage of the Popes (indeed all of Christianity traces its authority) all the way back through Peter to Jesus, primarily because of this verse. Of course, with that in mind it is quite interesting to note the words Jesus spoke but five verses later. "But [Jesus] turned and said to Peter, 'Get behind me, Satan! You are a hindrance to me; for you are not on the side of God, but of men" (Matthew 16: 23). According to Jesus (and Jesus does not err, right?), the Christian Church and its leaders (as traced through Peter) are not only a hindrance to Jesus (for they are on the side of men and not God), but the church and its leaders are, in fact, Satan!

O) "And Jesus answered them, 'Truly, I say to you, if you have faith and never doubt ... even if you say to this mountain, "Be taken up and cast into the sea," it will be done'" (Matthew 21: 21). Remember, literal interpretation means interpreting every word of the Bible as factual, especially the words of Jesus.

P) "Let a woman learn in silence with all submissiveness. I permit no woman to teach or to have authority over men; she is to keep silent. For Adam was formed first then Eve. Adam was not deceived, but the woman was deceived and became a sinner. Yet woman will be saved through bearing children, if she continues in faith and love and holiness, with modesty." (The apostle Paul writing to Timothy in 1Timothy 2: 11-15). Not only are women faulted for starting the whole cycle of sin, but they are commanded by one of the Christian Church's original founders to keep quiet and have no authority. The notion of women being saved by bearing children completely contradicts most of Paul's other writings on salvation by grace through faith. While this verse highlights faith as still necessary for salvation, faith is not the primary vehicle for salvation, bearing children is.

Q) "... Let those who have wives live as though they had none"(1Corinthians 7: 29b).

R) "A great crowd had gathered, and they had nothing to eat..." but someone had seven loaves and a few fish, and "[Jesus] commanded the crowd to sit down ... And he gave thanks and broke them and gave them to his disciples to set before his people ... And they ate, and were satisfied; and they took up the broken pieces left over, seven baskets full. And there were about four thousand people" (Mark 8: 1-9).

S) "Moses allowed a man to write a certificate of divorce, and to put [his wife] away," Jesus said to them. "But [I say], 'whoever divorces his wife and marries another, commits adultery against her; and if she divorces her husband and marries another she commits adultery,'" Jesus said (Mark 10: 11-12).

Ironically, many Christians will condemn homosexuality as a sin, saying, "Love the sinner, hate the sin." Yet, never once — not even one time — does Jesus ever mention homosexuality as a sin. In fact, he never mentions it, at all. In contrast, no less than four times Jesus is quoted as condemning divorce (Matthew 5: 31-32, 19: 1-12; Luke 16: 18). The Apostle Paul echoes Jesus' thoughts on divorce another two times (1Corinthians 7: 10-11; Romans 7: 2-3). But how many of the homosexuality-condemning Christians will just as vigilantly condemn divorce? Answer: Almost none.

Why? Not because they disagree with Jesus, per se, but because they know that naming divorce as a sin will offend and alienate a majority of Christianity's audience. Far too many people have gotten divorced for such a proclamation to be warmly received. While people might acknowledge that divorce can have negative effects, many would surely run from any church that named it a sin.[60]

T) "Lazarus is dead ... Now when Jesus came, he found that Lazarus had already been in the tomb four days ... And [Jesus] cried out with a loud voice, 'Lazarus, come out.' The dead man came out, his hands and feet bound with bandages and his face wrapped with a cloth. Jesus said to them, 'Unbind him, and let him go'" [italics mine] (John 11: 14-17; 11: 43-44).

U) When they had crucified Jesus 'It was now the sixth hour (noon), and there was darkness over the whole land until the ninth hour (3pm), while the sun's light failed" (Luke 23: 44-45). A three hour solar eclipse?

V) And, of course, there is the whole bit about a man being dead for three days and coming back to life (Matthew 27-28).[61]

5) CONTINUING THE OFFENSIVE, if you must, you can tell your Christian friend that no two Christians believe the exact same things. Then, you can launch into a series of questions: "I'll bet you and your wife, or you and your mother, don't agree on every single belief, do you? On what beliefs do you differ? So who is right? I'm sure you're convinced you are, but who is to say? Furthermore, is she going to hell because you two have different beliefs? No, she's probably not, is she? So, you concede that it is okay to have different beliefs. Christians can have different beliefs.

"I simply believe and follow Jesus' First and Greatest Commandment, *Love*

God and Love Neighbor. You say your beliefs are the one true faith. But I guarantee I could find 100 theologians on-line or in person who are far better educated than your pastor and more fluent in Biblical languages that would agree that there is no one exact Christian faith.

"So, do you have the guts to tell me to my face that I am not a Christian, even though I ardently strive to love both God and neighbor?"

This is the make or break point. If your Christian says it is not his job to judge you or your faith, you are dealing with someone who is, at least, semi-rational and semi-decent. This person likely recognizes the difficulties and limits of faithfulness to Jesus' message, and who recognizes when it is wisest to back off and entrust something or someone to God, even though he or she may disagree. With this person, the conversation is probably close to being done at this point. Be kind and walk away, if you can.

However, if he has the audacity to say you are not a Christian (believe it or not, this has happened to some people), first applaud his guts. It takes an awful lot of nerve to do that. Let him know you respect his strength.

Then, at that point, you have two choices: You can simply shake your head and walk away, recognizing that any well-versed, well-intentioned Christian would never make this mistake; or, if you feel so compelled, you can continue an aggressive attack. For, he has crossed into a world that is not his to enter — the world of judgment of another human being. His instructions as a Christian are clear, and now would be a fortuitous time to apprise him of them:

A) Matthew 7: 1: "Judge not, that you may not be judged."

B) Romans 14: 13: "Then let us no more pass judgment on one another, but rather decide never to put a stumbling block or hindrance in the way of a brothers."

C) Matthew 5: 22: "Every one who is angry with his brother shall be liable to judgment; whoever insults his brother shall be liable to the council, and whoever says, 'You fool!' shall be liable to the hell of fire."

D) Matthew 5: 43-44: "You have heard it that it was said, 'You shall love your neighbor and hate your enemy.' But I say to you, Love your enemies..."

E) Matthew 25: 40: "Truly, I say to you, as you did it to one of the least of these my brethren, you did it to me."

F) James 4: 11-12: "...There is one lawgiver and judge, he who is able to save and to destroy. But who are you that you judge your neighbor?"

G) Romans 12: 19-20: "Vengeance is mine...says the Lord."

Instruct your bold friend that your faith is between you and God, as is his between God and him. If you prefer sarcasm, you might say, "May God be as gracious to you as you have been to me. I did not judge you, but you have judged me. While I did disagree with you, I did not demean you. But you have demeaned me. Jesus brought love. You have not."

Or, you might bring the rhetoric back down a bit, remembering that no matter what you say or do, you probably cannot beat a pushy Christian at pick-a-verse Bible combat. You might just keep coming back to Jesus' *First and Greatest Commandment*: *Love God and Love your neighbor.*

Most importantly, no matter what happens you ought to never ever forget that *the real way to beat Christians at their own game is to* **extend to Christians and all people more love through words and actions than they ever extend to you.** That is the essence of Jesus' message. It is to love your neighbor even at great price to yourself, not because you have to, but simply because you can. It is to love indiscriminately, just as the rain indiscriminately falls on all and the sun indiscriminately shines on all. That is Jesus' love.[62]

A Final Question or Two

Is there someone who is in your spiritual home that you don't want there, or who just doesn't belong there? Is there someone cramping your spiritual space or molesting your spirituality? What is the worst part about that? Are you at the point where you are ready to simply not allow them into that part of your life anymore? Do you have the courage yet to make this happen?

On the other hand, who are the people that breathe life into your spiritual home? Why? Who are your spiritual influences, spiritual guides, and spiritual friends? Have you told them so? How can you better be a source of love, spiritual encouragement, and joy in the lives of others?

Conclusion

You will always gain more respect with radically loving actions than with Biblical knowledge or doctrinal perfection. That was Jesus' message. To "beat" the particular Christians who are judgmental requires simply excelling at life itself. In fact, to rescue God from Christianity and to re-school the Christians in how to be followers of Jesus requires simply remembering that Jesus was about love and that God is love. Then, it is to live that other-centered love as you draw closer to the Spirit of the Universe on your own personal spiritual journey.

I hope this chapter has given you some of the tools necessary to defend yourself and create space for your relationship with God to breathe. Lastly, just as God is the one who created self-deprecating humor, I hope this chapter has given you permission to laugh at the Bible, even as earlier chapters were intended to teach a new reverence for this book of great truths.

My intent with this book was to simultaneously convey the beauty and wisdom of the Bible while acknowledging its flawed and man-made nature. It is my belief that in doing so your own contempt for Christianity and its most favorite weapon might find voice. Yet, you might also then finally begin a new conversation with God (one rooted not in resentment, but in love and desire for greater intimacy), the Bible, and the many truths of love the Bible holds.

For in the end, the only way to ascend to the heights of spiritual fulfillment, or even simple fulfillment in life, is to find the fantastic joy, peace, power, hope, purpose, and so much more that come with being a bearer of self-sacrificial and other-centered love of God and neighbor. In the end, the only path to self-fulfillment is to abandon the quest for self-fulfillment, and to give your life in love and service to others.

[Epilogue]

"I have missed more than 9,000 shots in my career. I have lost almost 300 games. On 26 occasions I have been entrusted to take the game-winning shot . . . and missed. I have failed over and over again in life. And that is why I succeed."

— Michael Jordan, basketball legend

THE SPIRITUAL JOURNEY IS ABOUT WORKING through life's hard stuff as you grow closer to God. It is about moving forward despite life's constant setbacks and trials.

I'd like to be able to tell you that there is some sure-fire, linear way to get to God, to get to a higher state of living in love, and to get to that sense of joy, peace and true fulfillment in life that you seek. I'd love to tell you that the steps of this book are all you need to get to God.

And the truth is I can tell you that . . . .and I can't. The greatest thinkers, poets, mystics, and spiritual leaders of history agree that the most fulfillment, contentment, joy, and sense of purpose come from:

1) Bringing love to others, even though love is always accompanied by pain;

2) Taking yourself out of the center of the universe and compassionately putting those in need (which really is all people you encounter) in your place, not because you have to but because you can. We do this by throwing out the Golden Rule we were all taught as children. While you pursue in life that which brings you joy, to truly love others is not to love them as you would like to be loved, but to discover how *they* like and need to be loved, and to strive

to love them in those ways. That is other-centered love;

3) Ironically enough, walking directly into and through that which hurts, not forcing it to go away, but reading it to see what gems of truth it bears;

4) Mastering the challenge, best stated by the rock group *38 Special,* to "hold on loosely." It is to fight for life and truth just as willingly as you effortlessly let life come and go through your open hands. Yes, things, stuff, job, power, leisure, exercise, and so on can bring some great joy. That is indisputable. But, seeking more and more, as Madison Avenue tells us we should, won't bring greater joy. Soon the cost, whatever it may be, outweighs the profit, whatever it may be. We must have the wherewithal (or good horse-sense) and the guts to, first, recognize that our needs are for "higher" things not more things; and second, have the guts to let go of the quest for more stuff. Neither is a small feat.

5) Finding the beauty in every person and thing you encounter every day. It is a cliché, but it is true. Just as you have a dream that pulls you forward, to find joy and contentment is to balance that dream with the love for today.

6) Lastly, unifying yourself with your spiritual center — God — and pursuing that vision God has put inside you.

Those are the truths of time. They are the paths to God. Those are what the masters have taught, in some form or another.

Yet, even as these are paths to God and love, most masters taught that there is, paradoxically, no guaranteed way. Further, there is no path that exempts you from suffering. Anyone who tells you otherwise is lying in order to sell you something, or still has more life to experience. And, any teacher who tells you to avoid your pain is a teacher who has not yet discerned how to read suffering for its worth.

Additionally, there is no way to avoid the feeling of Divine Absence. There will be times in life when you feel like God has abandoned you. Maybe God has, maybe God hasn't. Rather than cower in fear, trust the gifts and mind God has given you, not to mention your spiritual brothers and sisters around you. The mother cannot walk for the child. The child must fall on its own in order to learn balance and forward movement on its own.

You will get lost. You will fail. If you find your guts, you will take steps off the accepted and beaten path. There others will question and mock you.

You will love and be loved. And, as with your life and your successes (which will also come and go), your loves will never end up looking like you imagined. For, what we want is never as good as what we didn't expect.

I fully believe the Bible can be a powerful tool on the spiritual journey. You can simultaneously embrace its wisdom and reject Christianity, if you desire. And I hope this book has helped you understand how to find its wisdom beyond the black-and-white, and re-think common theological misconceptions.

I cannot stress enough: No matter which path you take, you will suffer; you will suffer; you will suffer. God bless Buddhism for helping the Western World to fully understand and accept this. The trick of life is to learn to walk through the pain and find the truths in it and the joy anyway.

God is in you. God is around you. All of life bears God and speaks of God. Learn to listen for the truths. Love God and love your neighbor, and, as time goes on, joy and peace will come. You will discover heaven today insofar as you create heaven today for others.

Then, as it all comes to an end you can die with the deep satisfaction that comes from knowing you gave more love and life than you took, and thereby achieved some measure of nobility. You can live and die knowing that somewhere, somehow, sometime in someone your spirit will live on. You will have resurrection because you died to yourself.

So, begin your dance with God!

To life!

"I have come that you might have life, and have it abundantly!"

— Jesus

Comments and questions can be sent to sven_erlandson@hotmail.com

[Appendix A]

Metaphor sermon on a Jesus miracle, based on John 6: 1-15, which reads:
 "After this, Jesus went to the other side of the Sea of Tiberias. And a multitude followed him, because they saw the signs which he did on those who were diseased. Jesus went up the mountain, and there sat down with his disciples. Now the Passover, the feast of the Jews, was at hand. Lifting his eyes, then, and seeing that a multitude was coming at him, Jesus said to Philip, 'How are we to buy bread, so that these people may eat?' This he said to test him, for he himself knew what he would do. Philip answered him, 'Two hundred denarii would not buy enough bread for each of them to get a little.' One of his disciples, Andrew, Simon Peter's brother, said to him, 'There is a lad here who has five barley loaves and two fish; but what are they among so many?' Jesus said, 'Make the people sit down.' Now there was much grass in the place; so the men sat down, in number about five thousand. Jesus then took the loaves, and when he had given thanks, he distributed them to those who were seated; so also the fish, as much as they wanted. And when they had eaten their fill, he told his disciples, 'Gather up the fragments left over, that nothing may be lost.' So they gathered them up and filled twelve baskets with fragments from the five barley loaves, left by those who had eaten. When the people saw the sign which he had done, they said, 'This is indeed the prophet who is to come into the world!' Perceiving then that they were about to come and take him by force to make him king, Jesus withdrew again to the mountain by himself."

Sermon

Do you buy it? Do you buy this story — this whole bit of Jesus feeding thousands of people with a few loaves and fish?

I'll be totally honest with you. I don't. Or, at least, I don't know for sure. I mean, I don't doubt that God *could* do it. God has done things far more strange and far more amazing than that. But it is just really hard for me to buy into. It is a hard, hard story.

And I know that some of you here today also have problems buying into other miracles of the Jesus story. Water into wine, people dying and coming back to life, cripples being healed, and now thousands of people being fed with some kid's school lunch. It ain't an easy one.

The real problem, however, in the long history of Christianity has not just been the story itself, but the belief that the point of the story *is* the miracle. The point has always been that Jesus is so powerful that he can even feed thousands of people with almost nothing. Many of us learned this in Sunday School, and have heard it preached from pulpits this way all our lives. Thus, if you don't buy the miracle, there is really no point to the story.

The point of God, in this whole way of thinking, is that God can do really big things. Either you believe it, or you don't. Believers can come into the church. Disbelievers can't.

But, what if the power of God *isn't* the point this time? What if believing that God can do really big things isn't what it is all about? What if there are a whole bunch of truths going on in this story that really have nothing to do with the actual fish and bread? In fact, what if believing that this story literally happened as it is written is a hindrance to understanding these other truths about God and life?

I'm telling you right now, there are a whole lot of other truths about God and life being conveyed in this story that you will never see if you get caught up in whether the miracle actually happened. So, let's just put the facts aside. Let's assume, just for today, that the facts and the truths are two different things. Let's separate them. We can't know if the facts really happened, so let's not worry about them. Just entrust them to God. We'll look at the story, but you don't have to believe it literally happened as told.

The writers of the Bible were not journalists. They were more poets than anything. You can read nearly any book of the Bible and find this to be clear. Journalists tell what happened. Poets allude to the main story that is going on, when there is really so much more going on that is not being said. It's a form of magic. It is getting you to look at this hand, when this other hand is doing all the tricky stuff. It is getting you to look at what appear to be facts, when really there are so many unspoken truths being conveyed.

So, let's follow the other hand. Let's look for the truths that are not tied up in the facts.

Have you ever noticed how the kid in this story is always forgotten? Now if that ain't gratitude. Actually, if that ain't a metaphor for life in America, I don't know what is. We claim to be so child-centered, at times we are even child-obsessed, but we forget kids on the really important stuff.

The KID here is the one with the loaves and the fishes. The KID saves the day as much as Jesus did. But we don't hear any mention of the kid. His food is taken, and then he is forgotten.

This is one of those times when the movie would be better than the book. I think a movie director could do a much better job of conveying an entire story by simply showing the boy's face after his food is taken and he is forgotten in the story. A simple look of dejection and abandonment would speak volumes.

And don't we forget our kids? I don't mean all the other people in America, I mean you and me. You and I forget the kids in our lives. We get so wrapped up in life. We get so wrapped up in the task at hand. We get so wrapped up in feeding the mouths that depend on us, that we forget the people attached to the mouths, especially the little people.

That's one point of this story. The child in life is too often forgotten.

But the really hard part comes after that. We realize who it was that did the forgetting. We realize that it was Jesus who forgot him. Jesus forgot the child. Ouch. That is a tough one. But, why then? Why would the man who is the very embodiment of love and wisdom, the man who so loves children, choose to turn his focus from the child?

This is where the warm and fuzzy gets a bit harsh.

See, sometimes in life (and this is going to hurt to hear, as much as it hurts to say) we have to turn our focus off the child. Sometimes, we have to forget the child, even if only for awhile. Sometimes we have to do the hard thing. Sometimes, some things are more important than the child.

5000 people, or more, need to be fed. The child has to be left aside, for now. The needs of the masses must be tended to. And isn't this the story of Jesus' crucifixion, as well? This is God's boy, and God let him be killed, because he knows that the needs of the people, right now, are more important. Sometimes, the needs of the majority are more important than the welfare of the boy.

And if that isn't a brutal, just brutal, thing to hear, then what is? And here you are getting it in church. Pastor is preaching a spiritual brutality to children and abandoning of children.

And y'know what? I am. I am saying that one great, very hard truth of life is that sometimes the children must be forgotten, in order for bigger tasks to be tended to. And that is brutal.

But that is the brutality that occurs every morning in your home, or every morning in the home you grew up in. Every morning, some parent has to, in a soft brutality, walk away from his or her not-even-two year-old boy, as the boy stands at the door in his pajamas holding his teddy bear in the air with one hand.

And the movie director focuses in on the face of the small boy who is not even a boy yet. "Dejected and abandoned" are written all over his face.

And that is the sermon right there, folks. That look. The entire sermon is summed up in the tight shot on that boy, teddy bear in the air, sorrow filling his little heart, missing daddy as he leaves.

How many of us feel that look when we think back on our own childhood? How many of us feel that brutality when we think about our own parents, our fathers in particular, because most often it was them who were leaving? Most often we think of our fathers as brutal or not as tender as mom, or as not being there, like mom was.

Every morning, Dad brutalizes the child. And everyday, our mothers and our society add salt to the wound when we hold men at fault for doing the thing that demands courage. We put the man down for doing the thing that would rip out any mother's heart. And isn't that what women have found? As more women have ventured into the business world in the last forty years, they have discovered how searing the anguish is of having to walk away from your own child, when all he wants is to be with you and play with you.

But, we condemn our dads (and now our moms) for doing what somebody had to do. Like Jesus, somebody had to feed those people. Maybe you think your dad took it too far, this "doing what had to be done." And maybe he did. But maybe he was just doing his best in the same circumstances you are in right now in your life. Maybe he loved you, even more than you wanted to be with him. Maybe his drinking or his keeping you at arm's length was his way of numbing himself to what he had to do everyday — walk away from his beautiful, tender, so soft and dear one, and walk away from the little son that he and she created.

Just as walking away everyday becomes routine for the child, so also does it become so for the parent. But the sorrow never really goes away, even while we justify it more and more.

But that is the tension we all live in, and the balance we must all create. We live in the balance between staying and tenderly loving our children all day, every day, as other primates do, and going and foraging for money and food to nourish and protect those children. If that is not a balance of sorrow, then I don't know what is. Yet, we all live it every day.

Even if you don't have children, you live it. The artist must every day walk away from her work, the work that feeds her soul, in order to go work a job to pay the bills that feed her mouth and roof her head. That artist's child is her work.

And so it is, somehow, for all of us. Part of adulthood is having to walk away from the people and things we most love. The college graduate must move away from family to take her first corporate job. The transferred corporate exec must move away from a community that he and the family just moved into. Constantly... it never ends. The tearing away from those we love.

That balance. That balance we must all live. Staying and playing with those little ones we love; and going and providing for those little ones we love.

That's the hard balance of life.

But, I must take this in a new direction.

First, before I do that, I want to ask one question, a question that will be the point of this week's Bible study on Tuesday night. This Jesus story says that no one had anywhere near enough food to feed these people. We are left to assume that people were traveling light, not even caring to bring along a little sandwich for the walk to see the Jesus guy. But after they have all eaten, it says the disciples went around and picked up twelve baskets full of leftovers. 12 baskets full!!!

I'm not concerned with the food. We already discussed that. My question is: Where did they get the baskets? No one is bringing so much as a coke and a bag of chips, but somehow they can magically come up with twelve baskets? Someone want to explain that one to me?

Well, I'll give that and more to you on Tuesday, if you come back for Bible study. Otherwise, you'll be forever left wondering about those doggone baskets. Every time you hear this story from now 'til death; every time you read it to your kid, and the little whippersnapper asks, "Where did they get the baskets?" AAAAARRRRRGGGHHHH! You're going to be screaming and cursing my name. "Why didn't I go to the Bible study? I should've gone. I should've gone!" Have I coerced you enough?

Back to the main story, if living in that balance between providing and being with those we provide for is point number one, then the second point I want to make today comes by looking farther into that boy in the story.

I can recall as a kid having to go to my older brother's basketball practice in the school gymnasium. I would go because mom had to get other things done, and it was probably easier to have two of her six kids in one place at one time. So I would sit on the sidelines and watch. Now, going to a game is one thing. But going to a practice is, well, boring. So I would daydream. All the while I would be imagining that, just once, the coach of my brother's team would look over to me and say, "Hey kid, you wanna play? Let's see what ya' got." And I would get to play with the big boys. I would get to play on the team.

Maybe it is not so bad that the child in this Jesus story is no longer mentioned after he contributes his food. For, really, what did he do? He did what every kid wants to do. Even if only for a very brief time, he got to play on the team with the big boys, and shoot the winning basket!! This kid got to be part of something great! This kid got to be a part of something far greater than himself. Jesus, the man, the religious equivalent of Tiger Woods or Barry Bonds, looked over to him and said, "Hey kid, whattya' got?"

Other than Jesus, this small boy was the critical piece that enabled 5000 men (not to mention all the women and children) to be fed. And you don't think this kid loved it!?! HE LOVED IT!!!! What kid wouldn't? He loved just being included and having a job to do!!

And THAT is what it's all about. THAT is what we all crave. THAT, my friends, is the real point of the sermon.

Life ain't about just living to play with the child or even just feeding the child. Life ain't about living in the balance between being with our loves and providing for our loves. Life is about the context it is all in. The context that surrounds it all. Life is about the question, "Yeah, but does the balance of my life have any purpose? Am I playing on a team greater than myself and the best interests of those who are close to me?"

Do you have a context for your life? Is life just about finding the food ... and eating the food? Or, are you in the game? Are you that boy? Are you serving a purpose far greater than yourself?

I'm here to tell you that there is joy in balancing between providing for your love and being with you love; but there is joy you ain't never known in serving a cause greater than yourself. There is a quote by novelist Willa Cather that reads, "That is happiness; to be dissolved into something complete and great."

181

That spiritual ache you feel; that longing; that aimlessness; that wishing for more, I am telling you, is only satisfied by living in some great and grand purpose that you are willing to live and die for, that something that expands way beyond foraging for food and eating it.

The great calling in life that God makes to each of us is to have the guts to follow that thing inside of us that is our calling. That is God turning to us and saying, "Let's see what ya' got." Or, to quote Shakespeare, "Come, show us your greatness!"

There is no more grand adventure, as it will take you to great valleys of loss and sorrow, and to great peaks of joy and accomplishment. That is the cause that devours us. It is that cause greater than ourselves. It is that calling from within that has long been nagging you. It is THAT, not the scrounging for your next paycheck, your next toy, your next meal, or your next day off, that will bring you joy.

If you want communion with God (and I can only presume that your simple presence in church today says that you do want to get closer to God) then you must follow that calling, no matter where it leads.

If you have not begun to follow it, you MUST begin, or you will never live.

If you are already following it, you MUST continue, or you will never know what might've been if you hadn't quit.

If you can feel the momentum of all your work of following your dream and calling, then you MUST ride it, and you MUST make sure you are doing everything in your power to make it work for the most amount of people possible. Your excellence must not be squandered.

If you have followed the calling, and exhausted it, you MUST go into a period of rest to allow God to replenish your energy and resources.

If you have been fallow and resting, recuperating from a well-followed calling, you MUST begin to listen again for what God is calling you to next. I know callings can be exhausting and can exact a mighty price, but you MUST find it and follow it. You MUST, or you will certainly die. Even as you live into old age, you will be dead inside.

My friends, the point of life is to find that which moves you from within, and to have the courage to follow it. That is the voice of God. That is what it means to be on the team, even if you are alone in your efforts. That is what it means to have a purpose far greater than yourself for which to live, such as the improvement of society or the world. That is what it means to have something greater than yourself, something to believe in.

That is what it means to be that kid with his lunch, who happens to be pulled into the Jesus traveling show, and is asked to play on the team. That it's a kid is a metaphor for the fact that no gift is too small. You NEVER know where your small gifts can lead. All you have are a few loaves and fish. That is all God gave you. But God has mighty plans for those loaves and fish you have been holding on to. God can do great things with all you have. You just have to have the guts to step into the ring and do what you can. Then watch how it all multiplies.

You must play the cards God has given you to play. You must ask yourself,

"Who am I, really? What am I about? What has God given me? What, really, are my gifts and what are my interests? Now, what is the itch I have been thinking about scratching?"

And then the last question is: Do you have the guts to follow the calling that is speaking to you from within?

See, I believe God has very great things planned that you are to work for and accomplish. I truly believe that. The only questions are:

1) What is God calling you from within to do? And

2) Do you have the guts to follow?

Amen.

PS. These 5000 people were on a spiritual journey, following the master. As the book *Jonathan Livingston Seagull*, by Richard Bach, so clearly illustrates, when you are on the serious spiritual path you are only concerned with the task at hand, so much so that you often forget to eat and forget all the practical matters of daily living. These 5000 not bringing food is a great metaphor for the spiritual path and forgetting to even eat when you are soaking in the master's teaching. The food is not just food, but also spiritual food, as mentioned above. And spiritual food is far more important than food for the belly.

The baskets are, then, no more than a metaphor for the dedicated disciples themselves. Note: There were 12 baskets, just as there were 12 disciples. 5000 people were spiritually fed by the master's teaching. But the master's teaching is so meaty and fulfilling that even 5000 people couldn't take it all in. There was plenty left over, and the 12 disciples were eager to gather it up. For, the avid disciple still has room to take in more of the master's teaching. The spiritually hungry person, whether in Jesus' day or in ours, gathers and gathers every morsel that drops from the master, because the disciple is so spiritually hungry. Thus, the mysteriously appearing baskets are the disciple's spiritual hunger that, just when you think it is fed, appears out of nowhere still longing for more.

[Appendix B]

Metaphor sermon based on Deuteronomy 23: 1, which reads:
"Any man who has had his testicles crushed or his penis severed from his body shall not be allowed into the assembly of the LORD."

Sermon[63]

I lost a bet.

A buddy of mine once asked me what the single hardest verse of the Bible would be to preach on. I told him, off the top of my head, that the single scariest text for most clergy to preach on would easily be Deuteronomy 23: 1, because of the touchy subject matter, and because most clergy think they wouldn't have much use for it. Apart from going into some lengthy historical analysis, most clergy wouldn't see the value of the text as outweighing the risk.

So, at a later date, when he and I happened to be betting on a Minnesota Vikings playoff game (a bet I lost), he said I had to write a sermon on Deuteronomy 23: 1. Never mind what kind of odd guy he is that he would ask for a sermon as payment for a bet. Never mind what kind of fool I was for betting on the Vikings to win a second-round playoff game.

So, let's be honest. This verse is just plain weird. It's off the hook. There are odd verses in the Bible, ones that deal with killing your own unruly children, not mixing fabrics in your clothing, people coming back to life after dying, and plenty dealing with sex. But this one . . . .

This one just stands alone. It's in its own category for weirdness.

Most Christians, I think, hate this verse, cuz they don't know what to do with it. Actually, many don't even know it exists. But if they do, they are not real fond of it. It's an embarrassing verse. It just doesn't seem to fit.

185

Christians would prefer to hide such a verse, because they think it robs from the Bible's venerability and preciousness.

Non-Christians love it, cuz it shows the vulnerability of the Bible. It is almost farcical. It allows the Bible to be self-deprecating. Thus, to the non-Christian this verse has the simultaneous effect of making the Bible laughable yet somehow endearing. Teenage Christians really love it, cuz ... well ... it's just funny; but also it opens their eyes to a side of the Bible they didn't know existed.

So, let's get the history out of the way first. This was one of the 600+ laws of the Israelite people (from long before Jesus came around), most of which dealt with purity. Basically, the priesthood (the people who were also the judicial system) sought to keep the lineage clean, intact, and continually bearing fruit. To allow a non-reproductive male or female into the temple was to render the temple unclean. This was bad. The point was to do nothing to defile the temple, the people, or the God. Then and only then, when they are completely pure will the God show favor on the people.

As an aside, the obvious question is how would they know? While some might like the job of checking, that was almost unnecessary. The Israelites were to a very large degree a closed society. Everyone's organs would be known from birth by the priests, as they would have put children through purification rituals.

Overtaken and assimilated peoples would likely not be allowed into the temple, anyway, and certainly not without ritual circumcision. At the point of circumcision the genitals would be inspected. Lastly, genitals of Israelites that had been harmed or lost, say in battle, would very likely be known about, if for no other reason than they would've required medical attention. This would've been administered by, overseen by, or reported to the priesthood. Further, when any man's wife didn't produce offspring he would have been exposed, so to speak.

So, that is the historical context for such a peculiar verse. In fact, that is the historical context for all of the Laws of Moses.[64] Now let's get on to the meat of the text.

I can recall from my days working at Starbucks that one old gal, Betty, who was a regular, gave me her order one day only to moments later change her mind, informing me she would get her coffee somewhere else that day. For, when I had responded to her drink order she could hear that I had a cold, and she did not want my germs.

I, of course, was mildly offended. But, I could see her point. So I blew it off. But Betty is so symbolic of what we've become. We are so germ-obsessed in this culture. We want no diseases. No impurities. No microbes. No MSG.

Nothing but:

Free-range chickens,

Hormone-free beef,

Organic vegetables,

Anti-bacterial soap,

Soy hamburgers,

Neurosis-free relationships,
Baggage-free partners,
No-bully schools,
900-blocking phones,
Crime-free cities,
Immigrant-free welfare,
High-octane gas,
Lactose-free dairy,
Non-inhaling politicians,
Filtered email, and
Super-sized problem-free lives.
We want no impurities in our lives!

Our levels of wealth, leisure, and sophistication have gotten so monstrous that our reality has become divorced from the reality of our 2nd and 3rd World neighbors, whose lives are about mere survival. In our collective wealth we so seriously navel-gaze that our lives have become to a very large degree about filtering out impurities of every kind. Where, in contrast, other peoples will eat our rotten and discarded food, microbes and all, just to survive one more day.

This is what we've become, an impurity-obsessed culture. We have become, in an equally ritualistic way, precisely what the Israelites of 2500 or 3000 years ago were. The purification of the "American Race" has become, in legislation and in daily living, the ultimate drive of the American people. And we are only getting worse.

Now, am I condemning it? Well, some parts yes, and some parts no. Poking fun at it? Yes, definitely. And trying to take it with a hearty dose of salt? Of course.

I poke fun at it simply because it is time to take the focus off our own purity, cleanliness, and (by extension) holiness. It is time to take yourself and your own well being out of the center of the universe, and instead invest that mental energy and physical action into the affairs of someone or some ones who can repay you in no possible way. I am encouraging you to put God and neighbor in the center of the universe, and go and mingle with the commoners. I am encouraging you to make your life about the service of those people outside the walls — the walls of your everyday life and the walls of America.

But let's play with this verse a little bit more, because there is far more to this verse than the obvious purity discussion. There is a second, deeper meaning.

What if we went just one layer below the surface and viewed the genitalia not as genitalia, but as a metaphor for simply the ability to create? And I don't mean the ability to create babies. I mean create with your mind and your hands . . . as in creativity, as in create something new, something of value, and something lasting.

And what if, in reading this Deuteronomy text, we viewed "assembly of the

LORD" not as a physical place, but instead as "relationship with God" and in the receivership of the fruits such a relationship brings — peace, hope, power, purpose, love, joy, etc. For, to be in the temple was to be establishing right relationship with God so that such fruits would come to your life.

Taken as such, this verse can be understood with far greater impact. "Any man who has lost his ability to create, any man (or woman) who as stopped creating, any man who has stopped expressing and pushing out the creative life spirit inside him shall not know the peace, power, joy, hope, love, and fruits which come from union with the creative energy of the universe."

A totally different read, isn't it? Kinda cool, huh?

"Stop creating and you will never know God or the fruits of God. Never." God made you to push out the little creations God puts inside you.

Did you know that the Dead Sea is dead and cannot sustain life NOT because there is no water flowing into it, but because there is no water flowing out of it? Interesting, isn't it? The sea is fed, but has no outlet. Hence, it is dead.

It is not enough to take in newness. Newness and oldness must be constantly pushed out.

Did you know that after a woman bears a child her breasts naturally produce milk for the child? Of course you did. But, did you know that if that milk is not used (for instance, if the child does not waken for a mid-night feeding) the breasts become, what is called, *engorged*. And this, any mother will tell you, is not a nice thing. In fact, it is downright painful. The breasts become so swollen with untapped milk that they become huge and aching.

And so, new mothers are often taught to, what is called, *express* their milk. That's the official term. And the Latin root of that word is fascinating in this context: *ex* means *out*, and *press* means *to push*. To *express* means *to push out*.

In order to relieve her pain and keep the milk flowing, the mother must *push out* the unused milk. If she stops breastfeeding and no longer expresses the milk, the milk will simply stop flowing.

The milk is the source of life for the child. It is the very energy of life. And unless the energy of life is drawn out of the mother and ingested in the child, the energy of life will cease to flow and the child will die.

Are you beginning to see the point?

An old seminary professor of my father's used to say that if a pastor is not preaching regularly (if he is not pumping God out) he will become spiritually constipated!

Back to testicles and penises. These are just a metaphor for your creative inner force. Stop creating and you will dry up! You will never know the fruits of communion with God and God's voice inside you — the fruits of peace, joy, hope, power, purpose, deep love, and so on.

The challenge before you in life is to tap into that creative inner spirit. It is what I call the voice of God. If you do not listen for, heed, and act on the creative voice of God inside you, you will forever either ache, as if with engorged breasts (you will spiritually ache for more in life), OR, you will simply dry up. If you stop listening or cut yourself off from that creative voice you will live, but be dead

inside. As Bob Dylan said, "He not busy being born is busy dying."
Are you listening and creating?
Are you engorged and aching?
Or have you dried up?
If you feel alive and full up, it's flowing.
If you're aching and longing for more in life, you're engorged and in need of creative expression of the life energy inside you.
If you feel numb, you've cut yourself off; you've cut off the creative outlets.
To live again you must risk. You must *choose* self-expression. You must re-find yourself. You must stop much of your life as you know it, and start listening for God's inner voice.
But, what if there's something even deeper than this to this odd Deuteronomy text?
This third understanding of the Deuteronomy text is going to be a bit graphic, but I think by this point we've already stepped well beyond socially acceptable. Further, the text itself is graphic and cannot be honestly addressed without graphic discussion.
I can recall as a ten or twelve year-old occasionally sharing the very boyish dialogue with my buddies:
"Question: What is the definition of pain?"
"Answer: Sliding down a forty foot razor blade and using your testicles for brakes."
Yeah, kinda graphic, isn't it?
A collective wince just went over the men in the congregation. Now, yes, I know that is very juvenile and most certainly unfit for church. But, well, it's out there now. So, let's deal with it, and you can fire me on Monday. See, this little kid conversation is the perfect illustration for our purposes here.
At a very young age, a boy knows that the harshest physical pain he can endure is to get hit in the private parts. That's why boys in sports wear nut cups, or "athletic protectors." That is also why it is just wrong for a man's sexual partner to take him to the point of near-peak arousal and then not allow for release. It is akin to breast engorgement in a woman, but in the most sensitive and painful section of a man's body.
So what does all of this have to do with Deuteronomy 23: 1? What is the redeeming value of this vulgar discussion and low-brow humor?
Some say that man (and woman) was created for community, for relationship, for gathering, for assembly. Humans, it is believed, are not meant to exist alone.
But Deuteronomy 23: 1 says "Any man who has had his testicles crushed or his penis severed from his body shall not be allowed into the assembly of the LORD."
So, let's play with that verse again.
If humanity is meant to live in community, then when we read "assembly of the LORD" in this verse, it can be re-interpreted as "one way God intends us to live."

"Penis severed" equals pain, any man knows that. "Testicles crushed" equals pain, severe pain. Again, any man knows that. So think of them as simply metaphors for severe pain, of any sort, not just physical or sexual.

Then read Deuteronomy 23: 1. "Any person who lives in a permanent state of severe pain, whatever its physical or emotional source may be, shall never be able to live as God intended or as life is meant to be lived — in relationship with others."

Again, a powerful and rich meaning is found in an otherwise senseless text; metaphor offering the key.

Severe pain isolates us. We have no ability to step out into the lives of others. All of our energy is used up surviving and enduring our own pain.

Any person who is stuck or stays stuck in severe pain will be alone, period. It is unavoidable. You cannot simultaneously live in severe pain and be in relationship with others.

You might relate to others, but not in a two-way relationship. Instead, it will be more like a doctor-patient or therapist-client relationship, where one gives and another takes. You will suck the life out of others, and they'll either move on or burn out. Or, in the rare case, they will stick with you, because you have done the same for them at one point or another. In most cases, however, where a person relates from a position of extreme pain he or she tends to burn through a lot of people.[65]

One of the leading Jungian psychologists in the world, James Hillman (70+ years old) and one of the leading pop psychologists in the U.S., John Gray (of *Mars/Venus* fame), agree on a very important point: The trick to letting go, the trick of moving past your pain is NOT to try to move past your pain. The trick is NOT to try to let go. The trick is to try to hold on to it, feel it, and go deeper into it. Just as the trick to getting through a fever, according to some schools of medicine, is not to try to reduce the fever — i.e. run from it — but to try to spike the fever — i.e. go farther into it.

Quite simply, your body and soul grieve because they need to. Deny them that, and you'll never get past it. To will yourself to let go of pain is but an illusion that actually only keeps you stuck in your pain longer.

But if you go into it, live it, and feel it, eventually your body will run out of pain. The pain of holding on will scorch you, but eventually your system will run out of its need to grieve. By holding on as tightly as you can your hand, metaphorically speaking, eventually gets tired and lets go. The muscles that are holding on eventually grow exhausted. The hand then naturally opens and releases that to which it clung so tightly.

This is why, when children get hurt and start to cry or scream after being hurt, it is highly effective to simply let them. Inconvenient and socially awkward as this may be, it encourages the child to release the pain. Try it sometime. I guarantee that if you say, "Go ahead and cry it all out; that was scary and did hurt" in a loving manner, rather than "Don't cry. It'll be okay" in a dismissive way, you will find that your child is soon done and is tired of crying. If you stop everything (yes, everything; yes, every time your child cries)[66] and *patiently* wait until the child is finished releasing his or her pain (and even encourage the child to cry a little extra), you will find that in mere minutes the child has slipped out of your arms and is off, again, running and jumping.

The key to releasing the severe pain is to go further into it, to go further into isolation and pain, to feel more sharply the sting of aloneness and loss.

For, only when the pain is great enough (whatever that "great enough" point is for you) or painful enough will you be compelled to act, to move past it, to change, and to become something new . . . .

And with time, you will move back into human contact and give-and-take relationships. In other words, just as your severe pain is the source of your isolation, it also holds the seeds for your return to life-giving human relationship and community, which is itself a form of relationship with the Divine. To again know love, to again know the joy of relationship, to again savor the richness of shared community you must move into (not away from), through, and eventually past your pain.

And God promises to be with us there in that time of passing into and through the pain. It is never promised to us that we will feel no pain, or that God will take away our pain. Instead, relationship with God gives us a way to pass through the pain without being eaten alive by it. We are promised that we will be given new ways of dealing with pain. We will be stretched. Just as surely as God pulls us through, sometimes only by the skin of our teeth, God uses the pain to grow us into entirely new people. There is a saying of unknown origin that goes, "There is no birth without blood and the tearing of flesh."

That is God's promise to us. We will know pain in life, and God will help us pass through it. Yet, God also promises that we will be stretched and grown as a result of it, usually against our wills. And through that growth and movement through our pain we move into fuller relationship with God and fuller human community.

So, to sum all of this up, there are three points to work with in this Deuteronomy text:

1) The obsession with creating a purer and purer life is an insidious form of self-centeredness that keeps us from living in the richness of authentic human community;

2) Creative expression is the key to full relationship with God and enjoying the gifts God promises us (peace, power, purpose, joy, hope, love, etc.);

3) Severe pain simultaneously keeps us from full human relationship, and potentially moves us more fully into rich human community.

While it is a seemingly stupid and even vulgar text, this verse is just loaded with meaning . . . deep meaning and truths. But you gotta play with it a bit, like a boy plays with a bug. You gotta let it dance on your fingers. You gotta let it tickle you as it runs up your arm. You gotta scorch it with the sun through a magnifying glass. You gotta smash it with a rock.

Dealing with such oddball texts (in fact, dealing with life), as just literal, factual, one-to-one correlating things yields little fruit. That makes it nothing more than a law of a culture thousands of years old, a law that is completely inapplicable today. You gotta be willing to go deeper. Look below the surface. Turn it on its head, and just play with it. You will be amazed at what you unearth.

So what is this text saying to you? Play with it. And as you do, consider this poem by David Miller, author of the book *Gods and Games*, "Taking fun simply as fun/ and earnestness in earnest/ shows how thoroughly thou/ none of the two discernest."

May God bring peace, laughter, and growth to you this week. Amen.

[Endnotes]

1 *Gallup Poll*, May 2-4, 2004. Supporting this statistic, a FOX News/Opinion Dynamics Poll, Sept. 23-24, 2003, puts the percentage of those who believe in God in America at 92%.

2 *Religious Congregations and Membership in the United States 2000.* Copyright, Association of Statisticians of American Religious Bodies (ASARB).

3 *ABC News: 20/20: Lies and Myths with John Stossel: January 23, 2004.* In this same report Stossel points out that, even after inflation is accounted for, American families have tripled their disposable income over the last 50 years. "Fifty years ago, the average family in the United States had one car. Today the norm is two or three. Houses have more than doubled in square footage, and shoppers just seem to spend as much as they want." He goes on to report that most families do not have to have two parents working, but *choose* to do so in order to maintain a higher standard of living and have more luxuries [italics mine].

4 Religion fact: Technically, Buddhism is not a religion, because there is no mention of gods or the supernatural. Buddhism, at least originally, was a philosophy or ethic for living and a means for decreasing suffering and increasing peace. Buddhism grew out of the Hindu religion and its gods approximately six centuries before Jesus came onto the religious scene.

5 *Gallup Organization:* 2003 Aggregate of more than 12,000 interviews. Copyright 2004.

6 *Playboy* magazine ran an interview in 1999 with then-Governor of Minnesota, Jesse Ventura. In this interview Governor Ventura commented, "Organized religion is a sham for weak-minded people who need strength in numbers." In his home state, Governor Ventura drew sharp criticism from many religious leaders and people, who presumably heard of the interview second-hand or who buy said magazine "for the articles." He was asked to apologize for his statement, and eventually did.

However, in other parts of the country the news came and went, offering less than a week of material for Letterman and Leno. It was as if there was a sense of agreement

193

and delight visible in the American absence of response. Like the governor, America looks down on organized religion, particularly Christianity.

Far more interesting is the fact that many clergy came out swinging against the governor when, ironically, the very man their religion is founded upon (Jesus) said that God and religious community *are* for the weak! Jesus says all people are weak, afraid and unable to go through life alone, and therefore in need of God, neighbor, and community.

Parenthetically, Buddhism's teachings confirm this understanding of human nature in saying that life is full of illusions we embrace to mask our insecurities and fears. Islam teaches of humanity's need for total dependence upon God. Hinduism, too, teaches of the fears that underlie human existence.

Religion does not make men and women impervious to pain, setback, and heartbreak, as if such a thing was possible. Relationship with God and relationship in spiritual community simply give us the ability to move through life's losses and fears in confidence and peace. Thereby, we find lives of new joy, contentment, and love.

Thus, the joke is not on religion. The joke is not that religious people are weak. Instead, the joke is on anyone who thinks he or she isn't weak. The joke is on anyone who thinks he or she can do life without any power or purpose greater than him- or herself, or without the love of some form of (spiritual) community, and still feel fulfilled. History proves, time and again, the hollowness and fear men know when they live life solely on their own strength and strictly for self-service. Even the mightiest of leaders, captains of industry, and brawniest of professional wrestlers need more than just themselves. Oddly enough, former Governor Ventura has been a member of a Lutheran Church in Minnesota since long before his *Playboy* interview.

7 Rev. Gregory A. Boyd, a well-known conservative Christian pastor and writer, in his book *Repenting of Religion: Turning from Judgment to the Love of God* (Baker Books, 2004), with shocking insight and humility writes, "Perhaps the greatest indictment on evangelical churches today is that they are not generally known as refuge houses for sinners — places where hurting, wounded, sinful people can run and find a love that does not question, an understanding that does not judge, and an acceptance that knows no conditions.

"To be sure, evangelical churches are usually refuge houses for *certain kinds* of sinners — the loveless, the self-righteous, those apathetic toward the poor and unconcerned with issues of justice and race, the greedy, the gluttonous, and so on. People guilty of *these* sins usually feel little discomfort among us. But evangelical churches are not usually safe places for other kinds of sinners — those whose sins, ironically, tend to be much less frequently mentioned in the Bible than the religiously sanctioned sins."

8 "Have dominion over" is from the Hebrew word "rdh," which could be interpreted "caretaker." Thereby, the text offers a meaning implying responsibility and love for, rather than capricious use and misuse of the earth. However, even this nuanced change is all but negated by the very strong language in the remainder of these verses, which grants to humanity all of creation to use at its discretion. Further, it is a minute percentage of Christian Sunday School teachers who will have significant background in the Hebrew language or exposure to such a non-obvious interpretation, and thus be capable of teaching to children such a nuance. Therefore, recognizing that most theological foundational education occurs in the youngest years of life, it is the "dominion over" mindset that is nearly all-pervasive in Christian thinking.

9 In actuality, you can very often hear this preached in Christian pulpits, but the language is far more subtle and the point is usually implicit rather than explicit.

10 Even the most quoted and memorized verse of all Christian scripture, John 3:16, lends to this world-is-bad thinking. It states, "For God so loved the world that He gave his only begotten son that whoever believes in him shall not perish but have everlasting life." Now it does denote that God loved the world, but if God loves the world then why is the world about to perish? If God loved the world exactly as it is, then why would God destroy it or send it or us to everlasting hell? No, even here there is a connotation, or an implicit understanding, that we and the world are not good and not how God wants to be.

11 The old Christian saw goes, "An old priest was confronted by a young man who said, 'But Father, I don't believe everything in the Christian story.'" To which, the priest replied, "Dear boy, it doesn't matter what *you* believe," as if to imply that the beliefs of the church are unchanging and absolute. Our life task, per this thinking, is to grow in understanding of the church's truths, rather than bend them to suit us. And that would almost work, except the findings of Copernicus, Darwin, modern archaeology, church history, and chemistry, to name a few, seriously cripple the notion of the church's truths being absolute and unchanging. Examples of changing truths include the notions of transubstantiation, Biblical inerrancy, creation, sacraments, the Assumption of Mary, theodicy, free will, justification by works, and heaven, for starters.

12 Okay, I'll be totally honest. I realized that, in effect, at my core I am just lazy. That's why I have such respect for clergy who start their own churches. Doing so requires a massive amount of energy and sustained focus, not to mention sheer guts in risking constant rejection in the belief that you have something that will help people.

13 These two categories pair up roughly with the two types of Christianity mentioned in Chapter Two. The so-called "reasonable" Christians can generally be found in the old, white, dying Protestant churches. The literalist Christians are generally found in the slick, new, young congregations. Though, there is no shortage of old and dying literal-interpreting churches, either. In fact, all but a handful of the many, many denominations of Christianity have recognized a net decrease in membership over the last decade or three.

14 As a side note, this woman's denomination of Christianity, one that considers itself highly academic, considers false the argument that the New Testament explains and supersedes the Old Testament's discrepancies and difficulties, as if the Old Testament exists primarily to foretell what is coming in the New Testament. Honoring Jewish scripture as an entity unto itself and not simply a precursor to Christianity, her denomination objects to the argument of some denominations that the book of Second Peter in the New Testament explains that the creation process took much longer than seven days. Second Peter says, "With God, one day is as 1,000 years" (2Peter 3:8). Thus, creation did not take 7 days, but 7,000 years.

Her denomination's non-allowance of the 1=1,000 thinking is wise insofar as accepting it would bring more confusion to continued literal interpretation of the Bible. It would mean that not only did creation take 7,000 God-years, but Jesus was in the desert not for 40 days (Matthew 4:2), but for 40,000 God-years; and Jesus was dead not for 3 days, but for 3,000 years (which is actually somewhat believable, as no one has seen much of him lately); and the Israelites wandered with Moses in the desert not for 40 years (Exodus 16:35), but for 14,600,000 God-years (365 days/year times 1,000 times 40 years). That number swells dramatically for the Israelite canines to 102,200,000 dog-God-years.

Seriously, this act of reading New Testament verses into the Old Testament is a clear example of literal interpretation of scripture not making things easier, but, in fact, making scripture significantly more confusing. It also becomes far more difficult for the seeker to swallow. When you insist on literally interpreting all of scripture to cover the unbelievable nature of a few parts, matters can get quite muddy, and not necessarily more instructive, rather quickly.

15 *Spiritual But Not Religious: A Call To Religious Revolution in America*. Sven Erlandson. IUniverse Publishing, 1999.

16 The spiritual seeker or preacher could blend in resurrection figures from other religions and myth systems for greater wisdom and potency. Deities who died and came back to life include Dionysus (Greece), Osiris (Egypt), and Tammuz (Mesopotamia), to name a few.

17 Do not be afraid to draw from any non-Biblical source or conversation. There is truth in the words of Madonna in the song *Vogue*, "Beauty's where you find it." All truth is God's truth.

18 That's the same saint who said, "The church is a whore, but she's my mother."

19 Many Catholics and Orthodox Christians like to think there is a fourth door, marked "Mary, mother of Jesus," that is open to all who venerate her . . . much to the mortification of Protestants.

20 Some Biblical scholars assert that the Bible would not contradict these statements. Some would also assert that the Spirit is completely defined in the Bible, a particularly shaky proposition. The problem, however, is not the Bible. The problem is how Christianity is perceived to be interpreting the Bible. You would never hear conservative Christianity, which is Christianity's most vocal element, assert that other religions can bring people fully into a saving relationship with God, despite what the Bible says. Never. Rarely would you hear this asserted explicitly in moderate Christian churches either. Other religions, they might concede, can bring you to God, but Jesus is the only way to have the fullest, purest, bestest-ever relationship with God. It is easy to see that while Christian scripture may be quite tolerant of other religions, Christianity itself is perceived to be quite arrogant and intolerant.

21 *Repenting of Religion: Turning from Judgment to the Love of God*. Baker Books, 2004. Boyd shows a love, absence of judgmentalism, and progressive theology that boggle the mind when the reader considers his strong roots and leadership in the staunchly conservative Evangelical Christian community. His powerful excoriation of cowardly Christians in the section *Gluttony and Homosexuality* (pp 83-89) will tickle those critical of Christianity while shaking both Christians and their critics to their core.

22 *The Power of Myth* (Betty Sue Flowers, editor). Anchor Books, 1988. If you read no other book in your lifetime, this is the one.

23 *Repenting of Religion: Turning from Judgment to the Love of God*. Baker Books, Grand Rapids, MI. 2004.

24 *Every Second Counts*. Lance Armstrong and Sally Jenkins. Broadway Books, New York. 2003.

25 Ibid.

26 *New York Times*, Laurie Goldstein. Sept. 18, 2003.

27 Much, though certainly not all, of Christian theology asserts that God *does not* send bad, evil, hardship, or temptation, but redeems it, or turns it into good. However,

there are lesser-known segments of Christian theology that assert God is the sender of the bad, evil, and suffering that befall us.

The former way of thinking is rooted in a dualistic theology, where evil finds its roots in a devil/Satan figure then consequently in human nature, and all good comes from God. The latter is rooted in a belief that all of life was created by God, including any devil figure and including the human propensity to do "bad" things. If God created what we perceive to be evil (or even just the capacity for evil), then evil is part of God's plan (even if nothing more than a functionary in bringing about love and greater good) and is therefore inherently good. The challenge before humanity is to find the good, the learning, and the growth in what appears to be evil.

Further, there are just too many examples (in life, scripture, and nature) of bad bringing about good to deny that bad is sent by God. For that matter, there are just as many examples in life of good bringing about evil. There is no blessing in life that is absent of curse, nor curse absent of blessing. All of it is good insofar as it has the power to transform us, move us closer to God, and make us greater bearers of love in the world.

28 *New York Times: Reimagining a Downtown.* Adam Nagourney. May 10, 2002.

29 Ibid

30 Ibid.

31 *Good to Great: Why Some Companies Make the Leap . . . And Others Don't.* Jim Collins. HarperBusiness. 2001. This book is the must-read of this century for spiritual-religious people and leaders who specifically desire to radically improve the spiritual-religious climate in America. Oriented completely toward business, yet bearing enormous and obvious cross-over applicability, this book articulates well the gut-wrenching truths that set the great efforts apart from the merely good.

32 *Every Second Counts.* Lance Armstrong and Sally Jenkins. Broadway Books, New York. 2003.

33 Ibid.

34 While serving a 6 ½ year sentence in a Singapore prison, Mr. Leeson wrote a book, entitled *Rogue Trader* (Little Brown and Co., 1996), in which he states, "People at the London end of Barings were all so know-all that nobody dared ask a stupid question in case they looked silly in front of everyone else." This arrogance and fear of addressing the hard questions led to Barings' downfall.

In a *San Francisco Chronicle* article, entitled *Old-time religion on the decline* (July 21, 2004), writer Don Lattin quotes the National Opinion Research Center's most recent statistics, which indicate " . . . the number of Americans who say they are Baptist, Methodist, Lutheran, Presbyterian, Evangelical, or other varieties of Protestantism dropped from 63 percent in 1993 to 52 percent in 2002." (Subsumed under the Protestant umbrella are also the Mormon Church, Pentecostals, and the Jehovah's Witnesses, which are part of only a handful of denominations that are actually experiencing growth in numbers.) Lattin goes on to say, "Meanwhile, officials at the Manhattan-based National Council of Churches, a longtime bastion of American Protestantism, appeared unflustered by the latest news of their decline. 'We don't worry about it,' said Pat Patillo, the director of communications for [this] Protestant and Orthodox Christian ecumenical agency that still counts 50 million members in its member denominations."

This attitude bears a shocking similarity to the naïve optimism of Peter Barings and the leaders of his bank. In the case of the church, this ostrich-like behavior and

197

mindset are widespread and thinly veil an underlying terror at not having a clue about what to do to revive the Christian brand and reverse the tide of departures from the Christian Church.

The Lutheran Church alone, while claiming 8 million adherents in North America, had 82,000 people leave its ranks in just one year (2003). 82,000 people! That is 1% of its total population, and numbers from the previous decade show this is not a one time event. The exodus has been going on for quite some time, much to the befuddlement of its fearful leaders.

Lest any group consider itself immune, Lattin cites Tom Smith, author of *The Vanishing Protestant Majority*, who says that nominal Catholics "are less likely to stop calling themselves 'Catholic' because religion tends to be more of a part of their 'core identity' as Italians, Irish, Poles, Filipinos, Latinos, or people from other Catholic homelands" *even though these very same people may rarely go to church and may not adhere to church doctrine.*

35 *World Almanac and Book of Facts 2003*. Primedia Reference Inc., New Jersey 2003.

36 *Religious Congregations and Membership in the United States, 2000*. Copyright, Association of Statisticians of American Religious Bodies (ASARB). In this state there are now more Muslims than Jews, Presbyterians, or Episcopalians. In its largest city, ten years ago, there were a mere four mosques. Today, there are over sixty.

Yet still, of all the people in America as a whole who claim to be religious, 84% cite Christianity as their religion. 4% claim Judaism. Approximately 2% ascribe to Islam.

To offer some sense of perspective to this statistic, consider Budweiser, *The King of Beers*. Budweiser is the number one brewer worldwide with a 9% market share, nearly double the nearest competitor. Domestically, it commands only 45% market share, yet is *twice as large as its closest competitor*. Such market share is considered whopping in business. As a further point of reference, among the world's top soft drink makers, Coca-Cola Co. has 43.7% market share to Pepsi Cola Co.'s 31.6% (Market Share Reporter, 2003. Gale Publishing [Robert S. Lazich, Ed.].) .

While Christianity's 84% share is nothing short of astronomical (Worldwide it has a 32% market share, again twice as large as its nearest competitor, Islam.), the point of highlighting these numbers is not to say that bigger is better. Instead, the point is that Christianity is so big that change is very difficult. Further, Christianity's size contributes to its refusal to change. It doesn't think it has to.

Still, the greatest reason for Christianity's refusal and/or inability to change is its nearly all-pervasive fear of failure, mistake, embarrassment, and especially scandal and potential lawsuit. All it takes is one mistake (and the ensuing fallout) in a culture that is already largely biased against religion for the church to fear taking risks again. So, rather than take bold and creative steps, which by their very nature carry some measure of risk, the church opts for the low-risk, low-yield paths. These paths, by nature, lack the oomph to generate any measure of significant change. As a result, Christianity continues its slide into irrelevance.

37 Interestingly, many Americans outside the church (and many in the pews, even) already accept this fact.

38 *USA Today: George Soros putting his fortune behind a new cause: Ousting Bush*. Rick Hampson. June 1, 2004.

39 Ibid.

40 This begs the question, "Well, if we don't know Biblical events really happened, and if we don't know Jesus really said the stuff the Bible says he did, how can you quote them or listen to them now?" As discussed in Chapters Four and Five, it doesn't matter if these things literally happened or if Jesus even literally said the things the Bible says. The point is that the Bible bears much truth and wisdom, *whether it is factual or not*. Further, Jesus' teachings are worth following *not* because he said them, but because they are powerful truths that can challenge and transform your life.

41 The Daily Study Bible Series: The Gospel of John: Volume 2 [Revised Edition]. William Barclay. Westminster John Knox Press. 1975.

42 Quite unrelated to this discussion of hell, yet well worth noting, are the *Deep Thoughts* of author and humorist Jack Handy, who irreverently writes, "One good thing about hell, I think, is that you can probably pee wherever you want to" (*The Lost Deep Thoughts*. Hyperion, 1998.).

43 One of the underlying causes of the collective American spiritual crisis is the pervasive focus on happiness and fun, as opposed to joy and contentment. We have become a fun-seeking culture, obsessed with the new experience, ever-questing for a new high. To get off that never-satisfied ride, it is helpful to consider the difference between happiness and joy. This difference is best understood using two examples: Running a marathon and sex.

In preparation for a marathon a runner will spend anywhere from one month to one year training and getting in shape. This time of preparation and anticipation is, oddly, joy. It is the contentment of living and preparing, and being on a mission. It is the sense of being "in the zone," or having a purpose. It is a feeling that life has quality. It is spread out over time, and it infuses all aspects of life with a new spirit.

In contrast, happiness is the second, the minute, the hour, and the week after crossing the finish line. This is the high of accomplishment. It is the rush of seeing all your work come to fruition. Beyond the camaraderie, this is the fun part of marathoning. It is a great rush and release of energy packed into a small amount of time.

Similarly, during sex, the minutes or hours leading up to climax are joy and contentment. Foreplay is the working toward something special. It is the slow building of energy. It is the peace and power of being on a mission.

Whereas, climax is the ecstatic happiness of accomplishment and release. Climax is the seconds and minutes of wow, and the afterglow that follows. But the high of climax does not last. It is always chased, yet always fleeting.

Contentment and joy are long-lasting and deep. They are less of a high, and more of a long, slow crescendo. Joy is a sense of life's goodness, even amidst life's oddities, hardships and sorrows. Further, joy is the result of volition or choice. It is something we can create.

Happiness is compact, overwhelming, and also fleeting. While you can guarantee foreplay and joy, you cannot guarantee climax and happiness. In fact, the very word *happiness* has as its root the word *hap*, which means *circumstance, chance,* or *luck*. Happiness is rooted in chance. To be happy is to be lucky. It comes and it goes. It cannot be controlled or directly created. It can only be pursued. For the person who is centered it is in the pursuit of happiness that joy can be found.

Interestingly, the American Constitution says that all persons are guaranteed *the pursuit of happiness*. As if recognizing that happiness is elusive, and comes and goes with the wind, the Constitution implies that it is the *pursuit* of happiness, and the joy that pursuit brings, that people really want.

Early stages of spiritual existence are characterized by the constant foraging for (fleeting) happiness, new highs, and constant accomplishment. The move into advanced levels of spiritual growth is characterized by the creation of contentment and lasting joy, which spring from a sense of purpose or mission.

44 This is the shift that must happen to the Christian image! Before people will enter Christianity's doors the image of the Christian must shift from posturing, judgmentalism, and self-consciousness to a more Mother Teresa-like servant humility and love. Then will people see the honor in Jesus' path and want to follow.

45 My uncle, Rev. John Johnson, was a long-time missionary to Ecuador. He built an English-speaking school for the native people and continued the work of Christianizing that region. Uncle John and his family endured persecution of all sorts. He was stoned three times by people who did not want him there, his children were given poisoned candy, and years of in-bred resentment in the native people troubled his efforts in the early years, only to give way to mutual trust and respect years later.

46 Buddhism does speak of the path of compassion and other-centered-ness as a noble alternative to the strict focus on elimination of one's own suffering. In fact, this path of the Bodhisattva is a motif that has grown in popularity over time. But the fundamental drive of Buddhism is still the total elimination of one's personal suffering.

47 It is from one of the two books of the Bible that Christians most frequently call on to denounce homosexuality and other acts it deems social ills. The other commonly referenced book is Leviticus. Both are thought by modern scholars to be the priestly/societal laws of a culture 2500+ years old.

48 For a bit of fun, read Appendix B to see how Deuteronomy 23: 1 could realistically be used as a personal meditation or a sermon text in a church.

49 Not to be confused with Noah's Ark, which was a big boat, the Ark of the Covenant was more the size of a coffin. It contained the entire 613 Laws of Moses.

So sacred was the Ark of the Covenant that merely touching it brought instant death. Only the High Priest was allowed to do so without dying.

The Ark required four servants to carry it, using two long poles, running front to back. One story from the Old Testament tells how the four servants were carrying the Ark over a particularly treacherous stretch of ground. While doing so, one servant stumbled and reached up to catch the Ark from falling. As his hand stretched out to save the Ark he was instantly struck dead.

This horrible nature of God is echoed in the movie *Raiders of the Lost Ark*, in which Harrison Ford and Adolph Hitler go chasing after Ark, one to put it into a museum, the other to tap into its mythical power and rule the world, somehow. In the climactic scene, the bad guys (Hitler's) open the Ark and are met with the Angel of Death, who, it seems, is a bit grouchy after her 2500-year slumber. Call it, in the words of Rudolf Otto, *mysterium tremendum*, or call it a freshly-opened can of holy whoop-ass. Either way, it was not a pretty sight.

I recall first seeing the movie with my parents. Upon exiting, my mother, not prone to seeing, much less liking, action flicks remarked rather dryly, "Well, it sure did a good job of portraying the wrath of God."

50 This notion also makes apparent the obvious religious undertones and backhanded metaphors of the movie *The Wizard of Oz*. No one has ever seen the Wizard, but

everyone in the kingdom believes in his special powers (God). Only a select few can go and speak to the Wizard. There are lots of "smoke and mirrors." Don't look behind the curtain. But when you do it is just a frail old man running the Wizard (metaphor for the frail old men that run many religious institutions). Yet, in the end, the Wizard, as a simple man, helps others to see that they already have the gifts they seek from the Wizard (God and God's power are already in them).

51 *Salon.com*, Feb. 20, 2004, Patrick Smith writes that American Airlines is investigating a Feb. 6 incident involving a pilot on flight 34 from LA to NY. The pilot is reported to have asked over the airplane loudspeaker for "all Christians on board to identify themselves by raising their hands. He then urged them to engage their non-Christian seatmates, whom some witnesses say he referred to as 'crazy,' in a discussion about faith."

52 Or perhaps your very well-being depends upon listening to the proselytizer. I once had stitches pulled by a doctor who went into a quite lengthy and impassioned speech about why I should become a Christian. I didn't have the energy to get into a protracted discussion of how I am a follower of Jesus, but am definitely not his narrow idea of what a Christian is. I thought it would be less painful, conversationally-speaking, to just allow him to think I was a non-Christian. I also thought that he was less likely to be rough on a non-Christian with his suture-removing instrument than on a Christian who didn't see God his way.

53 Why is it that you can have a group of six friends over for a sumptuous dinner and get five telemarketer calls, but when you're in a Christian pinch there is never a furnace company that is going to be in your neighborhood?

54 To the Jew of Jesus' day, to say "all the law and all the prophets" implied that everything that was significant in life depended upon these commandments. It was another way of simply saying "everything."

55 It is worth noting, as stated earlier, that Jesus' teachings are a great guide not because Jesus said them, but because the teachings themselves are brilliant, powerful, and life-changing.

56 By the way, it also works on pushy Buddhists. Yes, believe it or not, they are out there. I've met some. There is always some group of people who can spoil a really good thing.

57 As I have attempted to show in this book, the Bible can be a powerful and exciting help on the spiritual journey, especially when read as metaphor. You must realize, however, that the book and the religion are two different things. You can have one without the other.

58 Even defining words, idioms, and colloquialisms *within* a language can be next to impossible. That is why many non-Americans often have such difficulty learning American English, even though they may already speak, say, British English. American English is so filled with idioms and "expressions." Perhaps the best example of the difficulty in defining/translating words within a language (not to mention into another language) is seen in the movie *From the Hip*. In this movie the lead character, played by Judd Nelson, in a courtroom scene articulately and humorously conveys the difficulty in attempting to define a particular word in American slang.

59 *New York Times* [opinion-editorial]: "Hug an Evangelical." Nicholas D. Kristof. April 24, 2004. While taking a few pokes at evangelical/conservative Christians (such as mentioning the T-shirt saying, "So many right-wing Christians, so few lions"), Kristof offers an insightful tweak of the hypocrisy of liberal views on right-

wing religiosity.

60 Yes, popular opinion *does* influence and determine theology, as do political, economic, and social struggles and pressures. One fascinating example of this is found in the Roman Catholic Church's veneration of Mary, the mother of Jesus. Bowing to worldwide popular legend and traditions, yet despite an absence of Biblical proof or allusion to the notion, the Roman Catholic Church in the 20th Century made into doctrine the belief that not only was Jesus born of a virgin, but Mary, herself, was born of a virgin. Interestingly, it is Mary's birth that is, in Catholic and Orthodox circles, known as the Virgin Birth.

One popular Catholic Holy Day is the celebration of the Assumption of Mary, the day that Catholics and Orthodox believe that Mary herself was lifted up into heaven (an assumption far too great for many Protestants because of its lack of Biblical mention). Mirroring the Ascension of Jesus, this event makes Mary one of only two people in Christian lore who never died, the other being not Jesus (killed on a cross) but Elijah, who was whisked up to heaven on a flaming chariot behind flaming horses.

These doctrines grew out of grass roots pressure from Catholics in many parts of the world who prayed to and worshipped Mary, often as more than simply the mother of Jesus. In some South American and African countries, for example, right up into the middle of the 1900s, many Christians engaged in what most Protestant critics considered Mariolatry. This was the belief that Mary is the Savior of the world (not Jesus) and is, in fact, God. This belief was allowed to persist by Catholic missionaries for many years as a way of assimilating the native beliefs that often included female deities.

This practice of creating theology by majority vote, so to speak, dates all the way back to the earliest centuries of Christianity. In the debates and councils of Christian leaders that for centuries followed Jesus' death, theology was determined, often, by those who had power or money, or by those who could simply rally the most number of supporters. Even today, for example, Christianity as a whole is slowly adopting a far more tolerant stance toward other religions than it ever had in the past. This has grown out of worldwide pressure to create greater world harmony by reducing conflict and mutual judgment. It is an incontrovertible fact that Christian theology, in all of its forms, is and always has been the product of human imagination, intellect, struggle, consensus, and force.

61 An excellent supplement to this list of questionable Bible verses is offered in the book *Rescuing the Bible from Fundamentalism*, by John Shelby Spong. Bishop Spong goes into great detail and makes fascinating points on topics not mentioned here.

62 Going back to my teenage religious students mentioned earlier, I offered the above verses to them for contemplation. Much of the year was then spent exploring how something doesn't have to be factual to be truth-bearing. We would together explore the great beauty and deep wisdom in the majestic book — the Bible — they had grown up reading in a literal way. All the while they were given the freedom and responsibility, in an atmosphere of acceptance and love, to decide for themselves if they would most like the literalist path, the metaphor-seeking path, or some combination of the two.

63 Because of the semi-graphic nature of the following sermon, it might be best suited to more mature audiences. However, if the pastor is trusted and respected among his or her people, this sermon could be delivered with little editing and minimal fallout.

However, truth be told, any audience of mixed ages is likely going to be favorably affected by this sermon. Small children generally tune out sermons. And while they might pick up a socially uncomfortable word or two, they will be quite unaffected by it. Older children, who are more apt to be bored by church, will find the preaching of such a sermon to be both real and refreshing. Likely, only certain adults will take any offense or experience any discomfort, and then only if it is delivered by a poor preacher or a leader who is not respected for being able to find seriousness and depth even in frivolity, and visa-versa.

64 A brief aside can be inserted into the sermon at this point which might read: "The 'homosexuality is an abomination' verse found in Leviticus would be included in this historical-cultural context. In its proper 2500 year-old cultural context it is denounced, not because it is absolutely and divinely wrong, but because such a relationship does not contribute to the procreation of the race, as two men cannot reproduce.

65 Another interesting, yet only distantly related, aside can be offered at this point: "There is an old saying that goes, 'If you are going through hell . . . keep going.'"

66 Yes, I do have children. Two of them; one a teenager. Both of them were raised this way. Raising children to have as little baggage as possible when they reach adulthood is a discipline, in the same sense that going jogging every morning is a discipline. It requires doing even when you don't feel like it.

It is a discipline that will greatly contribute to healthier adult lives and relationships, as there is less unresolved pain — in other words, baggage. If a child is not allowed by you, the parent, to express anger and sadness, that child will retain those emotions and, quite often, express them in ways that are far more socially unacceptable later in life. To note, letting children cry whenever they get hurt is not the same as letting a child throw tantrums just to get what they want.

[Annotated Bibliography]

ARMSTRONG, LANCE AND SALLY JENKINS. *Every Second Counts.* Broadway Books, 2003.

One of the world's greatest athletes shares the gritty and insightful wisdom he has learned from life's sufferings and self-punishment on the road to becoming the best and becoming himself. A challenge to traditional Christianity's notion that suffering is bad.

BACH, RICHARD. *Illusions: The Adventures of a Reluctant Messiah.* Dell Publishing, 1977.

The perfect introduction for the adult beginner (and an excellent reminder for the longtime spiritual traveler) on the spiritual journey, which challenges inside-the-box thinking. Told in delightful story form.

Bridge Across Forever. Thorndike Press, 1984.

The spiritual seeker's love story.

Jonathan Livingston Seagull. Macmillan, 1990.

Brilliant; a child's introduction to the nobility and beauty of the compassionate hero's spiritual path.

BARCLAY, WILLIAM. *The Daily Study Bible Series.* Westminster John Knox Press (Revised Edition), 1975.

The best Biblical commentary series available for the moderate-to-left-leaning Christian seeking strong spiritual guidance. Perfect as a daily devotional, packed with quotes, poetry, historical references, and excellent Biblical scholarship.

BARTH, KARL. *Epistle to the Romans* (Edwyn C. Hoskyns, trans.). Oxford Press (6th ed.), 1968.

205

One of the most influential 20th Century theologians. Dismisses theologies based in feeling, trust in church, and spirituality, and stays completely focused on God's supremacy and human sinfulness.

BERGER, PETER L. *A Rumor of Angels: Modern Society and the Rediscovery of the Supernatural.* Doubleday, 1969.

Wryly argues that God is not dead, but is very much at work and alive; speaks through sociological lenses.

BONHOEFFER, DIETRICH. *The Cost of Discipleship.* Macmillan, 1959.

One of the few pastor-theologians who stood up to the Nazi regime, he offers his theory on how religious conversion that is not followed by "works" cheapens the grace offered by God.

BOYD, GREGORY A. *Repenting of Religion: Turning from Judgment to the Love of God.* Baker Books, 2004.

Brilliant, rich, and challenging. The most insightful call to Christian love I've read in a long time. This book and his church in St. Paul, MN, offer genuine hope for Christianity's branding and future.

BRANCH, TAYLOR. *Parting the Waters: America in the King Years, 1954-63.* Simon and Schuster, 1989.

A Pulitzer Prize-winning thorough analysis of the shaping of American society by the non-violent protest of Black America, and how this movement took on mythic proportions largely out of the theology of one man, Martin Luther King, Jr.

BUBER, MARTIN. *I and Thou.* Scribner, 1970.

Almost as hard a read as Kierkegaard (below), because of its density and complexity. Pushes for treating whomever you may interact with not as an "it," but as a "Thou," as a bearer of the divine; thereby is life infused with greater reverence.

BULTMANN, RUDOLF KARL. *Jesus Christ and Mythology.* Scribner, 1958.

One of the seminal works on questioning literal translation of the Christian story; coined the term "demythologizing." A must-read.

BUSCAGLIA, LEO. *Loving Each Other: The Call of Human Relationships.* Ballantine, 1984.

Expositions on love as the highest calling of humanity.

CAMPBELL, JOSEPH. *Hero With a Thousand Faces.* Princeton University Press (Reprint Edition), 1972.

The well-researched, extremely thorough academic precursor to the popular *The Power of Myth*. It shows the significant similarities of religions and myth systems around the world and in history. Explores religions as outgrowths of the age-old hero myth.

The Power of Myth (Betty Sue Flowers, editor). Anchor Books, 1988.

The one religion must-read of the 20th Century! It completely revolutionizes religious thought by putting it in a world-history/myth context. Extremely popular because it is a broadly-accessible, absolutely intoxicating read.

A Joseph Campbell Companion **(Diane K. Osbon, editor). Perennial (Reprint), 1995.**

A poetic synopsis of his work to be always kept on hand for the advanced Campbellite.

CAMPOLO, ANTHONY. *Following Jesus Without Embarrassing God.* **Word Publishing. 1997.**

As with all of his works, he puts Christianity's feet to the fire to continually strive for cultural relevancy.

COLLINS, JAMES C. *Good to Great: Why Some Companies Make the Leap . . . And Others Don't.* **HarperBusiness, 2001.**

Based on hard research of the long term, very-top producing companies in America, this book hammers out a solid formula for the successful advanced growth of any organization. Obvious religious as well as personal spiritual crossover applicability. New York Times Bestseller. If you desire relevant religion, you must read this book.

ERLANDSON, SVEN. *Spiritual But Not Religious: A Call To Religious Revolution In America.* **IUniverse, 2000.**

Articulates the roots of the American spiritual crisis, and, and what must be done to solve the crisis.

FORDE, GERHARD O. *Christian Dogmatics* **(Carl E. Braaten and Robert W. Jensen, editors). Fortress Press, 1984.**

A classic Lutheran exposition of grace, faith, and Christian doctrine.

GAWAIN, SHAKTI. *Creative Visualization: Use the Power of Your Imagination to Create What You Want in Your Life.* **Nataraj Publishing, 1978.**

A New Age classic.

Living in the Light: A Guide to Personal and Planetary Transformation. **Nataraj Publishing, 1986.**

Challenging insofar as it offers spiritual seekers and Christian leaders who are searching for new words for Christian themes a stripped-down and redressed version of many Christian truths (whether intentional or unintentional on the author's part). Also, delves into the inherent societal-global-responsibility of the spiritual journey.

HAMILTON, J. WALLACE. *Ride the Wild Horses: The Christian use of our untamed impulses.* **Abingdon (Reprint), 1980.**

12 of the best sermons you will ever read. Argues not for a change in human instincts, but for a harnessing of them for use in God's work.

HANDY, JACK. *The Lost Deep Thoughts: Don't Fight the Deepness.* **Hyperion, 1998.**

An off-the-wall, funny-as-hell break from the over-serious world of theology.

HILLMAN, JAMES. *Loose Ends: Primary Papers in Archetypal Psychology.* **Spring**

Publishing, 1975.

A brilliant, dense read. The perfect mate to Joseph Campbell's research; uses a psychology perspective and application.

We've had a Hundred Years of Psychotherapy --- and the World's Getting Worse. **HarperCollins, 1992.**

A challenging and entertaining series of conversations and letters exploring the decline of American society as it fits in a psycho-religious context.

Soul's Code: In Search of Character and Calling. **Warner Books, 1996.**

The most accessible of his writings (though still very dense) for those on the spiritual journey. He explores archetypal patterns of spiritual seekers.

JUNG, CARL. *Portable Jung* (Joseph Campbell, editor; R.F.C. Hull, trans.). **Viking Press (Reprint Edition), 1976.**

The man whose thought cleared the way for the work of Joseph Campbell, James Hillman, Thomas Moore, and many others. The son of a Protestant pastor, he sought to give fresh language to Christian themes of death, resurrection, love, etc. This book makes his thinking accessible to the layman.

KEEN, SAM. *Fire in the Belly: On Being a Man.* **Bantam, 1992.**

Pushes for males to develop spiritually beyond traditional stereotypes to a new definition of man as passionate in the heart and fired in the belly.

KENNEDY, DAN. *Loser Goes First: My Thirty-something Years of Dumb Luck and Minor Humiliation.* **Crown Publishers, 2003.**

The one book every pastor and theologian should read, but won't. Essential for a realistic look into the mind and spiritual journey of today's un-churched. Far from the pretty people Christianity tries to attract to its churches, Kennedy is the consummation of the American masses under age 40 — brilliant, witty, skeptical, spiritual, and wanting to find his place in the world.

KIERKEGAARD, SOREN. *Philosophical Fragments by Johannes Climacus.* **Princeton University Press, 1936.**

A painstakingly thorough exposition of truth being delivered ultimately by grace.

LOWRY, EUGENE L. *Homiletical Plot: The Sermon as Narrative Art Form.* **John Knox Press, 1980.**

While addressing the issue of creating radically better sermons, he offers great insight into some of the fundamental religious question of the day, such as what does it take to be religiously relevant today?

LUTHER, MARTIN. *Martin Luther's Basic Theological Writings* (Timothy F. Lull, editor). **Fortress Press, 1989.**

A compilation of works of perhaps the single most pivotal Christian figure since Jesus. Offers a deep understanding of the underpinnings of much of Protestantism, as well as the spirit of fighting for societal change, and the heart of a man torn and strengthened by his own spiritual struggles.

MAXWELL, ROBERT. *The 21 Irrefutable Laws of Leadership: Follow Them and People Will Follow You.* **Thomas Nelson Publishers, 1998.**

A brilliantly insightful and powerful look into the natural laws of who humans follow and why.

MERTON, THOMAS. *The Seven Storey Mountain.* **Harvest Books, 1989.**

Merton's greatest work telling his own spiritual journey from successful writer to monk to inspiring Catholic pastoral influence in the world.

MILLER, DAVID. *Gods and Games: Toward a Theology of Play.* **World Publishing, 1970.**

An entertaining, thought-provoking cross-analysis of religion and gaming; particularly poignant in the early 21st Century as video-gaming becomes potentially the biggest form of entertainment in America.

The New Polytheism: Rebirth of the Gods and Goddesses. **HarperCollins, 1974.**

A fascinating exploration of recent trends in theology.

MOORE, THOMAS. *Soul Mates.* **HarperPerennial, 1994.**

On the book shelf of many a spiritual seeker. Moore excellently gels the spiritual and psychological worlds, offering deep insights into the actualization of self and the finding of love.

NIEBUHR, REINHOLD. *Moral Man and Immoral Society: A Study in Ethics and Politics.* **Westminster John Knox Press, (Reprint Edition) 2001.**

A classic; necessary for understanding all American theology in the second half of the 20th Century. Offers a delineation of modes of Christian existence in contemporary culture.

OTTO, RUDOLF. *The Idea of the Holy.* **Oxford University Press, 1923.**

A classic academic treatise on the many modes of the human experience of the Divine.

PAGELS, ELAINE. *The Gnostic Gospels.* **Random House, 1979.**

Documentation on the growth (and death) of various "heretical" interpretive movements that have grown out of Christian scripture over the last 2000 years and the scripture that drove the movements. Fascinating.

RAHNER, KARL. *Foundations of Christian Faith: An Introduction to the Idea of Christianity* **(William V. Dych, trans.). Herder and Herder, 1983.**

Dense and highly academic, Rahner articulates the multiple aspects of being human as those aspects interact with God.

SCHALLER, LYLE E. *Leading Beyond the Walls: Developing Congregations with a Heart for the Unchurched.* **Abingdon Press, 2002.**

Asserts well his theory that churches do not have to deny their theological or liturgical roots in order to provide relevant religion today.

SCHMEMANN, ALEXANDER. *Introduction to Liturgical Theology* (Ashleigh Moorhouse, trans.). **American Orthodox Publishing, 1966.**

Traditional theology seeks to guide actions after establishing beliefs. Coming from the Christian Orthodox tradition, Schmemann turns theology on its head and offers a Christian self-understanding by asking, how does what we do indicate what we believe? Academic and liturgical in scope.

SPONG, JOHN SHELBY. *Rescuing the Bible From Fundamentalism: A Bishop Rethinks the Meaning of Scripture.* **HarperSanFrancisco, 1991.**

Provocative! In the spirit of Bultmann, a thorough de-literalization of critical pieces of Christian scripture, in response to Christian fundamentalism. "Biblical literalists must postulate supernatural miracle after supernatural miracle to keep their fundamentalism intact" (p.211).

Why Christianity Must Change or Die: A Bishop Speaks to Believers in Exile. **HarperSanFrancisco, 1998.**

Where Spong's *Rescuing the Bible* de-literalizes the Bible, this one begins to offer new interpretations of scripture and Christian symbols.

WARREN, RICHARD. *The Purpose Driven Church: Growth Without Compromising Your Message and Mission.* **Thomas Nelson, 1995.**

A dead-on assessment of the methodological, if not theological, changes necessary for church relevancy today.

WARREN, RICHARD. *The Purpose Driven Life: What on Earth am I Here For?* **Zondervan, 2002.**

A great personal devotional book, effective in re-orienting you to God and God's purpose for your life.

WHITEHEAD, ALFRED NORTH. *Process and Reality.* **Free Press, 1978.**

A brilliant mind-blower for the intelligent seeker, offering a radical new concept for understanding the nature of God.

X, MALCOLM. *The Autobiography of Malcolm X.* **Grove Press, 1965.**

The story of an American hero's intense spiritual journey that led him from Baptist roots through prison and the Nation of Islam, to Mecca and traditional Islam, ending in a martyr's death. Also an excellent insight into religious institutions and their change-resistant nature.